Encyclopaedia of Mushrooms
Volume 1

Encyclopaedia of Mushrooms
Volume 1

D. Yashwant Kumar

RANDOM PUBLICATIONS
NEW DELHI (INDIA)

Encyclopaedia of Mushrooms
Volume 1

ISBN 978-93-5111-317-1

Published in 2014 in India by

RANDOM PUBLICATIONS

4376-A/4B, Gali Murari Lal, Ansari Road
New Delhi-110 002
Phone : +91-11-43580356, +91-11-23289044
e-mail: randomexports@gmail.com, sales@randompublications.com,
info@randompublications.com

Type Setting by : Keystoneprintads, Delhi-110051
Printed at : Sanat Printers

Preface

Mushrooms are the fruiting bodies produced by some fungi. Not all fruit bodies are true mushrooms. Puffballs and morels are edible fruit bodies that are sometimes called "mushrooms".

There are three different groups of mushrooms. Selecting the right type of mushrooms to be cultivated must be based on climatic conditions and market demand. Mushrooms offer a wide range of proteins, vitamins and minerals necessary for the body and are becoming more popular and in demand.

Mushrooms are the fruiting bodies produced by some fungi. Not all fruit bodies are true mushrooms. Puffballs and morels are edible fruit bodies that are sometimes called "mushrooms". The function of this visible part of some fungi is to produce and disperse the largest possible number of spores in the shortest possible time. Spores create new individuals after being carried away on the wind and landing in a good place for growth.

People have been eating mushrooms for a long time. They used to go the forests and other wild places and based on their personal knowledge of edible and poisonous mushrooms they used to collect the edible ones. Even now some people collect wild mushrooms from the forest and eat them. Sometimes they turn out to be poisonous and have harmful effects. In India the 'Guchhi' mushroom was a delicacy known to the people prior to the 1950's. It came mostly from Kashmir. Around the early 1950's the government of Himachal Pradesh appointed Shri S.S.Jain as its first Asstt. Plant Pathologist and Mycologist for the state. He worked in the Wild Flower Hall in Chharabra, Shimla. He was touring the interior areas of Himachal to help the apple orchardists and the farmers control the diseases of apples, other fruits and crops like potatoes and wheat. He noticed the poor hand to mouth condition of the poor farmers in the hilly state of HP. He wanted to help them.

A mushroom is the reproductive structure produced by some fungi. It is somewhat like the fruit of a plant, except that the "seeds" it produces are in fact millions of microscopic spores that form in the gills or pores underneath the mushroom's cap. The spores blow away into the wind, or are spread by other means, such as animal feeding. If they land on a suitable substrate (such as wood or soil) spores will germinate to form a network of microscopic rooting threads (mycelium) which penetrate into their new food source. Unlike the mushroom, which pops up then passes away quickly, the mycelium persists, often for many years, extracting nutrients and sending up its annual crop of mushrooms.

Most mushroom-producing fungi are members of the phylums Basidiomycota or Ascomycota. The technical difference between these groups has to do with how the spores develop, which can be detected only by using a microscope. However, the "ascos" (ascospores) are less frequently noticed and are often shaped like small cups. Probably the best-known ascos are the highly prized morels (genus Morchella), which typically fruit in the spring and are often mycorrhizal, or the true truffles (genus Tuber), all of which are mycorrhizal.

Cultivated exotic mushrooms are grown in a controlled environment and are very safe to eat. They are sometimes more expensive than button mushrooms but, as an occasional treat, are worth the extra money and effort to find them.

This Encyclopaedia is intended to provide knowledge of pests and pathogens to all those who are associated with mushroom production, so that by careful observation and description of the disorders it could be possible to make an identification and then apply the appropriate measures to combat the problem.

I would like to thank my team for standing beside me throughout my career and writing this book. My special thanks go to "Random Publications" who have published the book.

— D. Yashwant Kumar

Contents

1

Introduction

A mushroom (or toadstool) is the fleshy, spore-bearing fruiting body of a fungus, typically produced above ground on soil or on its food source. The standard for the name "mushroom" is the cultivated white button mushroom, Agaricus bisporus; hence the word "mushroom" is most often applied to those fungi (Basidiomycota, Agaricomycetes) that have a stem (stipe), a cap (pileus), and gills (lamellae, sing. lamella) or pores on the underside of the cap.

"Mushroom" describes a variety of gilled fungi, with or without stems, and the term is used even more generally, to describe both the fleshy fruiting bodies of some Ascomycota and the woody or leathery fruiting bodies of some Basidiomycota, depending upon the context of the word.

Forms deviating from the standard morphology usually have more specific names, such as "puffball", "stinkhorn", and "morel", and gilled mushrooms themselves are often called "agarics" in reference to their similarity to Agaricus or their place Agaricales. By extension, the term "mushroom" can also designate the entire fungus when in culture; the thallus (called a mycelium) of species forming the fruiting bodies called mushrooms; or the species itself.

A mushroom is described as the "fruiting body of a fungus plant that typically appears above the ground and contains spores". It is this fleshy bracket (fruiting body) that is commonly eaten and which reproduces by dispersing spores in the same way that other plants disperse seeds. Instead of drawing nutrients through the roots, fungi are sustained by a network of fine, microscopic threads known collectively as the "mycelium". This network can extend over vast distances, implanting into rotting wood, soil, or other preferred medium. Fungi are more akin to molds and yeasts than to vegetable plants. Although mushrooms are technically part of the plant kingdom, they are very different organisms since they do not contain chlorophyll or have a root system.

Mushrooms must also rely on organic material for their nutrition and do so in three ways:

- As saprophytes (living on dead wood or dead tissue of living trees or dung)

- As parasites (attacking living plant or animal tissue), or
- As mycorrhizae (having a symbiotic relationship with plants).

To separate some of the confusion as to what is a simple fungus and what is a mushroom, scientists now generally use the term 'mushroom' to encompass fungi of either the order Agaricales or the order Boletales.

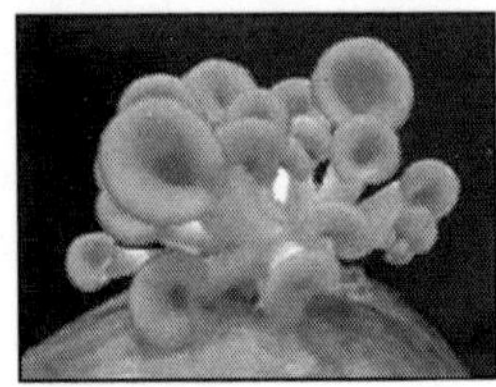

MUSHROOM PRODUCTION

Paddy Straw Mushroom - Bed Preparation and Cropping

The cultivation of paddy straw mushroom can be done in a thatched house and also under the shade of a tree. Fresh, disease free paddy straw is the ideal substrate . Ten –fifteen kg paddy straw is necessary for preparing one bed. In recent years, it is cultivated inside plastic film houses to maintain the temperature of around 25 -35 ° C and relative humidity of 75-80 %.

Paddy Straw Bundle Method

Procedure:

- Prepare a raised platform of about I m in length and 0.75 m in breadth with a deal wood flanks and keep it over a support by arranging bricks on all four corners.
- The paddy straw is bundled into to weigh about kg each.
- Soak the straw bundles in water for 12-18hr.
- Ten bundles are taken out and drain the excess water
- Place the bundles over the platform with their butt end on one side.
- Build the second layer by placing the butt end towards the other direction. (These 8 bundles make one layer of bed)
- Place the a small quantity of spawn 8-12cm inside the margin at an interval of 10- 15cm all along the periphery.
- Apply a spoonful of coarsely powdered dhal powder before placing spawn.
- Place the straw bundles at right angles to the previous layer in cris-cross fashion to make the third layer.
- Place the straw bundles with opposite butt ends to make fourth layer.
- Spawn this layer as stated above.

- Place another layer of straw bundles over this and do not apply spawn.
- Pressure the bed to make it as compact as possible and cover it with a transparent polythene sheet.
- Keep the beds undisturbed for for a few days.

Note: Usually the bed will have the necessary humidity, if the straw bundles are properly soaked. If moisture is found to be less, it may be watered using a rose can. On the other hand, if the moisture is found to be excess, polythene cover is to be partly to regulate the moisture. The success of cultivation depends upon the temperature and moisture in the bed. The optimum temperature of 30- 35°C is necessary for developing buttons.

The mushrooms start appearing from all sides in 6-10 days as tiny buttons, which can be harvested in another 4- 5 days. The harvesting is to be done at the button stage itself, since the opened sporocarp will be more fibrous. Usually, 1-2 kg of mushroom can be harvested from 10 kg substrate.

Paddy Straw Twist Method

Instead of bundled straw, twisted paddy straw can also be used for cultivation

Procedure:

- Make the straw into twists of about 5-8 m long and 5-10 cm diameter.
- Immerse the twists in water for 12 hr.
- Take out the straw and drain the excess water.
- Place the place them lengthwise over a platform on a zigzag manner.
- Place a second over this in an opposite direction.(This forms the first layer of the bed)
- Sprinkle the coarsely powdered dhal and place small bits of spawn all along the periphery as above.
- Build another layer as described above and spawn the layer.
- Build up 4-5 layers and spawn as usual.
- Compact the bed by pressing and cover it with a polythene sheet.

OYSTER MUSHROOM - CROPPING, HARVESTING & PACKAGE

The fully spawn run beds should be transferred to cropping room in the thatches shed, where the diffused light and good ventilation are necessary for the button development. There are different methods to handle the spawn run bed to initiate button development.

They are:

- Open bed method, wherein the polythene cover is completely removed and allowed for cropping.
- Closed bed method, wherein the polythene cover is intact and buttons will come out through the holes made on the cover.

- Half cover open method, wherein the one half of the polythene cover is removed for
- cropping and second half after first harvest.
- Stripe method, wherein the polythene cover as longitudinal strips of 5-cm breadth at 4-5 places in the bed.
- Tear method, wherein the polythene cover is teared longitudinally at several places.
- Round opening method, wherein the round shaped openings of 5 cm diameter are made at random.

However, among all the methods of opening of beds, complete removal of the polythene cover is found to give more yields than others. The steps followed in full opening of bed are described below

Procedure:

- Use a new blade and cut the polythene covers and remove fully.
- Allow the bed to dry for a day, as freshly opened beds contain more moisture.
- Spray water on the beds from second day of opening using an atomizer.
- Observe the beds regularly, if any bed showing contamination should be removed.
- Two to three days after opening pinheads of mushroom button develop which will be ready for harvest with in another 4 days
- Harvest the entire bunch of mushroom gently in the early hours of morning.
- Remove the straw bits adheres to the mushroom and cut off the bottom portion of the stalk.
- Pack neatly in a polythene cover @ 200 g per bag and put a few ventilation holes.
- Keep them in an icebox and send to sales unit immediately. (The freshly harvested and packed mushrooms can be kept in a refrigerator, if mushroom to be sold next day)
- After harvest, scrap out the mushroom bed with a new comb to remove dried and rotten buds of mushroom.
- Spray the beds daily, based on the conditions of the beds two to three sprays may be needed.(Second harvest can be done 7-10 days after the first harvest)
- After second harvest, scrap out the outer layers as above and spray water regularly. (Third harvest can be had after a week or ten days).
- Dispose the beds after third harvest as it is uneconomical to keep the beds further.

Precautions to be observed:

- Always maintain the optimum temperature of 23-25° C
- and relative humidity of 80-85% inside the shed.
- Never pour water on the beds, which leads to complete rotting of young developing buds.
- Spray water on the beds only after harvesting the mushroom.
- Always harvest the mushroom in the morning and pack them immediately.

If the closed bed system or other partial opening methods is followed, it is better to wet the sand layer frequently to maintain the temperature and relative humidity.

Milky Mushroom

The cultivation of milky mushroom is usually carried out in transparent polythene covers. The size of the cover should be 60 × 30 cm, with a thickness of 80 gauge.

Procedure:

- Wash hands thoroughly with antiseptic lotion.
- Take the polythene cover and tie the bottom end wit a thread and turn it inwards.
- Mix the dried straw thoroughly to get a uniform moisture level in all areas.
- Take out well-grown bed spawn, squeeze thoroughly and divide into two halves. (Two beds are prepared from the single spawn bag)
- Fill the straw to a height of 3″ in the bottom of polythene bag, take a handful of spawn and sprinkle over the straw layer, concentrating more on the edges.
- Fill the second layer of the straw to a height of 5″ and spawn it as above.
- Repeat this process to get five straw layers with spawns.
- Gently press the bed and tie it tightly with a thread.
- Put 6 ventilation holes randomly for ventilation as well as to remove excess moisture present inside the bed.
- Arrange the beds in side the thatched shed, (Spawn running room) following Rack system of hanging system.

- Maintain the temperature of 22-25°C and relative humidity of 85-90% inside the shed.
- Observe the beds daily for contamination, if any. The contaminated beds should be removed and destroyed.
- Similarly, observe regularly for the infestation of insect pests viz., flies, beetles, mites etc., If noticed, the pesticide like Malathion should be sprayed in side the shed @ 1 ml per litre of water.
- The fully spawn run beds can be shifted to blue coloured tent after casing for initiation of buttons.

Precautions to be observed:

i. Keep the spawn running room dark so that spawn running will be faster.

ii. Periodically place Rat-baiting to kill rats as they are attracted by the spawn.

iii. Periodically sprinkle water on sand layer to maintain the required conditions.

iv. Never spray any insecticides on the mushroom beds.

MILKY MUSHROOM - CASING AND CROPPING

In the case of milky mushroom, an extra process called casing has to be done to induce button formation. After casing operation the beds should be arranged inside the Blue polythene covered pit tent for the growth of the mushroom. The fungus requires an optimum temperature of 30-35° C and relative humidity of 80-85 per cent for the better growth and production of sporocarp. In addition, the fungus needs a light intensity of 2500- 3000-lux for production of buttons, and the cased beds should be kept inside the blue tent.

Casing

Casing nothing but application of thin layer of sterilized soil on the surface of mushroom bed to induce buttons formation. For casing, garden land soil rich in calcium is preferable. Instead of that soil and river sand, mixed in equal proportion can also be used. Sometimes the soil is mixed with Calcium carbonate @ 100g/kg and used as a casing medium. The soil used for casing process should be free of stones and stubble and has to be sterilized before casing. The soil is taken in a mud pot or a vessel and steamed in an autoclave or pressure for 45 minutes. (Soil can also be mixed with a little quantity of water and sterilized for this purpose). The soil is used for casing after cooling.

Procedure:

- Take the fully spawn run bed and cut horizontally into two equal halves.
- Compact the beds as much as possible by pressing firmly with hand.

- Apply casing soil to a height of 1 cm and press it gently.
- Spray the water sufficiently to wet the cased soil.
- Place the beds inside the blue tent.
- Observe the beds daily and spray water, if necessary, to keep the beds wet.
- Watch for any contamination and insect pests. If noticed take necessary steps. (Ten after casing the small pin head buttons develop and with in another 7 days mushrooms are ready for harvest)
- Harvest the mushroom, clean it and pack it in a polythene bag for sales. Stir the top of the bed after first harvest and spray water regularly. (Second harvest can be obtained in another 10 days)
- Disturb the topsoil after second harvest and spray water as regular. (Third harvest can be done after 10 days and for commercial cultivation a maximum of three harvests is recommended).
- The mushroom yield of 350 –400 g can be obtained from 250 g dry weight of the straw, providing all optimum conditions inside the mushroom shed.

Base Spawn/Nucleus Culture

Tissue culture technique is used to bring the edible mushroom to pure culture so that the mushroom fungus can further be used to prepare spawn, which is an essential material for mushroom cultivation. This nucleus culture is grown on Potato Dextrose Agar medium in test tubes. A small tissue from a well-grown mushroom is aseptically transferred to agar medium in a test tube in a culture room. The test tubes are incubated under room temperature for 10 days for full white growth of fungal culture. This is further used for preparation of mother spawn.

Procedure:

1. Select well grown, disease free button mushroom early in the morning and keep it on a clean paper for 2-3 hr, to get certain amount of moisture present in the mushroom to get evaporated.
2. Clean the culture room/ laminar flow chamber with antiseptic solution.
3. Keep the sterilized PDA slants, razor blades, forceps etc. inside the chamber and put on he UV light.
4. After 20 minutes put off the UV light and start working after 5 minutes.
5. Sterilize all the instruments to be used by exposing to Bunsen burner.
6. Take in the mushroom and split open the mushroom longitudinally into two halves.
7. Using a blade cut a small piece of tissue from the centre of the spilt mushroom at the junction of pileus and stipe.

8. Remove the cotton plug of the agar slant and the tissue is aseptically placed inside the slant by using a sterilized forceps and closes it immediately.
9. After transferring tissues from the mushroom, the tube are arranged in a wire basket and kept in a clean room at room temperature for the growth of the fungus
10. Observe the tube at periodical intervals and remove the contaminated ones. The tubes will be ready for further use within another ten days. The base spawn is used for preparation of mother spawns.

Precautions to be observed:

- Wash the hands with antiseptic lotion before start working inside the chamber. If possible, it is better to use hand gloves while operation.
- It is better that the maximum of two persons may work inside the room at a time. Avoid unnecessary talking while working inside the room.
- While separating the tissue from the centre of the mushroom it should not touch the bottom or sides of the mushroom.

Mother Spawn

Mother spawn is nothing but the mushroom fungus grown on a grain based medium. Among the several substrate materials tested by TNAU, Coimbatore, sorghum grains are the best substrate for excellent growth of the fungus. Well-filled, disease- free sorghum grains are used as substrate for growing the spawn materials. The various steps involving in preparation of mother spawn are listed below here under.

Procedure:

1. Wash the sorghum grains in water thoroughly to remove chaffy and damaged grains.
2. Cook the grains in an autoclave/ vessel for 30 minutes just to soften them.
3. Take out the cooked grains and spread evenly over a Hessian cloth on a platform to remove the excess water.
4. Mix Calcium carbonate (CaCO3) thoroughly with the cooked, dried grains @ 20g/kg.
5. Fill the grains in polypropylene bags up to ¾ th height (approximately 300-330 g/bag), insert a PVC ring, bold the edges of the bag down and plug the mouth tightly with non-absorbent cotton wool.
6. Cover the cotton plug with a piece of waste paper and tie tightly around the neck with a jute thread.

7. Arrange the bags inside an autoclave and sterilize under 20 lbs. pressure for 2 hours.
8. Take out the bags after cooling and keep them inside the culture room and put on the UV light.
9. After 20 minutes put off the UV light and start working in the culture room. Cut the fungal culture into two equal halves using a inoculation needle and transfer one half portion to a bag. Similarly, transfer another half portion of the culture to an another bag.
10. Incubate the inoculated bags in a clean room under room temperature for 10 days for further use to prepare bed spawn.

Bed Spawn

The method of preparation of bed spawn was same as that of mother spawn. The cooking, filling and sterilization were similar to that of mother spawn. After sterilization, the bags are taken for inoculation.

Precautions to be observed:

- Avoid over cooking of sorghum grains on the floor. Always dry over hessian cloth spread on a raised platform.
- Don't dry the cooked grains on the floor. Always dry over hessian cloth spread on a raised platform
- Use only recommended dose of CaCo3 for mixing with the cooked grains. Mixing over dose reduces the fungal growth in the inoculated bags.
- Avoid further sub culturing of the second-generation bed spawns. This leads to lose of virulence of the spawn lead to reduced yield and repeated sub culturing lead to complete lose of virulence wherein the fungal growth may be noted in the beds but no buttoning is completely arrested.

Procedure:

1. The sterilized bags are placed inside the culture room and put on the UV light.
2. After 20 minutes put off the UV light and take in the well-grown mother spawn.
3. Transfer spawn from the mother spawn to sterilized bags @ 10 g per bag.
4. After inoculation the spawn bags are kept in a clean room for fungal growth. (This is first generation of bed spawn).
5. Use the bed spawn after 10 days of inoculation for bed preparation.
6. Sub culture the first generation bed spawn as mother spawn to produce one more generation, which is second generation bed spawn.

Compost Preparation

The substrate for cultivation is specially prepared compost. The mushroom houses should have the facilities for temperature control and pasteurization. Buildings are constructed of wood or hollow cement bricks or double walls. The shed is partitioned into small compartments and provided with trays. Environmental conditions like temperature, relative humidity and ventilation are controlled inside the shed by installing suitable equipment.

Compost is the substrate in which the mushroom mycelium grows and on which it produces fruiting bodies. It is the product of a fermentation process brought out by a number of mesophilic and thermophilic microorganisms that decompose plant residues and other organic and inorganic matters. The quality of compost influences the yield of mushroom. Compost prepared out of horse manure and wheat straw is ideal one. Since these materials are not easily available, many substitutes are suggested and are in use. There are two methods of composting, Long method and short method.

The distinction is based on the time taken for composting and the long method needs three to four weeks, while the short method requires only 12-15 days, since the composting process is hastened by pasteurization. In the long method of composting, pasteurization is avoided, which will make the compost poor in quality and often gives variable yields.

BUTTON MUSHROOM – SPAWNING

Tray System of Cultivation

The compost when ready, is taken in trays leaving about 5 cm from the top.

There are different methods of spawning and are indicated below:

1. *Single layer spawning*: The grain spawn is scattered uniformly all over the compost surface in a tray which is then covered with a thin layer of compost 200 g of spawn for 1 m^2 beds.
2. *Double layer spawning*: The trays are half filled and spawn is scattered. Then the tray is filled completely compost and spawn is applied as above and covered with a thin layer of spawn.
3. *Through spawning/mixed spawning*: The required quantity of spawn is mixed with the compost and filled in trays or polybags
4. *Spot spawning*: The compost is filled in trays and holes of 2.5 to 5 cm deep are made with fingers about 8-12 cm apart in rows. About 5g of spawn if introduced into the cavities and covered with a thin layer of compost.

After spawning the beds should be covered with sterilized newspapers and water is sprinkled over the papers to maintain the moisture in the compost. The temperature should be around 25± 2° C with RH of 90 per cent. The spawn running will be completed in 15 days and it is ready for casing.

Bag System of Cultivation

In this method polythene covers of size: 35″×24″ with 150 gauge thickness are used. The spawn is mixed with the compost @ 500- 750g/ 100kg compost. Then mixed compost is filled in polythene bags @ 15-20kg/bag. Finally, the beds are covered with newspaper.

BUTTON MUSHROOM- CASING AND CROPPING

Casing is nothing but application of a thin layer of soil so as to induces buttoning. There are different materials are used for casing and some of the commonly used ones are given below:

Casing materials:

S.NO	Substrates	Ratio
1	Spent compost, Sand, Lime	4:1:1
2	Spent compost, FYM, Clay loam	2: 1:1
3	FYM, Clay Loam soils	1:1
4	Loam soil sand	1:1

Casing soil should have 80% water holding capacity, with a pH of 6-7-8.2(Best:7.7). In addition it should have high porosity to get good aerobic condition.

- *Treatment of casing materials*: The casing materials are to be sterilized before application. Chemical treatment and Pasteurization are the two important methods followed.
- *Chemical treatment*: Prepare formalin 2% solution by mixing 2 lit in 40 lit of water. Heap the case material and drench formalin @ 10 lit/ m^3 and cover it with polythene sheets for 3 days. After 3 days disturb the casing soil to remove excess formaldehyde and used for casing. It has to be done 15 days before casing.
- *Pasteurization*: Fill the casing soil in trays and steam at 65-70° C for 4 hours.

Procedure

Procedure for casing:

1. Remove newspaper and apply casing soil to a thickness of 3-4 cm and gently press it.
2. Keep the temperature around 24 and relative humidity of 100 for one week.
3. Reduce the temperature to 15-18 and relative humidity to 85-90 after one week.

(Pinheads appear 12-15 days after casing and cropping continues for 6-8 weeks. Mushroom ready for harvest in another 10 days and appear at weekly intervals.) Normally 4 kg of mushroom can be harvested from 20 kg compost in Polybag method. In the case of tray system, the yield varies from 6-8 kg/ Sq. m.

Mushroom can be harvested by gently twisting the fully-grown mushroom to avoid disturbance to young buttons. The following are the different stages of mushroom and the button stage is the correct stage of harvest and stages yield poor quality mushroom.

Stages of harvest:

Stages	Description
Buttons	Mushroom with closed membrane. Size- diameter of button will be 3-6 cm with a stem length of 2 cm.
Cups	Fully opened mushroom, which is "T", shaped with a stalk. The cap diameter may be 6-7 cm with a stalk length of 2.5 to 3 cm.
Opens/Flats	The harvested mushrooms are cleaned to remove dirt and soil particles adhering and packed in polythene bags and send for sales.

MUSHROOM POISONING

Mushroom possessing toxins that are harmful to living beings are called as poisonous mushrooms. Number of poisonous mushrooms is reported all over, in which few species are deadly poisonous. Identification of entire poisonous mushrooms is so difficult but it is most essential to know about the common features of poisonous mushrooms in general.

Few common attributes of poisonous mushroom are listed below:

i. Presence of warts and scales on pileus or cap
ii. Umbrella or parasol shaped cap
iii. Presence of bulbous or round ball at the base of stipe
iv. Attractive and brilliant coloured mushrooms
v. Presence of annulus or ring around stem
vi. Gill is thin and white
vii. Small sized, brown coloured mushrooms

The above features are general in nature. Many poisonous mushrooms resembles like edible mushrooms and vice versa. Hence don't eat mushrooms without knowing their details. Better identify through standard procedures or through recognized resource personals before eating wild mushrooms.

Classification of Poisonous Mushrooms

Based on toxin presence, poisonous mushrooms are classified as follows:

- *Amatoxin mushrooms*: Amanita ocreata, Conocybe filaris, Lepiota josserandii
- *Psilocybin mushrooms*: Psilocybe cyanescens, Paneolus cyanescens

- *Cylopeptid mushrooms*: Amanita phalloides, Amanita verna
- *Orellanine mushrooms*: Cortinarius orellanus, Cortinarius rubellus
- *Muscimol mushrooms*: Amanita gemmata, Amanita pantherina
- *Mushrooms*: Gyromitra esculenta
- Muscarine histamine mushrooms: Boletus luridus, Omphalotus olivascens, Inocybe fastigata
- *Coprine mushrooms*: Coprinus variegatus, Coprinus atramentarius
- *Gyromitrin mushrooms*: Gyromitra esculenta, Gyromitra infula

Folklore about Poisonous Mushrooms

Local people identify poisonous mushrooms by adopting certain keys or criteria of their own. These local keys and criteria are applicable to their own geographical regions alone. Hence these local keys and criteria are non reliable in general.

Few Myths are Given Below

- Poisonous mushroom exudes latex. Not so. Few latex exuding mushrooms are edible in nature.?
- Poisonous mushrooms are colourful and attractive. This is false as certain white coloured mushrooms are also poisonous.?
- Silver spoon turns yellow when cooking with poisonous mushroom. Few poisonous Amanita species do not change spoon colour.?
- Poisonous mushroom emits strong odour. Not true, certain poisonous mushrooms are less odorous.?
- Wild animals do not eat poisonous mushroom (False). Certain poisonous mushroom are very good food for certain animals, snails and insects.?

Mushroom Poisoning

Mushroom poisoning refers to the toxic condition caused by eating certain mushrooms due to the poisonous compound present in it. The toxic condition may be from mild pain or discomfort to death in human beings. These toxins are the secondary metabolites produced in mushrooms through specific metabolic pathways. The poisoning effect of mushrooms depends upon the type of toxin, quantum of ingestion, size and age of the consumer, presence of alcohol in human, mode of cooking and other factors.

Cause

The main cause of mushroom poisoning is eating poisonous mushroom by misidentification. It is also attributed to intentional ingestion of certain mushrooms for their hallucinogenic effects. Consumption of certain mushrooms with alcohol or specific drugs also leads to poisoning. In few cases, consumption of raw mushroom causes poisoning whereas cooked mushroom are non toxic as the water soluble toxins are removed while boiling and the mushroom become non toxic. Hence, better not to eat raw mushroom. In some cases, individual selectivity of particular mushroom causes allergy or some health mushrooms.

Symptoms

Toxins from different wild poisonous mushrooms vary in their toxicity. Symptom of mushroom poisoning varies according to the mushroom toxin. Toxicity may be simple allergy to causing death. First symptom expression is usually few hours after mushroom consumption to few days depending upon the toxin present in mushroom, quantum of mushroom consumed and human body nature. The most common symptom is gastrointestinal upset and irritation. These cause consequent vomiting and diarrhea under mild toxicity conditions. Under severe cases, mushroom toxins affect the specific human parts and cause its failures. This further leads to mortality.

Mushroom Toxins and Associated Symptoms

Mushroom Species	Toxin	Symptoms
Amanita ocreata, Conocybe filaris, Lepiota josserandii	Alpha amanitin	Gastrointestinal upset after 6 hours of eating i.e., vomiting and profuse, watery diarrhea. Damage to liver begins after 24 hours of ingestion.
Amanita phalloides	Phallotoxin	Gastrointestinal upset such as vomiting and diarrhea normally leads to death
Cortinarius orellanus	Orellanine	After 20 days of ingestion, symptoms such as pain in kidney area, thirst, vomiting and headache occurs
Boletus luridus, Omphalotus olivasceus, Inocybe fastigiata	Muscarine	Sweating, salivation, tears, blurred vision, palpitations and respiratory failure.
Gyromitra esculenta, Gyromitra infula	Gyromitrin	It blocks neurotransmitter leading to muscle cramps, loss of coordination, tremors, seizures and gastrointestinal upset such as vomiting and diarrhea. It also causes red blood cells to break down, leading to jaundice, kidney failure, and signs of anemia.
Coprinus variegate, Coprinus atramentarius	Coprine	It inhibits aldehyde dehydrogenase, which generally causes no harm. If alcohol is ingested, it prevents removal of alcohol in body leading to flushed skin, vomiting, headache, dizziness, weakness, apprehension, confusion, palpitations, and sometimes trouble breathing.

Amanita muscaria, Amanita pantherina	Ibotenic acid	Nausea, vomiting, confusion, euphoria, or sleepiness is possible. Loss of muscular coordination, sweating, and chills are likely.
Amanita gemmata, Amanita pantherina, Amanita muscaria	Muscimol	It alters neuronal activity and displays sedative, hypnotic and dissociative psychoactive effects including dissociation, synesthesia, auditory and visual distortions.
Psilocybe cyanescens, Paneolus cyanscens	Psilocybin	Euphoria, visual and religious hallucinations, and heightened perception.
Amanita pantherina, Hygrophoropsis aurantica	Arabitol	Gastrointestinal irritation
Boletus satanas	Bolesatine	It is a protein synthesis inhibitor and main symptoms include violent vomiting, which can last up to six hours

Treatments

It is necessary to take the concerned person immediately to nearby hospital if mushroom poisoning is suspected. If the consumption time is less than a hour, induce vomiting so as to remove the poisonous mushroom from stomach. Information on time of ingestion, time of first symptom noticed is to be noted and be given to the doctor towards better treatment along with mushroom information. Information on alcohol drinking also essential if the person is recently drunk.

The treatment for mushroom poisoning is not well known all over world. Initial treatment consists of gastric lavage in order to remove the toxins before they get absorbed in to body system (Anita Gautam et al., 2011). Benzyl penicillin is used as an anti-toxin based on the assumption that it decreases the uptake of toxin in to hepatocyte (Moroni et al., 1976). The toxin alpha-amanitin is excreted by the kidneys and are reabsorbed in the renal tubules, therefore forced dieresis may be useful (Vesconi et al., 1985). Antioxidant silymarin has also been used in the treatment of mushroom poisoning (Enjalbert et al., 1999).

Precautions:

- Avoid eating of unknown wild mushrooms
- Do not eat unknown raw mushroom directly
- Eat small amount of mushroom if you are eating unknown mushroom for the first time
- Avoid new mushroom dishes for elderly and diseased people besides children

- Use only firm, healthy, insect free mushrooms for culinary purposes
- Keep a small part of wild mushroom whose identification may help in identifying type of poisoning

MAJOR DISEASES OF MUSHROOM

FUNGAL DISEASES

Dry Bubble

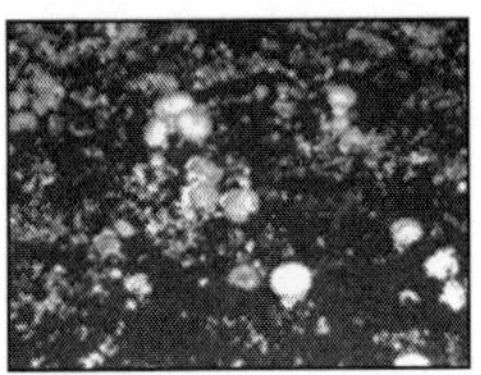

- Verticillium fungicola
- Muddy brown, often sunken spots on the cap of the mushrooms
- Greyishwhite moldy growth seen on pileus
- Later stage mushroom becomes dry and leathery
- Initially infected one are not develop or remain small
- Main source of infection
- Debris
- Dust on floors of growing house
- Spread
- Water splashes on healthy mushroom
- Sciarid and phorid flies over long distance
- Favorable temperature 28o c
- Poor ventilation
- High humidity

Management of Dry Bubble

- Pick and destroy infected mushroom to prevent spread
- Sanitary conditions in growth house
- Lower the temperature to 14oc when disease noticed
- Use clean equipment
- Control flies and mites
- Bubble can destroy with salt

Management by using Salt

- Use of clean pasteurized casing media
- Properly maintained air filtering system.

- Water early infection centers with formaldehyde
- For protective measure use zineb
- Apply chlorothalonil at casing or mix into casing material

Dry bubble in Oyster

False Truffle

- Diehliomyces microsporus
- Competitor than a pathogen
- Appears as cottony weft of mycelium on bed surface
- Wefts turn to dense small reddish brown,wrinkled,stromatic bodies resemble a truffle
- Infected bed have peculiar disagreeable odour
- Reduced yield at mycelia exist
- Introduced through soil

Management

- Good sanitation
- Proper Pasteurization of casing material
- Low temperature during spawn run

Wet Bubble

Mycogone perniciosa:

- Malformed mushrooms with swollen stipes
- Reduced or deformed caps
- Undifferentiated tissue becomes necrotic and a wet, soft rot emit bad odor
- An amber liquid appears on infected mushrooms.
- Mushrooms become brown in color
- Bubbles may be as large as a grapefruit.
- The fungus is spread via airborne dust and contaminated casing.
- It is also a parasite of wild mushrooms.
- It produces two spore types,

- One which is small and water-dispersed like Verticillium,
- Second which is a large resting spore capable of persisting for a long time in the environment

Control:

- Sanitation in growth house
- Clean environment around cultivation area
- Incorporating benzimidazoles in the casing.
- Benomyl at the rate of 0.95 g/m2,
- Carbendazim and thiabendazole at the rate of 0.62 g/m2

Cobweb:

- Cladobotryum dendroides
- White silky growth grows over surface of casing soil
- It climb up and cover mushrooms comes in it's path

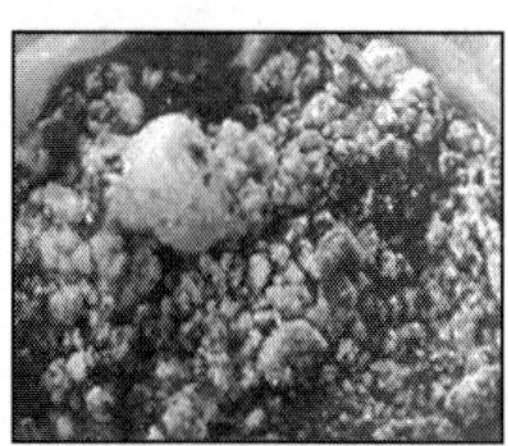

Older mycelium changes from silky to granular white:

- Infected mushroom become soft
- Later engulfed by cottony ball of mycelia
- Serious problem where year around growing is practiced
- Cobweb mold is darker than mycelium... almost grey as compared to white.
- Main source of infection is casing soil
- A cottony mycelium grows over casing
- the mycelium soon envelopes the mushroom with a soft mildewy mycelium and causes a soft rot.
- It is also a parasite of wild mushrooms.
- Cobweb mold is favored by high humidity.

Management of Cobweb:

- Identify disease symptoms early, not only the web but also cap spotting.
- Treat spotty infections with a alcohol drenched paper towel
- Cover infected areas with salt
- Change from light peats to heavy peat casing may encourage disease development, but heavy black peats are not responsible for initial infections.

- Heavier casing may require increased water applications, therefore may encourage the spread and development the disease.
- Heavily infected 2nd or early 3rd breaks should be steamed off to reduce the spore load on the farm.
- Control strategies include lowering humidity and/or increasing air circulation
- Increase hygiene of the harvesting and watering department.
- Judicious applications of Benzimidazole fungicides should be made
- Chlorothalonil should be included in the fungicide application program

Table. Common Chemicals used to Control Diseases in Mushroom

Fungicide	Against Pathogen	Doze
Benomyl and Carbendazim	Dactylium, Mycogone, Trichoderma, Verticillium	Mix 240 g/100m2 With casing or in water @ 240g/200 l/100m2
Chlorothalonil	Mycogone, Verticillium	200 ml/200 l/100m2 1st spary 1 week after casing & 2nd after 2 week
Prochloroz manganese	Dactylium, Mycogone,	300g/ 100 l/ 100 m2 for single spary Or 113 g/100 l/100 m2 if 2 spray
	Verticillium	Mix 240 g/100m2
Thiabendazole	Dactylium, Mycogone, Verticillium	With casing or in water @ 240g/200 l/100m2
Zineb	Dactylium, Mycogone, Verticillium	350 g/ 100m2, (dust) every week after casing. 1 kg/1000 l @ of 5 l/10m2 after casing & between flushes

BACTERIAL DISEASES

Bacterial Spot/Pit/Brown Blotch

- Pseudomonas tolaasii.
- Pale yellow spots on the surface of the piles later it turns to yellow
- In Sevier case mushrooms are radially streaked
- Damage at storage and transit

- Source of contamination may be soil or water
- High humidity and watery conditions are favorable for disease
- Vector: Tryoglyphid mite
- Lesions on tissue that are pale yellow initially, later become a golden yellow or rich chocolate brown.
- Discoloration is superficial (not more than 2 to 3 mm)
- Underlying tissue may appear to be water soaked and grey.
- Blotches appear in early button stage,
- Appear on any age - even on harvested refrigerated mushrooms
- At favorable moisture conditions spots enlarge and coalesce, sometimes covering entire cap
- Mushroom stems can also be blemished similarly
- Typical spotting is observed at or near the edge of mushroom caps wherever caps remain wet for a period of 4 to 6 hours or longer after water has been applied
- If very dry conditions occur after blotch has developed, infected caps may crack radially as the mushroom expands

- Casing and air-borne dust are primary source.
- The bacterial pathogen is probably present in most casing material, even after pasteurization.
- Occurrence of disease associated with the size of the bacterial population on the mushroom cap, rather than on the population in the casing, which explains why a prolonged wet period on the cap precedes disease occurrence.
- Spread by splash, tools, flies and nematodes.
- Moisture content of less than 62 percent at spawning preconditions mushrooms to blotch infection.

Management

- Sanitation
- Lowering humidity

- Watering with a 150 ppm chlorine solution (calcium hypochlorite products are used since sodium hypochlorite products may burn caps).
- If the mushroom stays wet, however, chlorine has little effect since the bacterial population reproduces at a rate that neutralizes the effect of the oxidizing agent.

Mummy Disease

- Pseudomonas spp.
- The disease was first described in 1942 by CM Tucker and JB Routien in the United States
- Fruit bodies have tilted caps,
- Early veil breaking,
- Base of the stem enlarged
- Curved stalk
- Tissue of the mushroom becomes
- Spongy,
- Dry and
- Brown
- Mummified appearance.
- Rapid rate of spread through the bed, up to 30cm (12 inches) daily.
- Infected mushroom is tough and dry texture
- Gritty texture appeared when cut.
- Water-soaked appearance and cavities in the mushroom tissue

Management

- Dig a trench to separate the diseased area from the healthy.
- Dug around 2m (6-8ft) ahead of the advancing disease and the trench itself to be several inches wide.
- All compost and casing has to be removed from the trench
- Gap thoroughly disinfected.
- If crop is growing in separate containers, the usual advice is to isolate or dispose of them.
- Good hygiene is strongly recommended.

VIRAL DISEASE

- Virus (several)
- Double-stranded RNA
- Reduced cropping,

- Bare patches on the beds,
- Long-bent stalks with small caps,
- Premature opening of mushrooms,
- Stalks tapering towards the base of stalk,
- Dying pinheads
- Infected mycelium grows slowly in the beds and fruiting bodies are not produced.
- Infection of the crop at spawning lead to a higher level of disease

Spread and Source of Infection of Virus

- Infected mushroom spores
- Mycelium from previous crops also survive in the trays
- Mushroom sheds can also release infected spores
- Dust from around the farm may introduce infected spores
- Only 10 infected spores are required for a disease outbreak.
- Farm hygiene
- Maintain 60oC temperature throughout the compost
- Filter air and seal rooms properly to prevent spores from entering during cool down phase of compost.
- Clean equipments
- Ensure workers have clean-spare clothes
- Ensure absolute filters are fitted to spawn-run buildings
- Clean trays to prevent infection from old-infected mycelia

Green Moulds

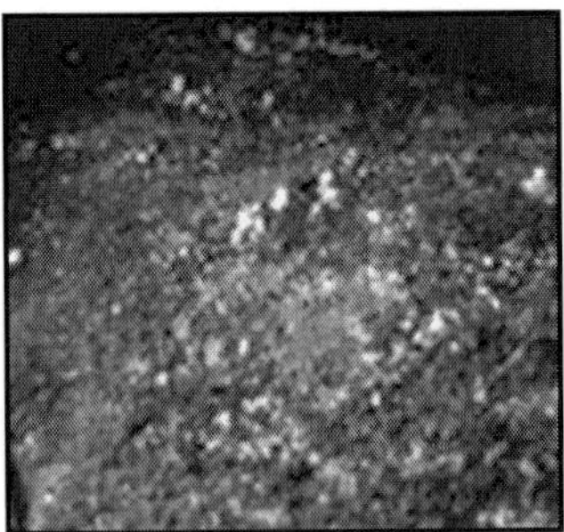

- Trichoderma koningii
- T.viride
- T.aggressivum f.sp.aggressivum
- Dark green mould patches on casing spreading to lesions on stems.

Control of green mould:

- Sanitation and hygiene programme, especially targeting post crop

- Cover spots with sodium hypochlorite solution, salt, lime or gypsum and lime mix.
- Good insect and mite control
- Personnel movement patterns further reduce the spread of the disease.
- chlorothalonil at casing or mix into casing material 254 mL formulation per 100 m2 of production
- Chlorothalonil is not effective against an established infection but lowering the infection

Cinnamon Mould:

- Chromelosporium fulva (Peziza ostrachoderma)
- The color of this mold ranges from yellow gold to golden brown to cinnamon brown.
- It grows rapidly in circular patches.
- It is very common in soil, and flourishes on damp wood.
- Areas in compost overheated during spawn run may be colonized.
- Improperly conditioned compost will also support growth,
- It often occurs on sterilized soil.
- Sexual fruiting bodies may appear several weeks after the first appearance of the mold.
- Spores are airborne

Pink Mold:

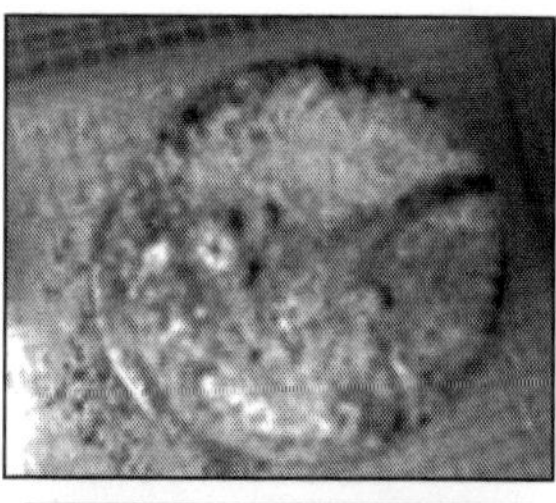

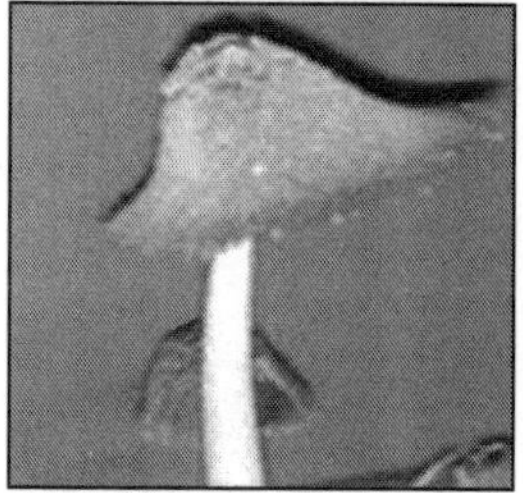

- Neurospora spp.
- Commonly to occasionally seen on agar and grain.
- It is ubiquitous in nature, occurring on dung, in soils and on decaying plant matter.

- Neurospora spores germinate more readily at elevated temperatures.
- The pink mold seen in mushroom culture is most frequently Neurospora sitophila, a pernicious contaminant that is difficult to eliminate.
- All infected cultures should be removed as soon as possible from the laboratory and destroyed.
- A thorough cleaning of the laboratory is absolutely necessary.
- If contamination persists, remove all spawn and start anew

Inky Cap:

- Coprinus spp.
- These are evidence of free ammonia in the compost.
- Their delicate gray caps autodigest quickly.
- Inky caps are indicators of nitrogen over supplementation or a poorly managed Phase II compost.
- If there is too much residual ammonia, Phase II thermophilic microflora may be unable to convert all the ammonia into microbial protein.
- fungus is strongly cellulolytic.

IDENTIFICATION OF MUSHROOMS

Identifying mushrooms requires a basic understanding of their macroscopic structure. Most are Basidiomycetes and gilled. Their spores, called basidiospores, are produced on the gills and fall in a fine rain of powder from under the caps as a result. At the microscopic level the basidiospores are shot offbasidia and then fall between the gills in the dead air space. As a result, for most mushrooms, if the cap is cut off and placed gill-side-down overnight, a powdery impression reflecting the shape of the gills (or pores, or spines, etc.) is formed (when the fruit body is sporulating). The color of the powdery print, called a spore print, is used to help classify mushrooms and can help to identify them. Spore print colors include white (most common), brown, black, purple-brown, pink, yellow, and creamy, but almost never blue, green, or red.

While modern identification of mushrooms is quickly becoming molecular, the standard methods for identification are still used by most and have developed into a fine art harking back to medieval times and the Victorian era, combined with microscopic examination. The presence of juices upon breaking, bruising reactions, odors, tastes, shades of color, habitat, habit, and season are all considered by both amateur and professional mycologists. Tasting and smelling mushrooms carries its own hazards because of poisons and allergens. Chemical tests are also used for some genera.

In general, identification to genus can often be accomplished in the field using a local mushroom guide. Identification to species, however, requires more effort; one must remember that a mushroom develops from a button stage into a mature structure, and only the latter can provide certain characteristics needed for the identification of the species. However, over-mature specimens lose features and cease producing spores. Many novices have mistaken humid water marks on paper for white spore prints, or discoloured paper from oozing liquids on lamella edges for coloured spored prints.

CLASSIFICATION

Fig. Trametes versicolor, a polyporemushroom

Typical mushrooms are the fruit bodies of members of the order Agaricales, whose type genus is Agaricusand type species is the field mushroom, Agaricus campestris. However, in modern molecularly defined classifications, not all members of the order Agaricales produce mushroom fruit bodies, and many other gilled fungi, collectively called mushrooms, occur in other orders of the class Agaricomycetes. For example, chanterelles are in the Cantharellales, false chanterelles such as Gomphus are in the Gomphales, milk mushrooms (Lactarius) and russulas (Russula), as well as Lentinellus, are in the Russulales, while the tough, leathery genera Lentinus and Panus are among the Polyporales, but Neolentinus is in the Gloeophyllales, and the little pin-mushroom genus, Rickenella, along with similar genera, are in the Hymenochaetales.

Within the main body of mushrooms, in the Agaricales, are common fungi like the common fairy-ring mushroom (Marasmius oreades), shiitake, enoki, oyster mushrooms, fly agarics, and other amanitas, magic mushrooms like species of Psilocybe, paddy straw mushrooms, shaggy manes, etc.

An atypical mushroom is the lobster mushroom, which is a deformed, cooked-lobster-coloured parasitized fruitbody of a Russula or Lactarius, coloured and deformed by the mycoparasitic Ascomycete Hypomyces lactifluorum. Other mushrooms are not gilled, so the term "mushroom" is loosely used, and giving a full account of their classifications is difficult. Some have pores underneath (and are usually called boletes), others have spines, such as the hedgehog mushroom and other tooth fungi, and so on. "Mushroom" has been used for polypores, puffballs, jelly fungi, coral fungi, bracket fungi, stinkhorns, and cup fungi. Thus, the term is more one of common application tomacroscopic fungal fruiting bodies than one having precise taxonomic meaning. Approximately 14,000 species of mushrooms are described.

ETYMOLOGY

The terms "mushroom" and "toadstool" go back centuries and were never precisely defined, nor was there consensus on application. The term "toadstool" was often, but not exclusively, applied to poisonous mushrooms or to those that have the classic umbrella-like cap-and-stem form. Between 1400 and 1600 AD, the terms tadstoles, frogstooles, frogge stoles, tadstooles, tode stoles, toodys hatte, paddockstool, puddockstool, paddocstol, toadstoole, and paddockstooles sometimes were used synonymously withmushrom, mushrum, muscheron, mousheroms, mussheron, or musserouns.

The word has apparent analogies in Dutch padde(n)stoel (toad-stool/chair, mushroom) and GermanKrötenschwamm (toad-fungus, alt. word for panther cap). Others have proposed a connection with GermanTodesstuhl (death's chair). Since Tod is a direct cognate to "death", in that case it would be a German borrowing. However, no common word akin to Todesstuhl is used in German referring to mushrooms, poisonous or not.

In German folklore and old fairy tales, toads are often depicted sitting on toadstool mushrooms and catching, with their tongues, the flies that are said to be drawn to the Fliegenpilz, a German name for the toadstool, meaning "flies' mushroom". This is how the mushroom got another of its names, Krötenstuhl (a less-used German name for the mushroom), literally translating to "toad-stool".

The term "mushroom" and its variations may have been derived from the French word mousseron in reference to moss (mousse). The toadstool's connection to toads may be direct, in reference to some species of poisonous toad, or may just be a case of phonosemantic matching from the German word.However, delineation between edible and poisonous fungi is not clear-cut, so a "mushroom" may be edible, poisonous, or unpalatable.

The term "toadstool" is nowadays used in storytelling when referring to poisonous or suspect mushrooms. The classic example of a toadstool is Amanita muscaria.

Cultural or social phobias of mushrooms and fungi may be related. The term "fungophobia" was coined by William Delisle Hay of England, who noted a national superstition or fear of "toadstools". He described the "fungus-hunter" as being contemptible and detailed the larger demographic's attitude toward mushrooms as "abnormal, worthless, or inexplicable".Fungophobia spread to the United States and Australia, where it was inherited from England. The underlying cause of a cultural fungaphobia may also be related to the exaggerated importance placed on the few deadly and poisonous mushrooms found in the region of that culture. In these regions, mushrooms were also sometimes regarded as magic or satanic, their fruiting bodies appearing quickly overnight from underground. Some believed they were the Devil's fruit, and others that mushroom rings were magical portals.

MORPHOLOGY

Fig. Amanita jacksonii buttons emerging from their universal veils

Fig. An image of the gills of Lactarius indigo.

A mushroom develops from a nodule, or pinhead, less than two millimeters in diameter, called a primordium, which is typically found on or near the surface of the substrate. It is formed within the mycelium, the mass of threadlike hyphae that make up the fungus. The primordium enlarges into a roundish structure of interwoven hyphae roughly resembling an egg, called a "button".

The button has a cottony roll of mycelium, the universal veil, that surrounds the developing fruit body. As the egg expands, the universal veil ruptures and may remain as a cup, or volva, at the base of the stalk, or as warts or volval patches on the cap. Many mushrooms lack a universal veil, therefore they do not have either a volva or volval patches. Often, a second layer of tissue, thepartial veil, covers the bladelike gills that bear spores. As the cap expands, the veil breaks, and remnants of the partial veil may remain as a ring, or annulus, around the middle of the stalk or as fragments hanging from the margin of the cap. The ring may be skirt-like as in some species of Amanita, collar-like as in many species of Lepiota, or merely the faint remnants of a cortina (a partial veil composed of filaments resembling a spiderweb), which is typical of the genus Cortinarius. Mushrooms lacking partial veils do not form an annulus.

The stalk (also called the stipe, or stem) may be central and support the cap in the middle, or it may be off-center and/or lateral, as in species of Pleurotus and Panus. In other mushrooms, a stalk may be absent, as in the polypores that form shelf-like brackets. Puffballs lack a stalk, but may have a supporting base. Other mushrooms, such as truffles, jellies, earthstars, and bird's nests, usually do not have stalks, and a specialized mycological vocabulary exists to describe their parts.

The way the gill's attach to the top of the stalk is an important feature of mushroom morphology. Mushrooms in the genera Agaricus, Amanita, Lepiota and Pluteus, among others, have free gills that do not extend to the top of the stalk. Others have decurrent gills that extend down the stalk, as in the genera Omphalotus andPleurotus.

There are a great number of variations between the extremes of free and decurrent, collectively called attached gills. Finer distinctions are often made to distinguish the types of attached gills: adnate gills, which adjoin squarely to the stalk; notched gills, which are notched where they join the top of the stalk; adnexed gills, which curve upward to meet the stalk, and so on. These distinctions between attached gills are sometimes difficult to interpret, since gill attachment may change as the mushroom matures, or with different environmental conditions.

Microscopic features

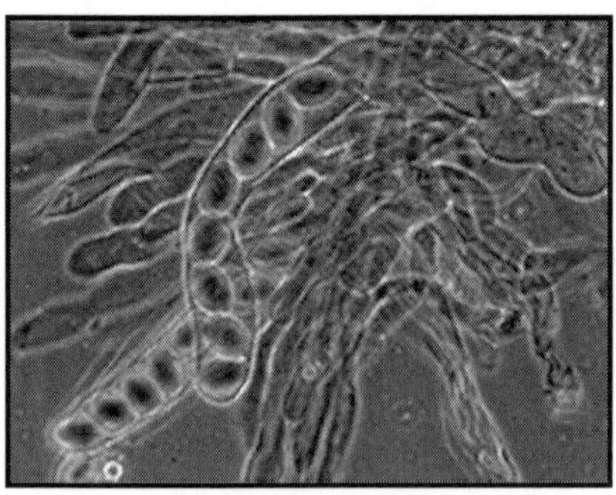

Fig. Morchella elata asci viewed with phase contrast microscopy

A hymenium is a layer of microscopic spore-bearing cells that covers the surface of gills. In the nongilled mushrooms, the hymenium lines the inner surfaces of the tubes of boletes and polypores, or covers the teeth of spine fungi and the branches of corals. In the Ascomycota, spores develop within microscopic elongated, sac-like cells called asci, which typically contain eight spores in each ascus. The Discomycetes, which contain the cup, sponge, brain, and some club-like fungi, develop an exposed layer of asci, as on the inner surfaces of cup fungi or within the pits of morels. The Pyrenomycetes, tiny dark-colored fungi that live on a wide range of substrates including soil, dung, leaf litter, and decaying wood, as well as other fungi, produce minute, flask-shaped structures called perithecia, within which the asci develop.

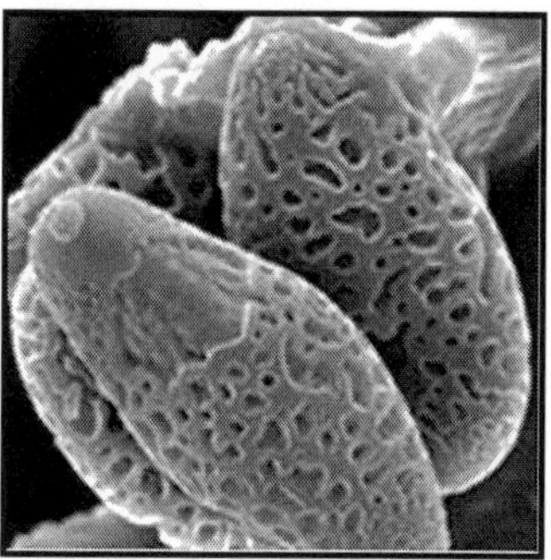

Fig. Austroboletus mutabilisspores viewed using electron microscopy

In the Basidiomycetes, usually four spores develop on the tips of thin projections called sterigmata, which extend from club-shaped cells called a basidia. The fertile portion of the Gasteromycetes, called a gleba, may become powdery as in the puffballs or slimy as in the stinkhorns. Interspersed among the asci are threadlike sterile cells called paraphyses. Similar structures called cystidia often occur within the hymenium of the Basidiomycota. Many types of cystidia exist, and assessing their presence, shape, and size is often used to verify the identification of a mushroom.

The most important microscopic feature for identification of mushrooms is the spores. Their color, shape, size, attachment, ornamentation, and reaction to chemical tests often can be the crux of an identification. A spore often has a protrusion at one end, called an apiculus, which is the point of attachment to the basidium, termed the apical germ pore, from which the hypha emerges when the spore germinates.

GROWTH

Many species of mushrooms seemingly appear overnight, growing or expanding rapidly. This phenomenon is the source of several common expressions in the English language including "to mushroom" or "mushrooming" (expanding rapidly in size or scope) and "to pop up like a mushroom" (to appear unexpectedly and quickly). In reality all species of mushrooms take several days to form primordial mushroom fruit bodies, though they do expand rapidly by the absorption of fluids.

Fig. Mushroom emerging through asphalt concrete in summer near Paris

The cultivated mushroom as well as the common field mushroom initially form a minute fruiting body, referred to as the pin stage because of their small size. Slightly expanded they are called buttons, once again because of the relative size and shape. Once such stages are formed, the mushroom can rapidly pull in water from its mycelium and expand, mainly by inflating preformed cells that took several days to form in theprimordia.

Similarly, there are even more ephemeral mushrooms, like Parasola plicatilis (formerly Coprinus plicatlis), that literally appear overnight and may disappear by late afternoon on a hot day after rainfall. The primordia form at ground level in lawns in humid spaces under the thatch and after heavy rainfall or in dewy conditions balloon to full size in a few hours, release spores, and then collapse. They "mushroom" to full size.

Not all mushrooms expand overnight; some grow very slowly and add tissue to their fruitbodies by growing from the edges of the colony or by insertinghyphae. For example Pleurotus nebrodensis grows slowly, and because of this combined with human collection, it is now critically endangered.

Fig. Yellow, flower pot mushrooms (Leucocoprinus birnbaumii) at various states of development

Though mushroom fruiting bodies are short-lived, the underlying mycelium can itself be long-lived and massive. A colony of Armillaria solidipes (formerly known as Armillaria ostoyae) in Malheur National Forestin the United States is estimated to be 2,400 years old, possibly older, and spans an estimated 2,200 acres (8.9 km2). Most of the fungus is underground and in decaying wood or dying tree roots in the form of white mycelia combined with black shoelace-like rhizomorphs that bridge colonized separated woody substrates.

It has been suggested the electrical stimulus of a lightning bolt striking mycelia in logs accelerates the production of mushrooms.

NUTRITION

Mushrooms are a low-calorie food usually eaten cooked or raw and as garnish to a meal. Dietary mushrooms are a good source of B vitamins, such as riboflavin, niacin and pantothenic acid, and the essential minerals,selenium, copper and potassium. Fat, carbohydrate and calorie content are low, with absence of vitamin C and sodium. There are approximately 20 calories in an ounce of mushrooms.

When exposed to ultraviolet light, natural ergosterols in mushrooms produce vitamin D2, a process now exploited for the functional food retail market.

HUMAN USE

Fig. The Agaricus bisporus, one of the most widely cultivated and popular mushrooms in the world

Edible Mushrooms

Mushrooms are used extensively in cooking, in many cuisines (notably Chinese, Korean, European,Japanese and Indian). Mushroom is called Khumb in Hindi. They are known as the "meat" of the vegetable world.

Most mushrooms sold in supermarkets have been commercially grown on mushroom farms. The most popular of these, Agaricus bisporus, is considered safe for most people to eat because it is grown in controlled, sterilized environments. Several varieties of A. bisporus are grown commercially, including whites, crimini, and portobello. Other cultivated species now available at many grocers include shiitake,maitake or hen-of-the-woods, oyster, and enoki. In recent years, increasing affluence in developing countries has led to a considerable growth in interest in mushroom cultivation, which is now seen as a potentially important economic activity for small farmers.

A number of species of mushrooms are poisonous; although some resemble certain edible species, consuming them could be fatal. Eating mushrooms gathered in the wild is risky and should not be undertaken by individuals not knowledgeable in mushroom identification, unless the individuals limit themselves to a relatively small number of good edible species that are visually distinctive. A. bisporus contains carcinogenscalled hydrazines, the most abundant of which is agaritine. However, the carcinogens are destroyed by moderate heat when cooking.

More generally, and particularly with gilled mushrooms, separating edible from poisonous species requires meticulous attention to detail; there is no single trait by which all toxic mushrooms can be identified, nor one by which all edible mushrooms can be identified. Additionally, even edible mushrooms may produce allergicreactions in susceptible individuals, from a mild asthmatic response to severe anaphylactic shock.

People who collect mushrooms for consumption are known as mycophagists, and the act of collecting them for such is known as mushroom hunting, or simply "mushrooming".

China is the world's largest edible mushroom producer. The country produces about half of all cultivated mushrooms, and around 2.7 kilograms (6.0 lb) of mushrooms are consumed per person per year by over a billion people.

Toxic mushrooms

Fig. Young Amanita phalloides, "death cap" mushrooms

Many mushroom species produce secondary metabolites that can be toxic, mind-altering, antibiotic, antiviral, or bioluminescent. Although there are only a small number of deadly species, several others can cause particularly severe and unpleasant symptoms. Toxicity likely plays a role in protecting the function of the basidiocarp: the mycelium has expended considerable energy and protoplasmic material to develop a structure to efficiently distribute its spores. One defense against consumption and premature destruction is the evolution of chemicals that render the mushroom inedible, either causing the consumer to vomit the meal, or to learn to avoid consumption altogether. In addition, due to the ability of mushrooms to absorb heavy metals, including those that are radioactive, European mushrooms may, to date, include toxicity from the 1986 Chernobyl disaster and continue to be studied.

Psychoactive mushrooms

Fig. Hallucinogenic Psilocybe mushrooms

Mushrooms with psychoactive properties have long played a role in various native medicine traditions in cultures all around the world. They have been used as sacrament in rituals aimed at mental and physical healing, and to facilitate visionary states. One such ritual is the velada ceremony. A practitioner of traditional mushroom use is the shaman or curandera (priest-healer).

Psilocybin mushrooms possess psychedelic properties. Commonly known as "magic mushrooms" or "'shrooms," they are openly available in smart shops in many parts of the world, or on the black market in those countries that have outlawed their sale. Psilocybin mushrooms have been reported as facilitating profound and life-changing insights often described as mystical experiences. Recent scientific work has supported these claims, as well as the long-lasting effects of such induced spiritual experiences.

Psilocybin, a naturally occurring chemical in certain psychedelic mushrooms such as Psilocybe cubensis, is being studied for its ability to help people suffering from psychological disorders, such as obsessive-compulsive disorder. Minute amounts have been reported to stop cluster and migraine headaches.

A double-blind study, done by the Johns Hopkins Hospital, showed psychedelic mushrooms could provide people an experience with substantial personal meaning and spiritual significance. In the study, one-third of the subjects reported ingestion of psychedelic mushrooms was the single most spiritually significant event of their lives. Over two-thirds reported it among their five most meaningful and spiritually significant events. On the other hand, one-third of the subjects reported extreme anxiety. However, the anxiety went away after a short period of time.

A few species in the Amanita genus, most recognizably A. muscaria, but also A. pantherina, among others, contain the psychoactive compoundmuscimol. The muscimol-containing chemotaxonomic group of Amanitas contains no amatoxins or phallotoxins, and as such are not hepatoxic, though if not properly cured will be non-lethally neurotoxic due to the presence of ibotenic acid. The Amanita intoxication is similar to Z-drugs in that it includes CNSdepressant and sedative-hypnotic effects, but also dissociation and delirium in high doses.

Medicinal properties

Fig. Ganoderma lucidum

Medicinal mushrooms are mushrooms or extracts used or studied as possible treatments for diseases. Some mushroom materials, including polysaccharides, glycoproteins and proteoglycans, modulate immune system responses and inhibit tumor growth in preliminary research, whereas other isolates show potential cardiovascular, antiviral, antibacterial, antiparasitic, anti-inflammatory, and antidiabetic properties. Currently, several extracts have widespread use in Japan, Korea and China, as adjuncts to radiation treatments and chemotherapy, even though clinical evidence of efficacy in humans has not been confirmed.

Historically, mushrooms have long been thought to hold medicinal value, especially in traditional Chinese medicine. They have been studied in modern medical research since the 1960s, where most studies use extracts, rather than whole mushrooms. Only a few specific extracts have been tested for efficacy in laboratory research. Polysaccharide-K and lentinan are among extracts best understood from in vitroresearch, animal models such as mice, or early-stage human pilot studies.

Preliminary experiments show glucan-containing mushroom extracts may affect function of the innate and adaptive immune systems, functioning asbioresponse modulators. In some countries, extracts of polysaccharide-K, schizophyllan, polysaccharide peptide, or lentinan are government-registeredadjuvant cancer therapies.

Other uses

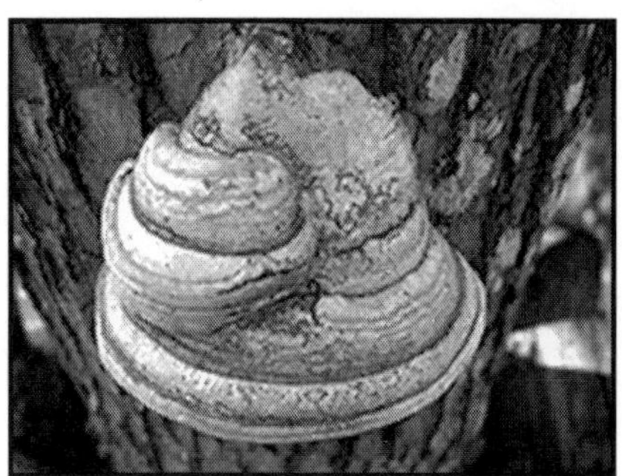

Fig. A tinder fungus, Fomes fomentarius

Mushrooms can be used for dyeing wool and other natural fibers. The chromophores of mushroom dyes are organic compounds and produce strong and vivid colors, and all colors of the spectrum can be achieved with mushroom dyes. Before the invention of synthetic dyes, mushrooms were the source of many textile dyes. Some fungi, types of polypores loosely called mushrooms, have been used as fire starters (known as tinder fungi).

Mushrooms and other fungi play a role in the development of new biological remediation techniques (e.g., using mycorrhizae to spur plant growth) and filtration technologies (e.g. using fungi to lower bacterial levels in contaminated water).

2

Edible Mushroom

Edible mushrooms are the fleshy and edible fruit bodies of several species of macrofungi (fungi which bear fruiting structures that are large enough to be seen with the naked eye). They can appear either below ground (hypogeous) or above ground (epigeous) where they may be picked by hand. Edibility may be defined by criteria that include absence of poisonous effects on humans and desirable taste and aroma.

Fig. White mushrooms ready for cooking. While common, they are just one of the many types of mushrooms cultivated and eaten.

Fig. Picked edible mushrooms in a basket

Edible mushrooms are consumed by humans as comestibles for their nutritional value and they are occasionally consumed for their supposed medicinal value. Mushrooms consumed by those practicing folk medicine are known as medicinal mushrooms. While hallucinogenic mushrooms (e.g. Psilocybin mushrooms) are occasionally consumed for recreational or religious purposes, they can produce severenausea and disorientation, and are therefore not commonly considered edible mushrooms.

Edible mushrooms include many fungal species that are either harvested wild or cultivated. Easily cultivatable and common wild mushrooms are often available in markets, and those that are more difficult to obtain (such as the prized truffle and matsutake) may be collected on a smaller scale by private gatherers. Some preparations may render certain poisonous mushrooms fit for consumption.

Before assuming that any wild mushroom is edible, it should be identified. Proper identification of a species is the only safe way to ensure edibility. Some mushrooms that are edible for most people can cause allergic reactions in some individuals, and old or improperly stored specimens can cause food poisoning.

Deadly poisonous mushrooms that are frequently confused with edible mushrooms and responsible for many fatal poisonings include several species of the Amanita genus, in particular, Amanita phalloides, the death cap. Mushrooms growing in polluted locations can accumulate pollutants such as heavy metals.

HISTORY OF MUSHROOM USE

Mycophagy, the act of consuming mushrooms, dates back to ancient times. Edible mushroom species have been found in association with 13,000 year old ruins in Chile, but the first reliable evidence of mushroom consumption dates to several hundred years BC in China. The Chinese value mushrooms for medicinal properties as well as for food. Ancient Romans and Greeks, particularly the upper classes, used mushrooms for culinary purposes. Food tasters were employed by Roman Emperors to ensure that mushrooms were safe to eat.

Mushrooms are also easily preserved, and historically have provided additional nutrition over winter.

Many cultures around the world have either used or continue to use psilocybin mushrooms for spiritual purposes as well as medicinal mushrooms in folk medicine.

CURRENT CULINARY USE

A fraction of the many fungi consumed by humans are currently cultivated and sold commercially. Commercial cultivation is important ecologically, as there have been concerns of depletion of larger fungi such as chanterelles in Europe, possibly because the group has grown so popular yet remains a challenge to cultivate.

Commercially cultivated

Fig. Commercial cultivated Japanese edible mushroom species. Clockwise from left,enokitake, buna-shimeji, bunapi-shimeji,king oyster mushroom and shiitake.

Mushroom cultivation has a long history, with over twenty species commercially cultivated. Mushrooms are cultivated in at least 60 countries with China, the United States, Netherlands, France and Poland being the top five producers in 2000.

Commercially harvested wild edibles

Fig. Chanterelles in the wild

Fig. A collection of Boletus edulis of varying ages

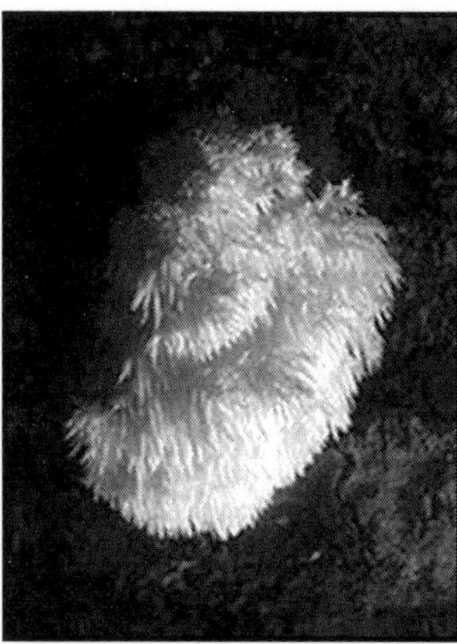

Fig. Hericium coralloides

Fig. Clitocybe nuda

Some species are difficult to cultivate; others (particularly mycorrhizal species) have not yet been successfully cultivated. Some of these species are harvested from the wild, and can be found in markets. When in season they can be purchased fresh, and many species are sold dried as well.

The following species are commonly harvested from the wild:

- Boletus edulis or edible Boletus, native to Europe, known in Italian as Fungo Porcino (plural 'porcini') (Pig mushroom), in German as Steinpilz (Stone mushroom), in Russian as "white mushroom", in Albanian as (Wolf mushroom) and in French the cèpe. It also known as the king bolete, and is renowned for its delicious flavor. It is sought after worldwide, and can be found in a variety of culinary dishes.
- Cantharellus cibarius (The chanterelle), The yellow chanterelle is one of the best and most easily recognizable mushrooms, and can be found in Asia, Europe, North America and Australia. There are poisonous mushrooms which resemble it, though these can be

confidently distinguished if one is familiar with the chanterelle's identifying features.

- Cantharellus tubaeformis, the tube chanterelle or yellow-leg
- Clitocybe nuda - Blewit (or Blewitt)
- Cortinarius caperatus the Gypsy mushroom (recently moved from genus Rozites)
- Craterellus cornucopioides - Trompette de la Mort or Horn of Plenty
- Grifola frondosa, known in Japan as maitake (also "hen of the woods" or "sheep's head"); a large, hearty mushroom commonly found on or near stumps and bases of oak trees, and believed to haveMacrolepiota procera properties.
- Gyromitra esculenta this "False morel" is prized by the Finns. This mushroom is deadly poisonous if eaten raw, but highly regarded when parboiled.
- Hericium erinaceus, a tooth fungus; also called "lion's mane mushroom."
- Hydnum repandum Sweet tooth fungus, hedgehog mushroom, urchin of the woods
- Lactarius deliciosus Saffron milk cap - Consumed around the world and prized in Russia
- Morchella species, (morel family), morels belong to the ascomycete grouping of fungi. They are usually found in open scrub, woodland or open ground in late spring. When collecting this fungus, care must be taken to distinguish it from the poisonous false morels, including Gyromitra esculenta.
- Morchella conica var. deliciosa
- Morchella esculenta var. rotunda
- Tricholoma matsutake the Matsutake, a mushroom highly prized in Japanese cuisine.
- Tuber species, (the truffle), Truffles have long eluded the modern techniques of domestication known astrufficulture. Although the field of trufficulture has greatly expanded since its inception in 1808, several species still remain uncultivated. Domesticated truffles include
- Tuber borchii
- Tuber brumale
- Tuber indicum - Chinese black truffle
- Tuber macrosporum - White truffle
- Tuber mesentericum - The Bagnoli truffle
- Tuber uncinatum - Black summer truffle

OTHER EDIBLE WILD SPECIES

Many wild species are consumed around the world. The species which can be identified "in the field" (without use of special chemistry or a microscope) and therefore safely eaten vary widely from country to country, even from region to region. This list is a sampling of lesser-known species that are reportedly edible.

Fig. Lactarius salmonicolor

AMANITA CAESAREA

Amanita caesarea, commonly known in English as Caesar's Mushroom, is a highly regarded edible mushroom in the genus Amanita, native to southern Europe and North Africa. This mushroom was firstdescribed by Giovanni Antonio Scopoli in 1772. This mushroom was a favorite of early rulers of the Roman Empire.

It has a distinctive orange cap, yellow gills and stem. Organic acids have been isolated from this species. Similar orange-capped species occur in North America and India. It was known to and valued by the Ancient Romans, who called it Boletus, a name now applied to a very different type of fungus.

TAXONOMY AND NAMING

Amanita caesarea was first described by Italian mycologist Giovanni Antonio Scopoli in 1772 asAgaricus caesareus, before later being placed in Amanita by Persoon in 1801. The common namecomes from its being a favourite of the Roman emperors, who took the name Caesar (originally a family name) as a title.

It was a personal favorite of Roman emperor Claudius. The Romans called it Boletus, derived from the Ancient Greek ß???t?? for this fungus as named by Galen. Several modern common names recognise this heritage with the English Caesar's mushroom and royal amanita, French impériale,Polish cesarski and German Kaiserling. In Italian, it is ovolo (pl. ovoli), due to its resemblance to an egg when very young. In Albanian it is kuqëlorja from its colour (< Albanian kuqe 'red'). Other common names include Amanite des Césars and Oronge.

It has also been classified as A. umbonata. A. hemibapha is a similar species originally described fromIndia, and this name has sometimes been applied to North American collections. The relationship of the similar North American species A. arkansana and A. jacksonii to A. caesarea is not clear. The edibility of some of these similar species is also unclear, though A. jacksonii is eaten by many and there have been no reports of illness from it. A. caesarea was first domesticated in 1984.

Description

Fig. Specimen of A. caesarea

This mushroom has an orange-red cap, initially hemispherical before convex and finally flat. The surface is smooth, and margins striated, and it can reach 15 cm (6 in) or rarely 20 cm (8 in) in diameter. The free gills are pale to golden yellow, as is the cylinder-shaped stipe, which is 8–15 cm (3–6 in) tall and 2–3 cm (around 1 in) wide. The ringhangs loosely and is lined above and smooth below. The base of the stipe is thicker than the top and is seated in a greyish-white cup-like volva, which is a remnant of universal veil. The spores are white.

It could be confused with the poisonous fly agaric (Amanita muscaria). Though A. muscaria has a distinctive red cap dotted with fluffy white flakes, these tend to fall off as the carpophor ages and the bright red tends to fade to a yellowy orange. The latter mushroom will always have white gills and stalk with a ringed volva rather than a yellow stalk and is typically associated with spruce (Picea), pine (Pinus) or birch (Betula).Certain varieties (e.g. Amanita muscaria var. guessowii) are close to yellow even at the juvenile stage.

Chemical properties

A study of isolates from the fruiting bodies of A. caesarea showed that the radial growth (increases in axon's diameter) of this species was possible at pH 6-7, and optimal growth was in a temperature of 24–28 °C (75–82 °F), depending on the isolate.

In another study, the quantities of heavy metals arsenic, cadmium, lead, mercury and selenium were investigated in mushroom samples. Cadmium amount was found to have exceeded in A. caesarea, Boletus edulis and Boletus pinophilus, which is not harmful. The study concluded that the concentrations of the metals may vary from species to species and may be playing a taxonomic role, but has no reliable part in the mushroom's ecology.

Organic acid compositions were noted in six mushroom species: Boletus edulis, Gyroporus castaneus, Lactarius deliciosus, Suillus collinitus andXerocomus chrysenteron. Each had at five acids in common - citric acid, ketoglutaric acid, malic acid, succinic acid and fumaric acid. In A. caesarea, malic acid and ascorbic acid were the most common compounds. Ergosterol has also been isolated from A. caesarea.

Fig. A. caesarea specimen from Italy.

Edibility

This mushroom is edible, and has been traditionally taken as food in Mexico. They consume it roasted with a bit of the herb Dysphania ambrosioides. International export market began from the 1990s. A. caesarea is also traditionally gathered and consumed in Italy, where it is known as ovolo or ovolo buono.

DISTRIBUTION AND HABITAT

This mushroom fruits in oak woodland, sometimes mixed with conifers, from early summer to mid autumn. It grows individually or in groups. Its natural habitat is pine, oak or fir forests at altitudes of 2,200–3,000 m (7,200–9,800 ft) above sea level. They prefer plains, and can occur at slopes of 20 degrees.

It is found in North Africa and southern Europe, particularly in the hills of northern Italy. It is thought to have been introduced north of the Alps by the Roman armies as it is most frequently found along old Roman roads. The mushroom is also distributed in Hungary, India, and China (Sichuan Province). Although the species is not known to exist in the United States and Canada, it has been collected in Mexico.

Amanita caesarea is listed in the Red Data book of Ukraine, and it is protected by law in Croatia, Slovenia.

ARMILLARIA MELLEA

Armillaria mellea, commonly known as honey fungus, is a basidiomycete fungus in the genus Armillaria. It is a plant pathogen and part of a cryptic species complex of closely related and morphologically similar species. It causes Armillaria root rot in many plant species and produces mushrooms around the base of trees it has infected. The symptoms of infection appear in the crowns of infected trees as discoloured foliage, reduced growth, dieback of the branches and death.

The mushrooms are edible but some people may be intolerant to them. This species is capable of producing light via bioluminescence in its mycelium.

Armillaria mellea is widely distributed in temperate regions of the Northern Hemisphere. The fruit body or mushroom, commonly known as stump mushroom, stumpie, honey mushroom, pipinky or pinky, grows typically on hardwoods but may be found around and on other living and dead wood or in open areas.

TAXONOMY

The species was originally named Agaricus melleus by Danish-Norwegian botanist Martin Vahl in 1790; it was transferred to the genus Armillaria in 1871 by Paul Kummer. Numerous subtaxa have been described:

Name	Authority	Year
var. viridiflava	Barla	1887
var. minor	Barla	1887
var. bulbosa	Barla	1887
var. camerunensis	Henn.	1895
var. exannulata	Peck	1893
var. flava	Peck	1897
var. glabra	Gillet	1874
var. javanica	Henn.	1900
var. laricina	(Bolton) Barla	1887
var. maxima	Barla	1887
var. obscura	Gillet	1874
var. radicata	Peck	1891
var. sulphurea	(Weinm.) Fr.	1879
var. tabescens	(Scop.) Rea & Ramsb.	1917
var. versicolor	(With.) W.G.Sm.	1908
subsp. nipponica	J.Y.Cha & Igarashi	1995
f. rosea	Calonge & M.Seq.	2003

DESCRIPTION

The basidiocarp of each has a smooth cap 3 to 15 cm (1 to 6 in) in diameter, convex at first but becoming flattened with age often with a central raised umbo, later becoming somewhat dish-shaped. The margins of the cap are often arched at maturity and the surface is sticky when wet.

Though typically honey-coloured, this fungus is rather variable in appearance and sometimes has a few dark, hairy scales near the centre somewhat radially arranged. The gills are white at first, sometimes becoming pinkish-yellow or discoloured with age, broad and fairly distant, attached to the stipe at right angles or are slightly decurrent. The spore print is white.

The stipe is of variable length, up to about 20 cm (8 in) long and 3.5 cm (1.4 in) in diameter. It is fibrillose and of a firm spongy consistency at first but later becomes hollow. It is cylindrical and tapers to a point at its base where it is fused to the stipes of other mushrooms in the clump. It is whitish at the upper end and brownish-yellow below, often with a very dark-coloured base.

There is a broad persistent skin-likering attached to the upper part of the stipe. This has a velvety margin and yellowish fluff underneath and extends outwards as a white partial veil protecting the gills when young. The flesh of the cap is whitish and has a sweetish odour and flavour with a tinge of bitterness. Under the microscope, the spores are approximately elliptical, 7–9 by 6–7 μm, inamyloid with prominent apiculi (short, pointed projections) at the base. The basidia (spore-producing structures) lack basal clamps.

The main part of the fungus is underground where a mat of mycelial threads may extend for great distances. They are bundled together in rhizomorphs that are black in this species. The fungal body is notbioluminescent but its mycelia are luminous when in active growth.

Similar species

Armillaria mellea once included a range of species with similar features that have since been reclassified.

DISTRIBUTION

Armillaria mellea is widespread in northern temperate zones. It has been found in North America, Europe and northern Asia, and It has been introduced to South Africa. The fungus grows parasitically on a large number of broadleaf trees. It fruits in dense clusters at the base of trunks or stumps.

ECOLOGY

Trees become infected by Armillaria mellea when rhizomorphs growing through the soil encounter uninfected roots. Alternatively, when infected roots come into contact with uninfected ones the fungal mycelium may grow across. The rhizomorphs invade the trunk, growing between the bark and the wood and causing wood decay, growth reduction and mortality. Trees that are already under stress are more likely to be attacked but healthy trees may also be parasitized. The foliage becomes sparse and discoloured, twig growth slows down and branches may die back. When they are attacked, the Douglas-fir, western larch and some other conifers often produce an extra large crop of cones shortly before dying. Coniferous trees also tend to ooze resin from infected areas whereas broad-leaved trees sometimes develop sunken cankers. A growth of fruiting bodies near the base of the trunk confirms the suspicion of Armillaria root rot.

In 1893, the American mycologist Charles Horton Peck reported finding Armillaria fruiting bodies that were "aborted", in a similar way to specimens ofEntoloma abortivum. It was not until 1974 that Roy Watling showed that the aborted specimens included cells of both Armillaria mellea and Entoloma abortivum.

He thought that the Armillaria was parasitizing the Entoloma, a plausible hypothesis given its pathogenic behaviour. However, a 2001 study by Czederpiltz, Volk and Burdsall showed that the Entoloma was in fact the microparasite. The whitish-grey malformed fruit bodies known as carpophoroids were the result of E. abortivum hyphae penetrating the Armillaria and disrupting its normal development.

EDIBILITY

Armillaria mellea mushroom are considered good edibles, although some individuals have reported "allergic" reactions that result in stomach upsets. Some authors suggest collecting mushrooms from the wood of various trees, including hemlock, buckeye, eucalyptus, and locust. The mushrooms have a taste that has been described as slightly sweet and nutty, with a texture ranging from chewy to crunchy, depending on the method of preparation. Parboilingmushrooms before consuming removes the bitter taste present in some specimens, and may reduce the amount of gastrointestinal irritants. Drying the mushrooms preserves and intensifies their flavour, although reconstituted mushrooms tend to be tough to eat.

Chemistry

Several bioactive compounds have been isolated and identified from the fruit bodies. The triterpenes 3ß-hydroxyglutin-5-ene, friedelane-2a,3ß-diol, and friedelin were reported in 2011. Indole compounds include tryptamine, L-tryptophan and serotonin.

BOLETUS BADIUS

Boletus badius, commonly known as the bay bolete, is an edible, pored mushroom. It is found in Europe and North America, where it grows in coniferous or mixed woods on the ground or on decaying tree stumps, sometimes in prolific numbers. Both the common and scientific names refer to the bay- orchestnut-coloured cap, which is almost spherical in young specimens before broadening and flattening out to a diameter of up to 15 cm (6 in). On the cap underside are small yellowish pores that bruise dull blue-grey when injured.

The smooth, cylindrical stipe, measuring 4–9 cm (1.6–3.5 in) long by 1–2 cm (0.4–0.8 in) thick, is coloured like the cap, but paler. Some varieties have been described from eastern North America, differing from the main type in both macroscopic and microscopic morphology.

First described scientifically by Elias Fries in 1818, the bay bolete was reclassified as Xerocomus badius in 1931, and it is still listed thus in several sources.

Modern molecular phylogenetics shows thatXerocomus is polyphyletic (not descended from a common ancestor), and the bay bolete is not particularly closely related to species in that genus. Often considered a poor relation of the cep (Boletus edulis),B. badius is nevertheless regarded as a choice edible mushroom by some authors, such as food expertAntonio Carluccio, and is sold in markets in Europe and central Mexico. Its mushrooms are less often infested by maggots than other boletes.

Several European studies have demonstrated that the mushroom can bioaccumulate some trace metals from the soil, such as mercury, cobalt, and nickel. Additionally, the mushroom contains a pigment that concentrates radioactive caesium; specimens collected in Europe following the 1986 Chernobyl disaster had Cs concentrations several times greater than those collected before the incident.

TAXONOMY

The bay bolete was first named as Boletus castaneus ß badius (i.e. a subspecies of Boletus castaneus) by Elias Magnus Fries in 1818. Fries later renamed it as a variety of Boletus castaneus in 1828,before assigning it distinct species status in his 1832 work Elenchus Fungorum.

The fungus has been transferred to several genera in its taxonomic history: Rostkovites by Petter Karsten in 1881; Viscipellisand Ixocomus by Lucien Quélet in 1886 and 1888 respectively; and Suillus by Otto Kuntze in 1898.In 1931, Edouard-Jean Gilbert reclassified it in the genus Xerocomus, and many sources still list it thus.

Review of Xerocomus strongly suggested it was polyphyletic, and the genus was not accepted by some mycologists. The stickiness of its wet cap distinguishes the species from others classified inXerocomus, and hence it has been left in Boletus pending further research.

Genetic analysis published in 2013 shows that Boletus badius is related to B. pallidus and B. glabellus; the three species form aclade known informally as the badius clade within a larger group (informally called anaxoboletus) in the suborder Boletineae. Other clades within the group include the Tylopilus, porcini (= Boletus sensu stricto) and Strobilomyces clades, as well as two other groups composed of members of various genera includingXerocomus (the taxa designated as Xerocomus species in this clade are not Xerocomus species and require new taxonomic designations) and Xerocomellus.

Fig. Both the common and scientific names refer to the bay cap colour.

The species Boletus limatulus, originally published by Charles Christopher Frost in 1874, was later redescribed, "with a slight tinge of irritation at the time, energy and gasoline spent", as a variety of B. badius by Wally Snell in 1945 (as Xerocomus badius var.limatulus). The taxon name comes from the Latin limatulus, "rather polished" or "refined". Varieties glaber and macrostipitatus were described from Nova Scotia, Canada, in 1976.

The starting date of fungal taxonomy had been set.as January 1, 1821, to coincide with the date of the works of Swedish naturalist Elias Magnus Fries, the "father of mycology".

Rolf Singer argued that setting the starting date earlier to Christiaan Persoon's 1801 publication ofSynopsis would make a name change necessary, as he had originally given what is now known as Royoporus badius the combinationBoletus badius Pers. and if the bay bolete was classified in the genus Boletus, the name would be unavailable and the names Boletus glutinosus Krombh. or B. spadiceus Krombh. (non Fr.) would have to be used instead.

The species name is the Latin adjective badius, meaning "chestnut brown". The common name is likewise derived from the colour of the cap, likened to the coat of a bay horse. Alternate common names of a similar derivation include bay-brown bolete and bay-capped bolete, and it is known as bolet bai in French. It is also known as the false cep. Variety glaber was named for its smooth (Latin: glaber, "without hairs") stipe, and macrostipitatus for its large (Latin: macro, "large") stipe.

DESCRIPTION

Fig. With wet and sticky cap

Fig. The pore surface stains bluish-grey when injured.

Boletus badius fruit bodies have a chestnut to dark brown cap, which is almost spherical in young specimens before broadening and flattening out to a diameter of up to 15 cm (6 in). The cap margin is acute, and cap surface velvety when young and slightly sticky when wet or old. The cap cuticle is difficult to separate from the flesh underneath. On the cap undersurface, the pores are initially cream to pale yellow, but become greenish yellow or olive with age. They stain dull blue to bluish-grey when bruised or cut, and are easily removed from the flesh. The pores are initially circular, becoming more angular with age, and number about one or two per millimetre. The tubes are 0.8–1.5 cm (0.3–0.6 in) long, and are adnate to depressed around the area of attachment to the stipe.

The flesh is mostly whitish or yellowish in some places; underneath the cap cuticle, it is brownish-pink or reddish brown. Initially firm, it begins to soften under the cap in older mushrooms. In some parts of the cap, such as the junction of the cap and the stipe, the flesh stains pale blue when injured or exposed to air, particularly in damp weather. This change is sometimes faint, and not persistent, as it eventually reverts to its original colour. The stipe is 4–9 cm (1.6–3.5 in) long by 1–2 cm (0.4–0.8 in) thick, and is similar in colour to the cap but paler, and sometimes with a rose-coloured tinge. Its surface has faint longitudinal ridges, a fine powdering, and fine reticulations (a net-like pattern of ridges) at the apex. It often has a whitish region at the base and the top, and white mycelium at the base. Unlike the bulbous stipe of many other boletes, the stipe of Boletus badius remains relatively slim and cylindrical. The flesh of the stipe gets tougher with age. Its smell has been described as fruity.

The spore print is olive to olive-brown. The smooth spores are somewhat oblong to slightly ventricose (fattened in the middle), and measure 10–14 by 4–5 μm.

The basidia (spore-bearing cells) are four-spored and measure 25–35 by 8–10 μm. Pleurocystidia (cystidia found on the faces of the tubes) are fuse-shaped and ventricose, with dimensions of 50–60 by 10–14 μm.

Variety macrostipitatus differs from the main form by its grey-orange cap, shorter stipe measuring 5–7 cm (2.0–2.8 in), longer spores (15–18 by 4–5 μm), and longer pleurocystidia (30–55 by 10–14 μm). The variety glaber has a smooth (glabrous) stipe, and smaller pleurocystidia (35–40 by 10–15 μm) and cheilocystidia (25–30 by 9–12 μm).

Several chemical tests can be used to help identify the mushroom. A drop of ammonium hydroxide solution (NH4OH) turns the cap cuticle a greenish to bluish colour. Application of iron(II) sulphate (FeSO4) solution causes the flesh to stain a dull bluish-green, while the pores turn golden brown with a drop of dilute potassium hydroxide (KOH).

Similar species

The similar colouration may cause confusion with Boletus projectellus, but the latter species is usually more robust, and has a reticulated stipe. Additionally, B. projectellus has the largest spores in the Boletaceae, up to about 30 μm in diameter. Another lookalike is Austroboletus gracilis, but this species does not have a blue bruising reaction, and its pore surface is initially white before turning pinkish.

Compared to B. badius, B. subtomentosusfruit bodies have narrower stipes, paler brown, dry caps, and wider pores that do not stain blue on bruising.

This latter species is not as good to eat.In western North America, B. badius is replaced by the similar B. zelleri, which also grows both on the ground and on rotten wood. The European species Xerocomus bubalinus can be mistaken for B. badius, but it has a paler yellow-brown cap flushed with pinkish-red, and is not sticky when wet.

ECOLOGY, DISTRIBUTION AND HABITAT

Although the bay bolete is predominantly a mycorrhizal species, it does have some saprophytic tendencies and may be able to utilise this lifestyle in certain circumstances. The ectomycorrhizae formed betweenB. badius and spruce (Picea abies) have active hyphal sheaths and a higher potential to store nitrogen,phosphorus, potassium, magnesium, iron, and zinc than other mycorrhizal types, indicating that the fungus is well adapted to acidic stands and that its mycorrhizae are very efficient in uptake and storage ofmacronutrients. Mycorrhizae with Monterey pine (Pinus radiata) have also been described.

Fig. The mushrooms often appear in huge numbers, allowing for large collections.

The bay bolete is common in coniferous and less commonly mixed woodlands in Europe, from the British Isles, where it is abundant throughout, east to the Black Sea Region in Turkey. In Asia, the species has been recorded from Jordan mainland China, and Taiwan. The North American distribution extends from eastern Canada west to Minnesota and south to North Carolina, where the mushroom fruits from July to November. It also grows in central Mexico.

The variety macrostipitatus is found from eastern Canada south to Maine and New York, while variety glaber is known from the Atlantic Maritime Ecozone of eastern Canada. Fruit bodies appear singly or scattered on the ground, or on decaying tree stumps, and can be well hidden by pine needles and ferns. Fruiting tends to peak generally three or four days after rain during warm weather. Numbers can be prolific, especially in highland areas that are humid and shady.

It is commonly found under white pine, spruce, and hemlock, although it also occurs under deciduous trees, especially beech. It also occurs in grassy or mossy areas at or near forest margins; Italian restaurateur and cook Antonio Carluccio recalled picking them in the grounds ofBlenheim Palace. It does not occur on calcareous (chalky) soils.

Boletus badius fruit bodies are less affected by insects than other boletes. Orbatid mites such as Carabodes femoralis, Nothrus silvestris andOribatula tibialis consume them, as do squirrels. Several microbial pathogens can damage the fruit bodies, and have had an effect on populations in China, including soft rot caused by Pseudomonas aeruginosa, and black mould caused by Mucor, Sepedonium, Paecilomyces and Diasporangiumspecies.

USES

Fig. Dried in Poland

Often considered a poor relation of the cep (Boletus edulis), the bay bolete is nevertheless highly regarded as a choice edible mushroom by some authors such as Carluccio. In central Mexico, it is collected from Izta-Popo Zoquiapan National Park and sold in neighbouring markets. It may cause an allergic reaction in some people,and the blue discolouration upon bruising can be offputting, although the staining disappears from white flesh when it is cooked.

The flavour is milder than its better-known relative. Younger specimens are best for eating, though more mature ones can be suitable for cutting up and drying. The tendency for the pores to absorb water means that wiping rather than washing is recommended before use in the kitchen. Unlike most boletes, B. badius can be eaten raw (though only young mushrooms should be used). Otherwise it can be fried in butter, or used with meat or fish recipes. Mushrooms can also be frozen, dried, or pickled in cider vinegar, wine or extra virgin olive oil, and later used in sauces or soups.

The fruit bodies can be used to make mushroom dyes. Depending on the mordant used, colours ranging from yellow, orange, gold, and green-brown can be obtained. Without mordant, a yellow colour is produced.

RESEARCH

In laboratory experiments, extracts of Boletus badius fruit bodies have been shown to have significant antioxidativeproperties in vitro. Fruit bodies contain the compound theanine, an amino acid and a glutamic acid analogue found in green tea. Efforts have been made to establish a protocol for producing theanine by growing the fungus mycelium using submerged fermentation. Several indole compounds have been detected in fruit bodies.

Unprocessed mushrooms contain tryptophan (0.68 milligrams per 100 g dry weight), tryptamine (0.47), serotonin(0.52), kynurenine sulphate (1.96), and kynurenic acid (1.57). Due to their temperature sensitivity, cooking significantly changes the contents and composition of indole compounds: cooked mushrooms contained tryptophan (1.74 mg/100 g dw), 5-methyltryptophan (6.55), melatonin (0.71), andindoleacetonitrile (2.07). Fruit body extracts have been shown to slow the growth of certain tumour cell lines in cell culture.

Polish studies found that although the mushroom bioaccumulates mercury and cobalt from the soil, occasional consumption of mushrooms should not cause maximum allowable intake doses to be exceeded. Similar conclusions about safety were made in a Polish study of the mushroom's ability to accumulate organochlorine compounds. Different methods of preparation for consumption affect the leaching rate of cadmium, lead, and mercury.After the 1986 Chernobyl disaster, several studies showed B. badius bioaccumulates radioactive caesium, 137Cs. 137Cs is produced in nuclear power plants following the chain decay of 235U to 137Te, and has a half-life of thirty years.

A German study showed that mushrooms collected from 1986 to 1988 had radiocaesium contents that were 8.3 to 13.6 times greater than mushrooms collected before the accident in 1985. This caesium-sequestering effect is caused by a brown pigment, the polyphenol compound norbadione A, which is related to a family of mushroom pigments known as pulvinic acids. Norbadione A has been investigated for its ability to provide a protective effect against the damaging effects of ionizing radiation. Tests with cell cultures and mice show that although it has some protective effect, it is toxic to cells in higher doses. A new series of alkali chelators based on the structure of norbadione A has been reported. The mushroom may have potential as a bioremediation agent to clean up contaminated sites.

CHROOGOMPHUS RUTILUS

Chroogomphus rutilus, commonly known as the brown slimecap or the copper spike, is a species of fungus in the Gomphidiaceae family. First described scientifically as Agaricus rutilus by Jacob Christian Schaffer in 1774, it was transferred to the genus Chroogomphus in 1964 by Orson K. Miller, Jr.. The fungus lives ectomycorrhizally with Pinus species, and is found in Europe and North America. The fruit bodies are edible but not highly regarded.

CALVATIA GIGANTEA

Calvatia gigantea, commonly known as the Giant puffball, is a puffball mushroom commonly found in meadows, fields, and deciduous forests worldwide usually in late summer and autumn. It is common throughout Europe andNorth America.

DESCRIPTION

Most giant puffballs grow to be 10 to 70 centimetres (3.9 to 28 in) in diameter, although occasionally some can reach diameters up to 150 centimetres (59 in) and weights of 20 kilograms (44 lb). The inside of mature Giant puffballs is greenish brown, whereas the interior of immature puffballs is white. The large white mushrooms areedible when young.

The fruiting body of a puffball mushroom will develop within the period of a few weeks and soon begin to decompose and rot, at which point it is dangerous to eat. Unlike most mushrooms, all the spores of the giant puffball are created inside the fruiting body; large specimens can easily contain several trillion spores. Spores are yellowish, smooth, and 3 to 5 micrometres (0.00012 to 0.00020 in) in size.

The classification of this species has been revised in recent years, as the formerly recognized classGasteromycetes, which included all puffballs, has been found to be polyphyletic. Some authors place the giant puffball and other members of genus Calvatia in order Agaricales. Also, the species has in the past been placed in two other genera, Lycoperdon and Langermannia. However, the current view is that the Giant Puffball is Calvatia.

COOKING

Fig. Old Giant puffball.

All true puffballs are considered edible when immature, but can cause digestive upset if the spores have begun to form, as indicated by the color of the flesh being not pure white (first yellow, then brown). Immature gilled species still contained within their universal veil can be look alikes for puffballs. To distinguish puffballs from poisonous fungi, they must be cut open; edible puffballs will have a solid white interior. Some similar mushrooms have the white interior (or yellowish) but also have the silhouette of a cap-type mushroom on the interior when cut open. These are young cap-type mushrooms and may be poisonous.

The meat of giant puffballs tastes very similar to tofu or melted cheese when cooked. To prepare, remove any brown portions and tough skin, which sometimes peels off easily. Do not soak in anything. Puffballs may be sauteed, broiled, or breaded and fried; they do not dehydrate well, but may be cooked and then frozen.

Resembles

Giant puffballs resemble the earthball (Scleroderma citrinum). The latter are distinguished by a much firmer, elastic fruiting body, and as an interior that becomes dark purplish-black with white reticulation early in development.

CLAVARIACEAE

The Clavariaceae are a family of fungi in the Agaricales order of mushrooms. The family contains 7 genera and 120 species. Collectively, they are commonly known as coral fungi due to their resemblance to aquatic coral, although other vernacular names including antler fungi, finger fungi,worm mold, and spaghetti mushroom are sometimes used for similar reasons.

Initially all classified in the genus Clavaria, they were later split out into many genera includingClavicorona, Clavulina, Clavulinopsis, Macrotyphula, Ramaria and Ramariopsis.

Some superficially similar species are not so closely related; the fairy club genus Clavariadelphus,Ramaria and Clavulina belong to the family Gomphaceae, Lentaria belongs in the Thelephorales order, while the genus Calocera is an entirely different organism of the class Dacrymycetes.

Coral fungi can be similar in appearance to jelly fungi. They are often brightly colored, mostly oranges, yellows, or reds, and usually grow in older mature forests. Some coral fungi are saprotrophic on decaying wood, while others are commensal or even parasitic.

CLAVULINACEAE

The Clavulinaceae are a family of fungi in the order Cantharellales. The family is not well defined, but currently comprises species of clavarioid (club and coral) fungi as well as some corticioid (crust- and patch-forming) fungi. These species are nutritionally diverse, some being ectomycorrhizal, others wood-rotting saprotrophs, others lichenized, and yet others lichenicolous (growing on or parasitizing lichens).

TAXONOMY

History

The Dutch mycologist Marinus Anton Donk first published the tribe Clavulinae in 1933 to accommodatespecies of clavarioid fungi in the genus Clavulina that had "stichic" basidia (basidia with nuclear spindles arranged longitudinally). He considered this feature placed the species concerned closer to thechanterelles (Cantharellales) than to other clavarioid fungi. In 1961, he raised the tribe to the rank of family, as the Clavulinaceae. In 1968, Estonian mycologist Erast Parmasto added the corticioid genusClavulicium to the family, noting that it had very similar basidia to those found in Clavulina.

Current status

Molecular research, based on cladistic analysis of DNA sequences, has confirmed the placement ofClavulina within the Cantharellales, but has not yet addressed the circumscription of the family Clavulinaceae. The corticioid genus Membranomyces (formerly referred to Clavulicium) is closely related. The lichenized clavarioid genus Multiclavula is also closely related and has been included within the family. Several species formerly referred to the corticioid genus Sistotrema may be included, but have not been formally renamed.

The genus Burgella, described for a probable anamorph of this latter group is, however, within the family. As such, the Clavulinaceae currently contain 4 genera and over 60 species.

HABITAT AND DISTRIBUTION

Fig. Clavulina amethystina

Species within the family are unusually diverse in habitat and ecology. Species of Clavulina areectomycorrhizal, forming mutually beneficial associations with the roots of living trees and other plants.Species of Multiclavula are lichens, their basidiocarps typically found scattered on sheets of their associatedalgae.

Species of Membranomyces and "Sistotrema" are presumed to be wood-rotting saprotrophs, typically forming corticioid basidiocarps on the undersides of dead, attached branches or fallen wood. Some of the latter group, however, (including the genus Burgella) often grow on and may parasitize lichens.Collectively, the Clavulinaceae have a cosmopolitan distribution.

COPRINUS COMATUS

Coprinus comatus, the shaggy ink cap, lawyer's wig, or shaggy mane, is a common fungus often seen growing on lawns, along gravel roads and waste areas. The young fruit bodies first appear as white cylinders emerging from the ground, then the bell-shaped caps open out. The caps are white, and covered with scales—this is the origin of the common names of the fungus. The gills beneath the cap are white, then pink, then turn black and secrete a black liquid filled with spores (hence the "ink cap" name). This mushroom is unusual because it will turn black and dissolve itself in a matter of hours after being picked or depositing spores.

When young it is an excellent edible mushroom provided that it is eaten soon after being collected (it keeps very badly because of the autodigestion of its gills and cap). If long-term storage is desired, microwaving, sauteing or simmering until limp will allow the mushrooms to be stored in a refrigerator for several days or frozen. Processing must be done whether for eating or storage within four to six hours of harvest to prevent undesirable changes to the mushroom. The species is cultivated in China as food. The mushroom can sometimes be confused with the Magpie fungus which is poisonous.

TAXONOMY

The shaggy ink cap was first described by Danish naturalist Otto Friedrich Müller in 1780 as Agaricus comatus, before being given its current binomial name in 1797 by Christiaan Hendrik Persoon. Its specific name derives from coma, or "hair", hence comatus, "hairy" or "shaggy". Other common names include lawyer's wig, and shaggy mane.

Coprinus comatus is the type species for the genus Coprinus. This genus was formerly considered to be a large one with well over 100 species. However, molecular analysis of DNA sequences showed that the former species belonged in two families, the Agaricaceae and the Psathyrellaceae. Coprinus comatusis the best known of the true Coprinus.

Coprinus comatus is a Nematophagous fungus capable of killing and digesting nematodes. A recent study has found the shaggy ink cap kills nematode species Panagrellus redivivus and Meloidogyne arenaria.

DESCRIPTION

The shaggy ink cap is easily recognizable from its almost cylindical cap which initially covers most of its stem. The cap is mostly white with shaggy scales, which are more pale brown at the apex. The free gills change rapidly from white to pink, then to black. It is deliquescent. The stipe has a loose ring and measures 10–37 centimetres (3.9–15 in) high by 1–2.5 centimetres (0.39–

0.98 in) diameter. Microscopically it lacks pleurocystidia. The spore print is black-brown and the spores measure 10–13 × 6.5–8 μm. The flesh is white and the taste mild.

Fig. Shaggy manes

Fig. Coprinus comatus

DISTRIBUTION AND HABITAT

It grows in groups in places which are often unexpected, such as green areas in towns. It occurs widely in grasslands and meadows in Europe and North America. It appears to have been introduced to Australia, New Zealand and Iceland. In Australia the species is sufficiently common to have been featured on apostage stamp issued by Australia Post in 1981.

Fig. Some Ink Caps of various ages

GROWTH

The left image below shows a young mushroom. The second image shows the same specimen 24 hours later. "Ink" can be seen dripping from the gills.

EDIBILITY

The young mushrooms, before the gills start to turn black, are edible. The taste is mild; cooking produces a large quantity of liquid. It can sometimes be used in mushroom soup with parasol mushroom. Large quantities of microwaved-then-frozen shaggy manes are delicious when used as the liquid component ofrisotto, replacing the usual chicken stock. The agent responsible for unpleasant symptoms when consumed with alcohol, coprine, which is found inCoprinopsis atramentaria, has not been isolated from C. comatus.

CORN SMUT

Corn smut is a plant disease caused by the pathogenic fungus Ustilago maydis that causes smut onmaize and teosinte (Euchlena mexicana). The fungus forms galls on all above-ground parts of corn species, and is known in Mexico as the food delicacy huitlacoche; it is eaten, usually as a filling, inquesadillas and other tortilla-based foods, and soups.

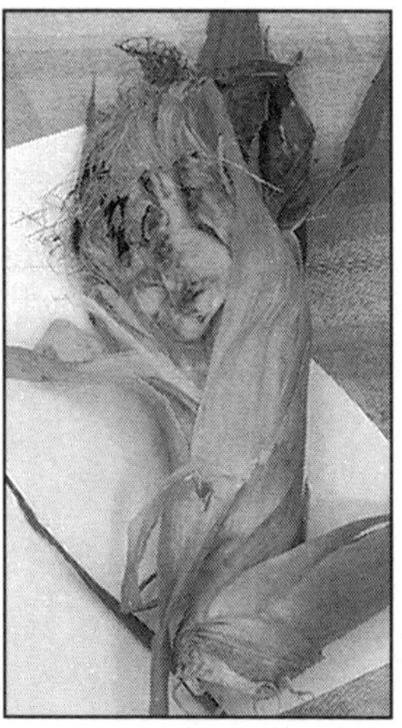

ETYMOLOGY

In Mexico, corn smut is known as huitlacoche, sometimes spelled cuitlacoche). This word entered Spanish in Mexico from classical Nahuatl, though the Nahuatl words from which huitlacoche is derived is debated. In modern Nahuatl, the word for huitlacoche is cuitlacochin, and some sources deem cuitlacochi to be the classical form.

Some sources give the etymology as coming from the Nahuatl words cuitla ("excrement" or "rear-end") and cochtli ("sleeping", from cochi="to sleep"), thus giving a combined meaning of "sleeping/hibernating excrement".

A second group of sources deem the word to mean "raven's excrement". These sources appear to be combining the word cuitlacoche for "thrasher" with cuitla, meaning "excrement". However, the avian meaning of cuitlacoche derives from the Nahuatl word "song" cuicatl, itself from the verb "to sing" cuica. This root then clashes with this reconstruction's second claim that the segmentcuitla- comes from cuitla ("excrement").

One source derives the meaning as "corn excrement", using cuitla again and "maize" tlaolli.This requires the linguistically unlikely evolution of tlaole "maize" into tlacoche.

CHARACTERISTICS

Although it can infect any part of the plant, it usually enters the ovaries and replaces the normal kernels of the cobs with large, distorted tumors analogous to mushrooms. These tumors, or "galls", are made up of much-enlarged cells of the infected plant, fungal threads, and blue-black spores The spores give the cob a burned, scorched appearance. The generic name Ustilago comes from the Latin word ustilare (to burn).

BIOLOGY

Life cycle

When grown in the lab on very simple media, it behaves like baker's yeast, forming single cells calledsporidia. These cells multiply by budding off daughter cells. When two compatible sporidia meet on the surface of the plant, they switch to a different mode of growth. First, they send out conjugation tubes to find each other, after which they fuse and make a hypha to enter the maize plant. Hyphae growing in the plant are dikaryotic; they possess two haploid nuclei per hyphal compartment. In contrast to sporidia, the dikaryotic phase of U. maydisrequires infection of the plant to grow and differentiate, and cannot be maintained in the laboratory.

Proliferation of the fungus inside the plant leads to disease symptoms such as chlorosis, anthocyanin formation, reduced growth and the appearance of tumors harboring the developing teliospores. Mature spores are released from the tumors and spread by rain and wind. Under appropriate conditions, aprobasidium is formed in which meiosis occurs. Resulting haploid nuclei migrate into elongated single cells. These cells detach from the probasidium to become the sporidia, thus completing the life cycle.

Host/pathogen conflict

Plants, in general, have evolved efficient defense systems against pathogenic microbes. A rapid plant defense reaction after pathogen attack is the oxidative burst, which involves the production of reactive oxygen species at the site of the attempted invasion.

As a pathogen, U. maydis can respond to such an oxidative burst by an oxidative stress response, regulated by gene yap1. This response protects U. maydis from the host attack, and is necessary for the pathogen's virulence. Furthermore, U. maydis has a well-established recombinational DNA repair system.

This repair system involves a homolog of Rad51 that has a very similar sequence and size to its mammalian counterparts. This system also involves a protein, Rec2 that is more distantly related to Rad51, and Brh2 protein that is a streamlined version of the mammalian Breast Cancer 2 (BRCA2) protein. When any of these proteins is inactivated, sensitivity of U. maydis to DNA damaging agents is increased.

Also mitotic recombination becomes deficient, mutation frequency increases and meiosis fails to complete. These observations suggest that recombinational repair during mitosis and meiosis in U. maydis may assist the pathogen in surviving DNA damage arising from the host's oxidative defensive response to infection, as well as from other DNA damaging agents.

USES

Model organism

The yeast-like growth of U. maydis makes it an appealing model organism for research, although its relevance in nature is unknown. The fungus is exceptionally well-suited for genetic modification. This allows researchers to study the interaction between the fungus and its host with relative ease. The availability of the entire genome is another advantage of this fungus as model organism.

U. maydis is not only used to study plant disease, but it also is used to study plant genetics. In 1996, a study on U. maydis genetics led to the discovery of synthesis-dependent strand annealing, a method ofhomologous recombination used in DNA repair. Other studies in the fungus have also investigated the role of the cytoskeleton in polarized growth. It is largely due to work with U. maydis that the function of the breast-cancer gene BRCA2 is now known.

Culinary uses

Fig. Huitlacoche corn taco

Fig. Quesadilla de huitlacoche, as it's often served in central Mexico

Fig. Huitlacoche for sale in the produce department of a Soriana store in Mexico

Smut feeds on the corn plant and decreases the yield. Smut-infected crops are often destroyed, although some farmers use them to prepare silage.

The smut is a delicacy in Mexico, where it is known ashuitlacoche, even being preserved and sold for a significantly higher price than uninfected corn. The consumption of corn smut originates from ancient Aztec cuisine. For culinary use, the galls are harvested while still immature — fully mature galls are dry and almost entirely spore-filled. The immature galls, gathered two to three weeks after an ear of corn is infected, still retain moisture and, when cooked, have a flavor described as mushroom-like, sweet, savory, woody, and earthy. Flavor compounds include sotolon andvanillin, as well as the sugar glucose. The fungus has had difficulty entering into the American and European diets as most farmers see it as blight, despite attempts by government and high profile chefs to introduce it. In the mid-1990s, due to demand created by high-end restaurants, Pennsylvania and Florida farms were allowed by the United States Department of Agriculture (USDA) to intentionally infect corn with huitlacoche.

Most observers consider the program to have had little impact, although the initiative is still in progress. The cursory show of interest is significant because the USDA has spent a considerable amount of time and money trying to eradicate corn smut in the United States. Moreover, in 1989, the James Beard Foundation held a high-profilehuitlacoche dinner, prepared by Josefina Howard, chef at Rosa Mexicano restaurant. This dinner tried to get Americans to eat more of it by renaming it the Mexican truffle.

Native Americans of the American Southwest, including the Zuni people, have used corn smut in an attempt to induce labor. It has similar medicinal effects to ergot, but weaker, due to the presence of the chemicalustilagine.

Recipes of Mexico

A favorite and simple Mexican-style succotash can be made from chorizo, onions, garlic, serrano peppers,huitlacoche, and shrimp with salsa taquera. The mild, earthy flavors of the huitlacoche blend nicely with the fats of the chorizo and bond to mellow out the heat from the peppers and salsa.

Another Mayan favorite on the Riviera Maya (Cancun to Tulum) is to add huitlacoche to omelettes. Once again, its earthy flavors bond with the fats that cook the eggs to mellow the flavors into a truffle-like taste.

An important thing to note about huitlacoche is that the blueish color transforms into the recognizable black color only with heat. Any dish with huitlacoche must include a slow simmer of the fungus until it becomes black which also removes most of the starch of the corn and what is left is a black oily paste.

Availability

In Mexico, huitlacoche is mostly consumed fresh and can be purchased at restaurants or street or farmer's markets throughout the country and, to a much lesser extent, can also be purchased as a canned good in some markets and via the internet. Farmers in the countryside have been known to spread the spores around intentionally to create more of the fungus. In some parts of the country, they call the fungus "hongo de maiz," i.e. "maize fungus."

FISTULINA HEPATICA

Fistulina hepatica (beefsteak fungus, also known as beefsteak polypore or ox tongue) is an unusualbracket fungus classified in the Agaricales, that is commonly seen in Britain, but can be found in North America, Australia,

North Africa, and the rest of Europe. As its name suggests, it looks remarkably similar to a slab of raw meat. It has been used as a meat substitute in the past, and can still be found in someFrench markets. It has a sour, slightly acidic taste. For eating it must be collected young and it may be tough and need long cooking.

DETAILS

Fig. Beefsteak fungus

The shape resembles a large tongue, and it is rough-surfaced with a reddish-brown colour. The spores are released from minute pores on the creamy-white underside of the fruit body. A younger Fistulina hepatica is a pinkish-red colour, and it darkens with age. It bleeds a dull red juice when cut, with the cut flesh further resembling meat.

The underside of the fruiting body, from which the spores are ejected, is a mass of tubules. The genus name is a diminutive of the Latin wordfistula and means "small tube", whilst the species name hepaticameans "liver-like", referring to the consistency of the flesh.

The species is fairly common, and can often be found on oaks andsweet chestnut, from August to the end of Autumn, on either living or dead wood. It has a tendency to impart a reddish-brown stain to the living wood of oaks, creating a desirable timber type. In Australia, it can be found growing from wounds on Eucalyptus trees. It causes abrown rot on the trees which it infects.

RELATIONSHIP TO OTHER FUNGI

Fistulina is classified in the family Fistulinaceae; molecular studies suggest close relations to the agaricmushroom Schizophyllum in the Schizophyllaceae (in the schizophylloid clade), but in the separate sisterfistulinoid clade. Fistulina is a cyphelloid genus, meaning that it is closely related to gilled fungi, but its fertile surface consists of smooth cup-shaped elements instead of gills. The underside (the hymenium) is a mass of tubules which represent a "reduced" form of the ancestral gills.

LACTARIUS SUBDULCIS

Lactarius subdulcis, commonly known as the mild milkcap or beech milk cap, is an edible mushroomin the genus Lactarius. It is brown in colour, with a large number of gills and a particularly thin layer of flesh in the cap. Mycorrhizal, the mushroom is found from late summer to late autumn at the base of beech treesin small groups or individually, where it is one of the two most common species of fungi.

Alternatively, it can be found in large groups in fields, sometimes with more than a hundred individual mushrooms. It is found in Europe, and, despite previous research to the contrary, is absent in North America. Although considered edible, it is not particularly useful as food due to its ivy-like taste and the fact that more choice mushrooms will be easily found at the same time.

L. subdulcis is known for its abundant, sweet-tasting milk that, unlike the latex of some of its relatives, does not stain fabric yellow.

TAXONOMY

Lactarius subdulcis was first described as Agaricus subdulcis by mycologist Christian Hendrik Persoon in 1801, before English mycologist Samuel Frederick Gray placed it in its current genus Lactarius in 1821 in his The Natural Arrangement of British Plants. The specific epithet is derived from Latin words sub"under", and dulcis "sweet", after the milk's delayed sweet taste. As well as mild milk cap, beech milk cap is an alternate common name.

DESCRIPTION

Fig. L. subdulcis is known for the large amounts of milk it produces.

Lactarius subdulcis has a convex cap of 3–7 cm (1.4–2.8 in) across that later develops a depression. It sometimes has a small umbo, and in colour can be a reddish-brown, rusty or dark-cinnamon, later paling to buff, though darker in the middle.

The cap can be fairly rigid to flexible, and smooth to slightly wrinkled. At first, the margin is incurved though it is sometimes slightly furrowed. The stem is 3–7 cm long and between 6 and 13 mm thick, and is generally cylindrical though can be club-shaped. The stem is sometimes furrowed lengthwise, and is generally the same colour as the cap, though paler at the top. The flesh is pale and there is only a thin layer in the cap. The crowded gills are adnate to slightly decurrent, and can be white or pink in colour. It has white, plentiful milk that does not stain fabrics yellow, differentiating it from other species of Lactarius, such as L. decipiens. It has a faint, oily scent.

Spores

Lactarius subdulcis has cream spore print with a slight salmon tinge. The spores are oval, with largish warts of around 1 micrometre (μm) which are joined by a well-developed network of mostly thin ridges.The spores measure 7.5–11 μm by 6.5–9 μm, and are amyloid or ellipsoid in shape.

DISTRIBUTION AND HABITAT

Lactarius subdulcis is found in Europe; it does not occur in North America, although a number of similar brownish-orange species were formerly classified under this species. It is found in broad-leaved woodland, especially on the floor at the base of beech trees. Along with L. vellereus, L. subdulcis is the most common fungi found on beech trees. The mushrooms can be found from late summer to late autumn, and are common. They are found individually, or in small groups. They can also be found in fields, generally appearing in large batches, with groups of over a hundred mushrooms not uncommon.

EDIBILITY

Lactarius subdulcis has a mild taste with a slightly bitter after-taste.

Though considered edible after cooking, it is not recommended, as it has a taste reminiscent of ivy. There are a number of other mushrooms that appear at the same time and in the same areas as L. subdulcis that are preferable to it, including L. mitissimus, meaning that L. subdulcis is not particularly useful as a foodstuff. The milk is one of distinguishing features, having a sweet taste that turns bitter in the mouth, with L. subdulcis being considered a sweet milk mushroom.

LACTARIUS VOLEMUS

Lactarius volemus is a species of fungus in the family Russulaceae. It is widely distributed in the northern hemisphere, in temperate regions of Europe, North America and Asia as well as some subtropical and tropical regions of Central America and Asia.

A mycorrhizal fungus, its fruit bodies grow on the ground at the base of various species of trees from summer to autumn, either individually or in groups.

It is valued as an edible mushroom, and is sold in markets in Asia. Several other Lactarius mushrooms resembleL. volemus, such as the closely related edible species L. corrugis, but these can be distinguished by differences in distribution, visible morphology, and microscopic characteristics. L. volemus produces a white spore print and has roughly spherical spores about 7–8 micrometres in diameter.

Fig. A collection from Wayne National Forest,Ohio, showing typical colour variations

Fig. Lactarius volemus var. flavus

The colour of the L. volemus mushroom varies from apricot to tawny, and the cap may be up to 11 cm (4 1/2 in) wide. The pale golden yellow gills on the underside of the cap are closely spaced and sometimes forked.

One of the mushroom's most distinctive features is the large amount of latex ("milk") that it exudes when the gills are damaged, leading to the common names weeping milk cap and voluminous-latex milky. It also has a distinctive fishy smell, which does not affect the taste. The fruit bodies have been chemically analysed and found to contain several sterols related to ergosterol, some of which are unique to this species.

The mushroom also contains a natural rubber that has been chemically characterized.Phylogenetic analysis suggests that Lactarius volemus represents several species or subspecies, rather than a single taxon.

TAXONOMY AND NAMING

The first mention of Lactarius volemus in the scientific literature was in Carl Linnaeus's 1753 Species Plantarum, under the name Agaricus lactifluus. In 1821, Swedish mycologist Elias Magnus Fries called it Agaricus volemus in his Systema Mycologicum. In this work he proposed a grouping of related species (called a tribus, or tribe) within the genus Agaricus, which he named Galorrheus.

Fries later recognised Lactarius as a distinct genus in his 1838 Epicrisis Systematis Mycologici, citing Galorrheusas a synonym; it was in this publication that the species was first called by the name it is known by today. Although Linnaeus had published the species before Fries, Fries's name is sanctioned and thus has nomenclatural priority. In 1871 Paul Kummer raised most of Fries's tribes to generic rank, and so renamed the species Galorrheus volemus.

The variety L. volemus var. subrugosus was identified byCharles Horton Peck in 1879, but is now classified as a separate species, L. corrugis. In 1891, Otto Kuntze moved the species into Lactifluus, a genus which has since been folded back into Lactarius.Another historical synonym is Lactarius lactifluus, used by Lucien Quélet in 1886, a renaming based on Linnaeus's Agaricus lactifluus. Lactarius wangii, reported by Hua-An Wen and Jian-Zhe Ying to be a new species from China in 2005, was synonymised two years later with L. volemus.

The specific epithet "volemus" is derived from the Latin vola, meaning "the hollow of the hand", suggestive of Fries's reference to the large amount of latex "flowing enough to fill the hand". Common names for L. volemus include the weeping milk cap, the tawny milkcap, the orange-brown milky,the voluminous-latex milky, the lactarius orange, the fishy milkcap, and the apricot milk cap. In theWest Virginian mountains of the United States, the mushroom is called a "leatherback" or a "bradley". The latter name may originate from its German name Brätling.

PHYLOGENY

Lactarius volemus is the type species of the sectionDulces in subgenus Lactifluus. This grouping includes species with a dry cap, abundant latex, and a white or pale cream spore print. Because the closely relatedL. corrugis has overlapping morphological characters, including similar colouration in the cap and stem, it has been difficult to reliably distinguish between the two species.

The difficulty in discerning the two is exacerbated by the fact that both species have several colour forms: Japanese specimens of L. volemus may have a red cap, a yellow cap with a long stem, or a velvet-like surface texture; the caps of L. corrugis may be either red, commonly rust-coloured.

In 2005, Japanese researchers clarified the relationships between these two species and others in section Dulces using molecular phylogenetics, and by comparing differences in fatty acid composition,morphology, and taste. The colour variants group phylogenetically into different subclades, suggesting that they might better be considered as "different species, subspecies, or varieties".

A 2010 molecular study of L. volemus of northern Thailand found that 79 tested specimens could be divided into 18 distinct phylogenetic species; six of these were described as new species: L. acicularis, L. crocatus,L. distantifolius, L. longipilus, L. pinguis and L. vitellinus.

DESCRIPTION

Fig. The profuse whitish latex may become brownish upon exposure to air, and stains tissues brown.

The fruit body of Lactarius volemus has a fleshy and firm cap with a velvety or smooth surface and a shape that changes with maturity: it starts off convex, with edges curved inwards, then later grows flat with a depression in the middle. With a typical diameter of 5 to 11 cm (2–4 1/2 in), its colour ranges from apricot totawny. The cap colouration, however, is somewhat variable, as has been noted in Asian, European,and North American specimens. The stem, whose height varies between 4 and 12 cm (1 1/2 and 5 in), and which is typically between 1 and 1.5 cm (0.4 and 0.6 in) thick, has a slightly lighter colouration than the cap. It is firm, with a velvety or smooth surface that sometimes has depressions running longitudinally up and down its length. The gills are adnate to slightly decurrent, brittle, narrow, quite closely spaced and sometimes forked. Normally a pale golden yellow colour, the gills turn brown when bruised. Interspersed between the gills are lamellulae, short gills that do not extend to the stem. The flesh is whitish and firm.

The mushroom smells somewhat fishy; one source suggests the odour is "like a dead shad, which anglers will tell you is probably the most malodorous freshwater fish". The odour is concentrated when the fruit bodies are dried. One of the mushroom's most distinctive features is the abundant latex, so plentiful that a small nick on the gills will cause it to "weep" the milky substance. The latex tends to impart brown stains on whatever it contacts.

The spore print is whitish. The spores are roughly spherical, translucent (hyaline), and typically measure 7.5–10.0 by 7.5–9.0 μm. The spore surface is reticulate—covered with ridges that form a complete network. The ridges are up to 0.8 μm high and have conspicuous projections up to 1.2 μm high. The spore-bearing cells of the hymenium, the basidia, are club-shaped, hyaline, four-spored, and have dimensions of 40–62 by 7.2–10.4 μm.

Interspersed among the basidia are sterile cells calledcystidia. The pleurocystidia (cystidia on the side of a gill) are roughly spindle- to club-shaped, and measure 48–145 by 5–13 μm.

The cheilocystidia (cystidia on the edge of a gill) may be spindle-, club-, or awl-shaped (subulate), or intermediate in between these forms, and measure 27–60 by 5–7 μm.Additionally, there are cystidia present on both the surface of the cap and the stem. If a drop of ferric sulphate (used as a chemical test in mushroom identification) is applied to the mushroom flesh, it will immediately stain dark bluish-green.

The variety Lactarius volemus var. flavus was described by Alexander H. Smith and Lexemuel Ray Hesler in their 1979 monograph of North American Lactarius species. This rare variety, found in the southeastern United States (ranging from South Carolina to Florida and extending west to Texas), has a cap that stays yellow throughout its development.

It also has slightly smaller spores than the regular variety: 6.5–9.0 by 6–8 μm. Some authors have considered the rarely collected L. volemus var. oedematopus, found in central and southern Europe, to be a distinct variety distinguished from the common variety by a darker reddish-brown cap and a swollen stem.

This assessment is not universally accepted, possibly because it falls within the range of morphological variation shown by the main variety. L. volemus var. asiaticus was named in 2004 based on Vietnamese specimens; associating with Khasi pine (Pinus khasya), it has small, dull brown, velvety fruit bodies. In general, little taxonomical significance has been ascribed to the several varieties of L. volemus that have been proposed.

Similar species

Fig. L. hygrophoroides (left) and L. corrugis (right) are lookalikes.

Lactarius volemus is closely related to L. corrugis, and generally similar in appearance. L. corrugis usually has more surface wrinkles, darker gills, weaker or absent scent, and less orange colouration; however, intermediate colour forms can be found.

The two can be distinguished more definitively by microscopic characteristics: L. corrugis has larger spores—typically 10.4–12.8 by 9.6–11.8 μm—with a coarser surface reticulum, and larger pleurocystidia. Lactarius hygrophoroides also resembles L. volemus, but differs in having widely spaced gills, and spores that lack surface reticulations.

The Zambian species L. chromospermus has a superficial resemblance toL. volemus, but the former species, in addition to its African distribution, can be identified by its cinnamon-brown spore print—unique in the Russulaceae.L. subvelutinus is also similar to L. volemus, but lacks the fishy odour, has a dull yellow-orange to bright golden orange cap, narrow gills, and a white latex that does not change colour. The species L. austrovolemus is closely related, but has more crowded gills, while L. lamprocystidiatus can only be reliably distinguished from L. volemus by microscopic characteristics: the reticulations on its spores are taller and more acute, and the meshes formed by the intersections of the reticulations are smaller. Both L. austrovolemus and L. lamprocystidiatus are known only from Papua New Guinea.

EDIBILITY AND OTHER USES

Despite the unappealing fishy scent that develops after the mushroom is picked, L. volemus is edibleand recommended for culinary usage, though, typical of Lactarius, it has a slightly granular texture that some may find unappetizing. The odor disappears during cooking. The latex only has a mild taste. The species is considered good for novice mushroom hunters to eat, and is best prepared by slow cooking to prevent it from becoming too hard; specimens that have been rehydrated after having been dried will require longer cooking times to eliminate the grainy texture.

The mushroom has also been suggested for use in casseroles and thick sauces. Pan frying is not a recommended cooking technique, due to the large amounts of latex it exudes. L. volemus is one of several species of Lactariusthat are sold in rural markets in Yunnan Province, China, and it is among the most popular wild edible mushroom species collected for consumption and sale in Nepal. In their 2009 book on Lactariusspecies of North America, Bessette and colleagues consider the mushroom "the best-known and most popular edible milk mushroom" in the eastern United States. A Turkish study of the nutritional composition of the fruit bodies concluded that L. volemus is a good source of protein andcarbohydrates.

Bioactive compounds

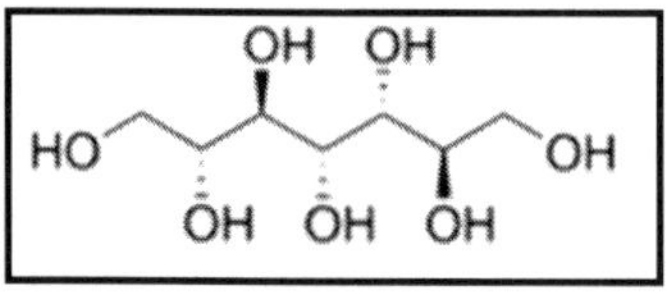

Fig. Volemitol

Fruit bodies contains a unique sterol molecule called volemolide, a derivative of the common fungal sterol ergosterol that may have application in fungal chemotaxonomy. A 2001 study identified a further nine sterols, three of which were previously unknown to science.

According to the authors, these types of highly oxygenated compounds—similar to sterols found in marine soft coral and sponges—are rare in fungi. The mushroom also contains volemitol (D-glycero-D-mannoheptitol), a seven-carbon sugar alcohol first isolated from the species by the French scientist Émile Bourquelotin 1889. Volemitol occurs as a free sugar in many plant and brown algal species.

Due to their natural polyisoprene content (1.1–7.7% by dry weight of fruit bodies), L. volemus fruit bodies can also be used to produce rubber. The chemical structure of rubber from the mushroom consists of a high molecular mass homologue of polyprenol, arranged as a dimethylallyl group, two transisoprene units, a long sequence of cis isoprenes (between 260–300 units), terminated by a hydroxyl or fatty acid ester.

Biosynthetically, the creation of the polyisoprene begins with the compound trans,trans-farnesyl pyrophosphate, and is thought to terminate by esterification of polyisoprenyl pyrophosphate. The enzyme isopentenyl-diphosphate delta isomerase has been identified as required for the initiation of rubber synthesis inL. volemus and several other Lactarius species.

ECOLOGY, DISTRIBUTION, AND HABITAT

Fig. Specimens in mixed forest, found in Bovec basin, East Julian Alps, Slovenia

Like all Lactarius species, L. volemus forms ectomycorrhizae, mutually beneficial symbioticassociations with various tree species. In this association, the fungal hyphae grow around the root of the plant and between its cortical cells, but do not actually penetrate them. The hyphae extend outward into the soil, increasing the surface area for absorption to help the plant absorb nutrients from the soil. It is found growing at the base of both coniferous and broad-leaved trees, although it is more common in deciduous woods. It may also sometimes be found in peat moss beds. The fruit bodies, which appear between summer and autumn, are common. They can be found growing solitarily or in groups, and are more abundant in weather that is warm and humid.

Fruit bodies can be inhabited by species of limoniid flies, such as Discobola marginata or Limonia yakushimensis, as well as several species of fungi-dwelling mites. The flies are hosts for the mites in asymbiotic association known as phoresis, whereby the mites are mechanically carried by its host. Mites are small and unable to migrate the relatively long distances between mushrooms without assistance; the insect hosts, in comparison, are large and can transfer the mites between their preferred feeding habitats.

Lactarius volemus is found in warm temperate regions and as well as some subtropical and tropical regions of the Northern Hemisphere. The fungus is widely distributed throughout Europe, although it is in decline in some countries, and has become rare enough in the Netherlands (and Flanders) to be considered locally extinct.

In the Americas, the northern limit of its distribution reaches southern Canada east of the Great Plains, and the species extends south to the East Coast of the United States and Mexico, and beyond into Central America

(Guatemala). It is also known from Asia, including China (Qinling Mountains, Guizhou Province, and Yunnan Province), Japan, India, Korea, Nepal, and Vietnam. Collections have also been made from the Middle East, including Iran and Turkey.

LECCINUM AURANTIACUM

Leccinum aurantiacum, is a species of fungus in the genus Leccinum. It is found in forests of Europe,North America and Asia and has a large, characteristically red-capped fruiting body. In North America, it is sometimes referred to by the common name red-capped scaber stalk. There are some uncertainties regarding the taxonomic classification of this species in Europe as well as in North America. It is considered edible.

Fig. L. aurantiacum in a Luxembourg wood

DESCRIPTION

The cap is orange-red and measures up to 8 in (20 cm) across. Its flesh is white, bruising at first burgundy, then grayish or purple-black. The underside of the cap has very small whitish pores that bruise olive-brown. The stem measures 4-7 in (10-18 cm) tall and to a ¾-1¼ in (2-3 cm) thick and can bruise blue-green. It is whitish, with short, rigid projections or scabers that turn to brown to black with age.

DISTRIBUTION AND HABITAT

Leccinum aurantiacum can be found fruiting during summer and autumn in forests throughout Europe and North America. The association between fungus and host tree is mycorrhizal. In Europe, Leccinum aurantiacum has been traditionally known to be associated with poplars (Populus). There exists some debate about the classification of L. aurantiacum and L. quercinum as separate species.

According to authors who do not recognise the distinction, L. aurantiacum is also found with oak(Quercus). Additionally, L. aurantiacum has been recorded with various other deciduous trees includingbeech (Fagus), birch (Betula), chestnut (Castanea), willow (Salix), and Tilia. L. aurantiacum is not known to associate with conifers in Europe.

North American populations have been recorded in coniferous as well as deciduous forests, though it remains uncertain whether collections from coniferous forests are not L. vulpinum instead. In addition, L. aurantiacum may be absent altogether from North America, with collections from deciduous forests being attributed to other North American species L. insigne, and L. brunneum.

USE

This is a favorite species for eating and can be prepared as other edible boletes. Its flesh turns very dark on cooking. Like most members of the Boletaceae, these mushrooms are popular with maggots. Due to a number of poisonings and the difficulty identifying species, Leccinum may not be considered safe to eat.

This species also needs to be cooked well (not parboiled) or else it may cause vomiting or other negative effects. It is commonly believed that this species can cause problems with digestion if not cooked properly. Portable kitchens and other simple solutions are therefore not recommended for cooking.

SIMILAR SPECIES

In Europe, several orange-red capped species exist, which differ mainly in habitat. L. quercinum grows with oak (Quercus) and other broad-leaved trees and bears red-brown stem scabers. In coniferous forests,L. vulpinum occurs with pine (Pinus), and L. piceinum with spruce (Picea). Not all authors recognise these as distinct species.

In North America, L. insigne grows in aspen or birch stands, while L. atrostipitatum grows in birch stands. Both are edible.

LECCINUM SCABRUM

The birch bolete (Leccinum scabrum) is an edible mushroom in the family Boletaceae, and was formerly classified as Boletus scaber. The birch bolete is widespread in Europe, as well as elsewhere, in theNorthern Hemisphere, occurring only in mycorrhizal association with birch trees. It fruits from June to October; its common names include rough-stemmed bolete, scaber stalk, and birch bolete.

DESCRIPTION

The pileus is 5–15 cm (2–6 in.) wide. At first, it is hemispherical, and later becomes flatter. The skin of the cap is light gray-brown to reddish gray-brown, later often more or less brown, smooth, bald, dry, and rather slimy when damp. The pores are white at a young age, later gray. In older specimens, the pores on the pileus can bulge out, while around the stipe they dent in strongly. The pore covering is easy to remove from the skin of the pileus.

The stipe is 5–15 cm (2–6 in.) long and 1–3.5 cm (3/8–13/8 in.) wide, slim, with white and dark to black flakes, and tapers upward. The basic mycelium is white.

The flesh is whitish, later more gray-white and does not change color when broken. In young specimens, the meat is relatively firm, but it very soon becomes spongey and holds water, especially in rainy weather. When cooked, the meat of the birch bolete turns black.

L. scabrum has been found in association with ornamental birch trees planted outside of its native range, such as in California.

SIMILAR SPECIES

Several different species of Leccinum mushrooms are found in mycorrhiza with birches, and can be confused by amateurs and mycologists alike. L. variicolor has a bluish stipe. L. oxydabile has firmer, pinkish flesh and a different pileus skin structure. L. melaneum is darker in color and has yellowish hues under the skin of the pileus and stipe. L. holopus is paler and whitish in all parts.

Fig. L. scabrum of different ages

USES

The birch bolete is edible and is especially enjoyable pickled in brine or vinegar. It is used also in mixed mushroom dishes, fried or steamed.

MACROLEPIOTA PROCERA

The parasol mushroom (Macrolepiota procera) is a basidiomycete fungus with a large, prominent fruiting body resembling a parasol. It is a fairly common species on well-drained soils. It is found solitary or in groups and fairy rings in pastures and occasionally in woodland. Globally, it is widespread in temperateregions.

DESCRIPTION

The height and cap diameter of a mature specimen may both reach 40 cm, a size truly impressive for the fruiting body of an agaric. The stipe is relatively thin and reaches full height before the cap has expanded. The stipe is very fibrous in texture which renders it inedible. The surface is characteristically wrapped in asnakeskin-like pattern of scaly growths. The immature cap is compact and egg-shaped, with the cap margin around the stipe, sealing a chamber inside the cap. As it matures, the margin breaks off, leaving a fleshy, movable ring around the stipe. At full maturity, the cap is more or less flat, with a chocolate-brownumbo in the centre that is leathery to touch. Dark and cap-coloured flakes remain on the upper surface of the cap and can be removed easily. The gills are crowded, free, and white with a pale pink tinge sometimes present. The spore print is white. It has a pleasant nutty smell. When sliced, the white flesh may turn a pale pink.

USES

It is a very sought after and popular fungus in Europe, due in part to its large size, seasonal frequency and versatility in the kitchen.

The parasol mushroom is difficult to mistake for any other, especially in regions like Europe where the poisonous look-alike Chlorophyllum molybdites does not occur. Nevertheless, as with picking any fungus for consumption, caution should be exercised at all times.

The parasol mushroom may not be eaten raw because it is slightly toxic. It is popular soaked in butter.

In central and eastern European countries this species of fungi is usually prepared similarly to a cutlet. It is usually run through egg and breadcrumbs and then fried on a pan with some oil or butter. Served with white bread, it makes a delicious meal of summer and early fall. A savory Slovak recipe is to bake caps stuffed with ground pork, oregano, and garlic. Italians and Austrians also serve the young un-flattened caps stuffed with seasoned minced beef, baked in the same manner as stuffed peppers.

SIMILAR SPECIES

Fig. Macrolepiota procera, the parasol mushroom

Smaller but similar in appearance is the common shaggy parasol(Chlorophyllum rhacodes.) Its edibility is suspect as it causes mild sickness in some people, especially when eaten raw. One must learn to distinguish the two as their geographical ranges overlap.

Differences from the parasol mushroom include its smaller dimensions, pungent (fruity) and reddening flesh when cut, lack of patterns on its stipe, and very shaggy cap surface.

Macrolepiota mastoidea, a European species, is yet another very large edible mushroom. Its dimensions are generally smaller than that of M. procera and the markings on its stipe less obvious. It is also much rarer.

Species of Agaricus have brown spores and the gills of mature specimens are never white.

There are a few poisonous species which can be mistaken for M. procera:

- Chlorophyllum molybdites, a species that causes the largest number of annual mushroom poisonings in North America due to its close similarity. Faintly green gills and a pale green spore print give it away. Furthermore this mushroom lacks the aforementioned snakeskin pattern that is generally present on the parasol mushroom. Its range is reportedly expanding into Europe.
- Leucocoprinus brunnea, also found in North America, slowly turns brown when sliced.
- White and immature species of Amanita are also a potential hazard. To be sure, one must only pick parasol mushrooms past their button stage. A general rule of thumb with the parasol mushroom as compared to amanita species is that the parasol mushroom has darker flakes on a lighter surface, whereas amanita species have the opposite, lighter flakes (if there are any) on a darker surface, such as the Panther cap.
- The Saffron Parasol Cystoderma amianthinum is very much smaller, and not often eaten.
- Lepiota brunneoincarnata is a lepiota species known to have caused mortal intoxications in Spain.

POLYPORUS SQUAMOSUS

Polyporus squamosus is a basidiomycete bracket fungus, with common names including Dryad's saddle and Pheasant's back mushroom. It has a widespread distribution, being found in North America, Australia, Asia, and Europe, where it causes a white rot in the heartwood of living and deadhardwood trees.

The name "Dryad's saddle" refers to creatures in Greek mythology called Dryads who could conceivably fit and ride on this mushroom, whereas the pheasant's back analogy derives from the pattern of colors on the bracket matching that of a pheasant's back.

TAXONOMY

The species was first described scientifically by British botanist William Hudson in 1778, who named itBoletus squamosus. It was given its current name in 1821 by Elias Magnus Fries in his Systema Mycologicum.

Description

This mushroom is commonly attached to dead logs or stumps at one point with a thick stem. Generally, thefruit body is 8–30 cm (3–12 in) across and up to 10 cm (4 in) thick. The body can be yellow to brown and has "squamules" or scales on its upper side. On the underside one can see the pores that are characteristic of the genus Polyporus; they are made up of tubes packed together closely.

The tubes are between 1 and 12 mm long. The stalk is thick and short, up to 5 cm (2.0 in) long. The fruit body will produce a white spore print if laid onto a sheet of paper. They can be found alone, in clusters of two or three, or forming shelves. Young specimens are soft but toughen with age. It is particularly common on dead elm and is also found on living maple trees.

Distribution and habitat

This organism is common and widespread, being found east of the Rocky Mountains in the United States and over much of Europe. It is also found in Australia and Asia. It commonly fruits in the spring, occasionally during autumn, and rarely during other seasons. Many mushroom hunters will stumble upon this when looking for morels during the spring as both have similar fruiting times, and this fungus can grow to a noticeable size of up to 50 cm (20 in) across. It plays an important role in woodland ecosystems by decomposing wood, usually elm, but is occasionally a parasite on living trees. Other tree hosts include ash,beech, horse chestnut, lime, maple, planetree, poplar, and willow.

Edibility and uses

Edible. Young tender squamosus is best with the edges thinly sliced and fried in bacon grease. Young specimens are preferred, as they can become infested with maggots and become firm and inedible as they mature. Cookbooks dealing with preparation generally recommend gathering these while young, slicing them into small pieces and cooking them over a low heat. Some people value the thick, stiff paperthat can be made from this and many other mushrooms of the genus Polyporus. The mushroom's smell resembles watermelon rind.

SUILLUS BOVINUS

Suillus bovinus, also known as the Jersey cow mushroom, is a pored mushroom of the genus Suillusin the Suillaceae family. It is an edible mushroom that often grows in a symbiosis (Mycorrhiza) with pine.

DESCRIPTION

The cap of Suillus bovinus is initially convex, then flat with a wavy margin and a grey-yellow in colour. The flesh is whitish or yellowish and the pores are irregular and grey- to olive-yellow and generally decurrent to the 4–6 cm tall stem, which is a similar colour to the cap and smaller towards the base. The flesh is very spongy and foam rubber like to the extent that it is often possible to bend the cap double without breaking it.

Distribution and habitat

It is found in coniferous woods across Europe, including subalpine regions in the Alps.

Edibility

Suillus bovinus tastes mild and is edible, although it was left for the medieval peasants while medieval French knights allegedly reserved the highly regarded Tricholoma equestre for themselves.

Ecology

The related Gomphidius roseus is found exclusively with this species, and is now thought to be parasitic upon the mycelium of Suillus bovinus.

SUILLUS GRANULATUS

Suillus granulatus is a pored mushroom of the genus Suillus in the Suillaceae family. It is similar to the related S. luteus, but can be distinguished by its ringless stalk. Like S. luteus, it is an edible mushroom that often grows in a symbiosis (Mycorrhiza) with pine. It has been commonly known as the weeping bolete, or the granulated bolete.

TAXONOMY

Suillus is an ancient term for fungi, and is derived from the word "swine". Granulatus means "fine grain".

Description

Fig. Suillus granulatus showing 'milky droplets' on pores.

The orange-brown, to brown-yellow cap is viscid (sticky) when wet, and shiny when dry, and is usually 3 to 9 cm in diameter. The stem is pale yellow, of uniform thickness, with tiny brownish granules at the apex. It is without a ring. The tubes and pores are small, pale yellow, and exude pale milky droplets when young. Theflesh is also pale yellow.

Distribution and habitat

Grows with Pinus (Pine trees) on both calcareous and acid soils, and sometimes occurs in large numbers. It is common in Britain, Europe, and North America. A native to the northern hemisphere, it has also been introduced into Australia under Pinus radiata.

Edibility

Suillus granulatus is Edible and fair. Like all Suillus species, the tubes are best removed before cooking. It is sometimes included in commercially produced mushroom preserves. Has been known to cause mild stomach upsets.

Toxicity

Suillus granulatus sometimes causes contact dermatitis to those who handle it.

SUILLUS LUTEUS

Suillus luteus is a basidiomycete fungus, and the type species of the genus Suillus. It is a common fungus indigenous to coniferous forests of Eurasia and North America, and introduced to southern Australia and New Zealand. Commonly referred to as slippery Jack or sticky bun in English-speaking countries, its names refer to the brown cap, which is characteristically viscid in wet conditions. The fungus fruits abundantly in autumn, and is harvested for food. The slime coating, however, may cause indigestion if not removed.

DESCRIPTION

The cap is brown and up to 12 cm in diameter at maturity. The cap is initially hemispherical, later flattening out. It is slimy to the touch, bare, smooth, and glossy even when dry and the cuticle is easily peeled off. The tiny, circular pores of the tubes are at first light yellow but turn olive to dark yellow with maturity.

The attachment to the stem is adnate. The stem attains a height of up to 10 cm and a width 3 cm. It is pale yellow and more or less cylindrical but may bear a swollen base. A white partial veil extends from the stem to the cap margin in immature specimens.

At maturity the veil detaches from the cap and its remnant forms a ring around the stem. The underside of the ring is characteristically dark brown to violet. This species is one of the few members of the genus Suillus that sport such a ring. The white flesh of the entire fungus does not discolour when damaged, and it is soft particularly in mature specimens. It is frequently infested with larvae.

Similar species

Suillus luteus is often confused with Suillus granulatus, which is another common mushroom occurring in the same habitat. S. granulatus is yellow-fleshed and exudes latex droplets when young but most conspicuously, it bears neither partial veil nor ring. Other than that, Suillus luteus is unlikely to be confused with other mushrooms, especially if its preferred home under pine trees and the whitish partial veil are taken into consideration.

Distribution and habitat

Suillus luteus can be found all over the northern hemisphere. It is found in coastal and montane pine forests and exhibits a tolerance of the northern latitudes. It is especially common in pine plantations and young pine forests. Suillus luteus forms mycorrhizal associations with various species of pine, which include Pinus sylvestris, Pinus nigra, and Pinus peuce in Europe, and Pinus resinosa and Pinus strobus in North America. It does not require a specific soil but seems to prefer acidic and nutrient-deficient soil. The fungus fruits in spring, summer and fairly prolifically in autumn, following periods of wet weather.

It has also been found under pine trees in introduced pine plantations in Australia, particularly in the Blue Mountains and Southern Highlands, as well as New Zealand and Argentinean Patagonia. There it can be picked around Easter.

Edibility

Suillus luteus is an edible mushroom. Although some authors regard it as one of low quality, slippery jacks are considered a delicacy in Slaviccultures (known as maslyata in Russian or maslaki in Polish, derived from the word for "buttery"). Slippery jacks are frequently marinated, fried, or stewed (used both fresh or dried), and are known for their tendency to maintain very light flesh color during cooking if the skin is peeled beforehand. S. luteus and other Suillus species may cause allergic reactions in some people. The fungus is better cooked before eating, and some authors recommend discarding the glutinous cuticle and tubes before cooking. However, some people may find them excessively slippery. Gastrointestinal symptoms could be due to high levels of arabitol.

SUILLUS TOMENTOSUS

Suillus tomentosus is a species of mushroom. The common names of the species are Blue-staining Slippery Jack, Poor Man's Slippery Jack, and Woolly-capped Suillus.

DESCRIPTION

The cap is pale to orange-yellow with grayish brownish or reddish tomentum. The tubes are yellow and become blue when bruised. The stipe is grandular dotted and the color is similar to the cap. The cap is scaly and has fibrillose. The spores are brownish when they are young. The spore print is dark olive brown to brown. The species stains fingers blue. Suillus variegatus and suillus reticulatus are similar to this species. The species can be distinguished between other species in this genus because fibrillose-scaly surface of the cap.

Edibility

The mushroom may be edible to some while others may find its taste acidic even after cooking. The species has been known to cause gastric upset such as diarrhea and vomiting.

The author David Arorasaid the species tastes the same as Suillus fuscotomentosus. Arora also said that on a blandness scale, this mushroom ranks at the bottom. Arora reports that one collector stated the mushroom smells and tastes like Tootsie Rolls when dried. The species have also been said to smell like almonds. Consumers have to be careful that when they look for this species, that they be careful to distinguish this between other species that stain blue but are poisonous.

Habitat

The species is commonly found in the Rocky Mountains of Idaho and the Pacific Northwest. It is less common in the lake states. The species fruits in thesummer in the Rocky Mountains. Also, the species fruits in autumn along the Pacific coast and in the lake states. The species is by itself or scattered inmixed forests. The species can commonly be found under lodgepole pines or other two-needle pines. It is rarely found under jack pines.

Suillus tomentosus forms tuberculate ectomycorrhizae (mycorrhizae that are nodular) with lodgepole pine (Pinus contorta var. latifolia). Recent work has shown that acetylene is reduced by the nodules which means that nitrogen is being fixed by bacteria within the nodules. This system is functionally similar to the root nodules in legumes like clover. Lodgepole pine can be found growing on gravel pits or other extremely nitrogen deficient soils. Lodgepole pine with its S. tomentosus symbiont is one of the most common pioneer species in northern forests. It colonizes highly disturbed soils and creates an environment suitable for other species to colonize.

TRICHOLOMA TERREUM

Tricholoma terreum, commonly known as the grey knight or dirty tricholoma, is a grey-capped ediblemushroom of the large genus Tricholoma. It is found in coniferous woodlands in Europe, and has also been encountered under introduced pine trees in Australia.

TAXONOMY

It was originally described as Agaricus terreus by Jacob Christian Schäffer in 1762, and as Agaricus myomyces by mycologist Christian Hendrik Persoon in 1794. It was given its current binomial name by German Paul Kummer in 1871. It is commonly known as the grey knight from its discoloured gills.According to some European mycologists, Tricholoma myomyces is a synonym, but this is not universally accepted.

Description

The cap is 4–7 cm (1.6–2.6 in) wide and evenly covered in fine grey scales. Convex with a slight boss, it is broadly conical in shape. The whitish stipe is 3–8 cm (1.2–3.2 in) high and 1.5 cm wide and has no ring. There is no ring or volva. The whitish flesh is thin, easily broken, and has a pleasant mild (not mealy) smell and taste. The widely spaced and uneven gills are free (unattached to the stipe). The spore print is white, the oval spores 6–7 μm long by 3.5-4.4 μm wide.

It could be confused with the larger (and poisonous) T. pardinum has a mealy smell and cap scales; the edible T. orirubens has fine dark scales and pinkish gills.

Distribution and habitat

Tricholoma terreum is found in Europe, where fruiting bodies appear under conifers, particularly pine and spruce, from late summer to late autumn. They may also arise in parks near these trees, and grow in fairy rings. They are generally in quite densely populated groups though not bunched. It has been recorded growing under exotic Pinus radiata plantations in Australia.

Edibility

With a mild taste, the species is regarded as a good edible. It is seen in markets in France, along withClitocybe nebularis and Tricholoma portentosum. However, some authorities recommend that inexperienced pickers avoid all grey tricholomas.

They need to be eaten within a day or two of picking since the gills and flesh yellow and spoil quickly:

- Armillaria mellea
- Boletus badius
- Chroogomphus rutilus (pine-spikes or spike-caps)
- Calvatia gigantea (Giant Puffball)
- Clavariaceae species (coral fungus family)
- Clavulinaceae species (coral fungus family)
- Coprinus comatus, the Shaggy mane. Must be cooked as soon as possible after harvesting or the caps will first turn dark and unappetizing, then deliquesce and turn to ink. Not found in markets for this reason.
- Corn smut
- Cortinarius variicolor
- Fistulina hepatica (beefsteak polypore or the ox tongue)
- Hygrophorus chrysodon

Fig. Auricularia auricula-judae

- Lactarius salmonicolor
- Lactarius subdulcis (mild milkcap)
- Lactarius volemus

- Laetiporus sulphureus (Sulphur shelf). Also known by names such as the "chicken mushroom", "chicken fungus", sulphur shelf is a distinct bracket fungus popular among mushroom hunters.
- Leccinum aurantiacum (Red-capped scaber stalk)
- Leccinum scabrum (Birch bolete)
- Lepiota procera
- Macrolepiota procera Parasol Mushroom - Globally, it is widespread in temperate regions
- Polyporus squamosus (Dryad's saddle and Pheasant's back mushroom)
- Polyporus mylittae
- Ramariaceae species (coral fungus family)
- Rhizopogon luteolus
- Russula, some members of this genus are edible.
- Sparassis crispa. Also known as "cauliflower mushroom".
- Suillus bovinus
- Suillus granulatus
- Suillus luteus
- Suillus tomentosus
- Tricholoma terreum

Conditionally edible species

Fig. Amanita muscaria, a conditionally edible species

There are a number of fungi that are considered choice by some and toxic by others.

In some cases, proper preparation can remove some or all of the toxins:

- Amanita muscaria is edible if parboiled to leach out toxins. Fresh mushrooms cause vomiting, twitching, drowsiness, and hallucinations due to the presence of muscimol. Although present in A. muscaria, ibotenic acid is not in high enough concentration to produce any physical or psychological effects unless massive amounts are ingested.

- Coprinopsis atramentaria is edible without special preparation. However, consumption with alcohol is toxic due to the presence of coprine. Some other Coprinus spp. share this property.
- Gyromitra esculenta is eaten by some after it has been parboiled; however, mycologists do not recommend it. Raw Gyromitra are toxic due to the presence of gyromitrin, and it is not known if all of the toxin can be removed by parboiling.
- Lactarius spp. - Apart from Lactarius deliciosus which is universally considered edible, other Lactariusspp. that are considered toxic elsewhere in the world are eaten in some Eastern European countries, and Russia after pickling or parboiling.
- Verpa bohemica - Considered choice by some, it even can be found for sale as a "morel", but cases of toxicity have been reported. Verpas contain toxins similar to gyromitrin and similar precautions apply.

Use in traditional medicine

Fig. Reishi, a well-known mushroom

Fig. Chicken of the Woods, a mushroom used as a susbtitute for chicken meat

Fig. Common Morel

Medicinal mushrooms are mushrooms or extracts from mushrooms that are thought to be treatments fordiseases, yet remain unconfirmed in mainstream science and medicine, and so are not approved as drugsor medical treatments. Such use of mushrooms therefore falls into the domain of traditional medicine.

Preliminary research has shown some medicinal mushroom isolates to have cardiovascular, anticancer,antiviral, antibacterial, antiparasitic, anti-inflammatory, and antidiabetic properties. Currently, several extracts (polysaccharide-K, polysaccharide peptide, lentinan) have widespread use in Japan, Korea and China, as potential adjuvants to radiation treatments and chemotherapy.

The concept of a medicinal mushroom has a history spanning millennia in parts of Asia, mainly as traditional Chinese medicine. Only a few mushroom extracts have been tested for potential efficacy. Preliminary research results for most other extracts are on isolated cell lines, animal research with rodents, or early-stageclinical human trials as pilot studies.

Preparing wild edibles

Fig. A collection of dried mushrooms

Some wild species are toxic, or at least indigestible, when raw. As a rule all wild mushroom species should be cooked thoroughly before eating. Many species can be dried and re-hydrated by pouring boiling water over the dried mushrooms and letting them steep for approximately 30 minutes. The soaking liquid can be used for cooking as well, provided that any dirt at the bottom of the container is discarded.

One recipe for Auricularia auricula-judae is to collect it while still soft, wash it thoroughly and cut it into thin slices. The prepared slices should be stewed in stock or milk for around three-quarters of an hour, and then served with plenty of pepper. The result is crispy and not unlike seaweed.

The difficult task of identifying mushrooms in the wild, for culinary or recreational purposes, can result in severe poisoning.

PRODUCTION

Vitamin D

Mushrooms that have been exposed to ultraviolet (UV) light contain large amounts ofvitamin D2. Mushrooms, when exposed to UV light, convert ergosterol, a chemical found in large concentrations in many mushrooms, to vitamin D2. This is similar to the reaction in humans, where Vitamin D3 is synthesized after exposure to UV light.

Testing showed an hour of UV light exposure before harvesting made a serving of mushrooms contain twice the U.S. Food and Drug Administration's daily recommendation of vitamin D, and 5 minutes of UV light exposure after harvesting made a serving of mushrooms contain four times the FDA's daily recommendation of vitamin D. High performance liquid chromatography analysis has also demonstrated the effect sunlight has on mushroom vitamin D2 content. The ergocalciferol, vitamin D2, in UV-irradiated mushrooms is not the same form of vitamin D as is produced by UV-irradiation of human skin or animal skin, fur, or feathers (cholecalciferol, vitamin D3). Although vitamin D2 clearly has vitamin D activity in humans and is widely used in food fortification and in nutritional supplements, vitamin D3 is often used in dairy products.

Mushroom	Sunlight exposure	Vitamin D2 content (IU/100g)
Shiitake	None	10 — 100
Shiitake	Gills down	11,000
Shiitake	Gills up	46,000
Reishi	None	66
Reishi	Pores up	2,760
Maitake	None	460
Maitake	Pores up	31,900

3

Mushroom Cultivation

INTRODUCTION

Mushrooms are a source of high quality proteins, essential minerals and vitamins. Being low in starch content, they are good for diabetic patients.

Mushroom is grown on agriculture residues like straw, leaves, and sticks which (after use) can be recycled back as organic manure.

Mushroom cultivation demands no land but closed structure, which can even be a thatch-hut. it can be a remunerative cottage industry for rural women.

CULTIVATION

TISSUE CULTURE METHOD

Select fresh mature mushrooms (straight from the bed), wash them gently under running water to remove surface dirt. Blot it dry. Wipe the surface gently with 70 per cent alcohol.

Using a sterile knife, cut a small slit at the bottom of the mushroom. Tear it into two halves and avoid touching the inner surface. Transfer a few pieces of tissue (Pseudoparen-chyama) from the centre of the mushroom to the media in plants.

Spore Culture Method

The surface of a mature (open) mushroom should be disinfected by wiping gently with 70 percent alcohol. Remove the spore and place the cap with gills downwards on a piece of sterile white paper.

Cut tiny piece of spore print and soak it in a few mi. of sterile tap water. Dip a sterile inoculating loop into this spore suspension and streak gently across the surface of an agar plate.

Incubate the plate for a few days and a white mycelial (white thread like structure) mass resulting form the growth of germinated spores becomes evident.

Preparation of Spawn

Cook the grains (rye/sorghum/maize/wheat) in water until they are ready to burst. Drain off excess water. Mix in 2 percent (w/w) lime (calcium carbonate), fill loosely into glass bottles and plug with cotton. Sterilize them in an autoclave for 30 minutes at 1210C and allow it to cool. Inoculate the bottles with the prepared pure culture and incubate at 25°C for 10-15 days. When the whitish mycelium has spread over the Surface, the spawn is ready for use.

MATERIALS OF MUSHROOM PRODUCTION

For 100 kg Mushroom production - Dry paddy straw (not more than one year old) -100 kg; gram powder-2 kg; spawn bottles-l0; polythene *bag-i* kg; water and a shady structure.

PREPARATION OF SUBSTRATE

Use Dried paddy straw, 500 gms per bed (Hulled maizecob, sugarcane bagasse, cotton waste, paper waste, etc., can also be used instead of paddy straw). Cut the paddy straw into small bits of 3 to 5 cm. and soak it in cold water for 6-8 hours.

Take it out and then immerse in boiling water for 15-30 minutes and drain off excess water. Dry the straw in the shade for 2 hours and then use. Remove the spawn from the bottle using a small iron rod with hook on one side. Dip the iron rod in antiseptic solution before use.

Separate the spawn into four lots. Fill the first layer with straw bits upto 5 cm height in the bottom of the polythene bag. Sprinkle spawn over the entire surface of the straw layer. Add second layer with the straw bits upto 10 cm height and sprinkle spawn as before. Similarly, repeat the spawning for third and fourth layers of straw bits. Then, fill the final layer with straw bits upto 5 cm height.

After spawning the beds keep the beds in the growing room for spawn running. Keep bags in the dark for a period of twenty days. White mycelial growth appears throughout the bed.

Cropping & Harvesting

After the spawn running period *(nearly* 15 days), remove the polythene cover and keep in the rack. The relative humidity is maintained above 75% by spraying water on the floor and gunny screens, but watering the beds is avoided for first two days.

After two days, sprinkle beds with water twice daily. Allow aeration and light for 20-30 minutes in morning and evening by opening windows of the growing room. First harvest can be made 24 to 26 days after spawning. Harvest fully-opened mushroom before the edge of the top rolls downward. Two to three harvests can be taken at 7-10 days interval. The yield is about 35 to 85 percent of the substrate (w/w).

HISTORY AND BACKGROUND OF MUSHROOM

FOLKLORE

Mushrooms, the plant of immortality? That's what ancient Egyptians believed according to the hieroglyphics of 4600 years ago. The delicious flavour of mushrooms intrigued the pharaohs of Egypt so much that they decreed mushrooms were food for royalty and that no commoner could ever touch them. This assured themselves the entire supply of mushrooms. In various other civilizations throughout the world, including Russia, China, Greece, Mexico and Latin America, mushroom rituals were practiced. Many believed that mushrooms had properties that could produce super-human strength, help in finding lost objects and lead the soul to the realm of the gods.

EARLY CULTIVATION

France was the leader in the formal cultivation of mushrooms. Some accounts say that Louis XIV was the first mushroom grower. Around this time mushrooms were grown in special caves near Paris set aside for this unique form of agriculture.

From France, the gardeners of England found mushrooms a very easy crop to grow which required little labour, investment and space. Mushroom cultivation began gaining popularity in England with more experimentation with spawn and publicity in journals and magazines.

In the late 19th century, mushroom production made its way across the Atlantic to the United States where curious home gardeners in the East tried their luck at growing this new and unknown crop. However growers had to depend on spawn imported from England which, by the time it reached the U.S. was of poor quality.

This industry text suggested that mushroom growing was perfect for florists. Since they grew flowers on benches, florists could just slide mushroom beds right under their flower benches and gain a profit in growing two crops in the area of one.

Falconer also thought that mushroom growing was ideal for farmers who had access to growing their own manure and spawn. At the time skilled labour was not a necessity of mushroom growing. It was recommended to house wives as well as a source of home income. Not only did Falconer's book develop target groups for which growing was suited. It also contained much practical advice on building beds for cultivation, the perfect growing temperature and where mushroom markets were developing.

The first producer of pure culture virgin spawn was the American Spawn Company of St. Paul Minnesota, headed by Louis F. Lambert, a French mycologist. He began the production of brick spawn and advertised it across the country as "Lambert's Pure Culture Spawn." It soon proved to be a very popular product. This spawn received a silver medal at the Universal Exposition in St. Louis in 1904. A measure of Lambert's success was that English spawn was soon being sold under the name "English Pure Culture Spawn."

By 1914, mushroom marketing began to play a much greater role in the industry. It was estimated in one publication that four to five million pounds of mushrooms were grown in the U.S. Cost to the mushroom grower was fifteen to twenty-five cents. At retail, the price was forty to sixty cents per pound. Marketing became very important with a popular theory being to bypass the middle man and aim directly at consumers. It was pointed out that attractive containers would move product and only good looking product would sell.

U.S. Mushroom Cultivation

In 1891, the first book on mushroom growing was published and it shed new light on the theory of cultivation. William Falconer, a mushroom grower and experimenter from Dosoris, Long Island agreed with the recommendations of agricultural journalists and compiled their theories in Mushrooms: How to Grow Them; A Practical Treatise on Mushroom Culture for Profit and Pleasure.

New Developments

At this time of budding industry developments, one problem continued to face farmers intent on perfecting the growing conditions–poor spawn quality. With such an important ingredient standing in the way of mushroom cultivation, the U.S. Department of Agriculture began work on manufacturing spawn as an alternative to the English product that had proven to be unreliable. In 1903, after much experimentation, two USDA scientists had produced the perfect pure-culture virgin spawn. The U.S. Mushroom Industry was finally freed from depending on imported spawn that had caused so many problems in the past.

Industry Growth

Moving from an easy back yard crop in the early days of cultivation, to a large money maker, the mushroom industry began to grow in certain parts of the country. Concentrated areas of industry growth were Long Island, Central Massachusetts, Chicago, Michigan and California. Southeastern Pennsylvania was (and still is today) the largest centre of mushroom production in the country. In 1924, the Pennsylvania Department of Agriculture boasted that 85% of U.S. mushrooms were grown in Pennsylvania. In 1930, the U.S. Census Bureau revealed that there were 516 growers in the U.S. and that 350 were in Chester County, Pennsylvania.

After 1930, the industry changed rapidly with better spawn production, the development of synthetic manure, and improvements of mushroom growing houses- hence the production of healthier crops. Organizations such as the Mushroom Growers' Cooperative Association were developed to assist and protect growers.

In attempt to find better marketing techniques for mushrooms, the Farm Credit Administration became involved. Pennsylvania State University also became a major factor in the growth of the U.S. mushroom industry helping improve productivity dramatically in the 70's and 80's allowing growers to produce more and more mushrooms per square foot of growing area.

Development of AMI

One organization was developed to coordinate the actions of independent growers and act on behalf of the mushroom industry as a whole. The American Mushroom Institute was brought to life by the Chester County, Pennsylvania growers.

Unfortunately, the first meeting for the development of the AMI was held December 4, 1941, only three days before the Japanese attack on Pearl Harbor. With America's involvement in World War II, this new mushroom growers' organization was put on hold. After the war was over and things began settling down for the nation, the American Mushroom Institute was finally officially organized with over 275 growers signed up to join. On January 14, 1955, AMI was legally incorporated as a non-profit organization.

Their goal was to promote the consumption of all cultivated mushrooms through research, advertising, publicity, merchandising, consumer education and government relations as well as to assist the industry in developing better growing and handling methods. Every broadcast medium was employed to promote mushrooms. Radio, television, magazines and newspapers told of different ways to eat them.

Even produce stores and supermarket chains were displaying mushroom merchandising posters. The American public was learning that mushrooms weren't something just used to garnish steaks. The AMI promoted recipes that used mushrooms in casseroles, appetizers, salads and other combinations. These were the first organized marketing efforts of the American Mushroom Institute.

THE NATIONAL MUSHROOM GROWERS ASSOCIATION

In 1985, the National Mushroom Growers' Association was established in Illinois to promote the sale of fresh mushrooms on a national basis. They developed a newspaper and magazine promotion programme. In spite of its small budget, the programme was very successful in receiving coverage from national women's magazines and newspapers.

THE MUSHROOM COUNCIL

In 1990, the Mushroom Promotion, Research and Consumer Information Act was passed by Congress to strengthen the mushroom industry's position in the marketplace, maintain and expand existing markets and uses for mushrooms, and develop new markets and uses for mushrooms. In 1993, the Mushroom Council was established to carry out the direction of this act. The Council started out with a meager budget and a lot of inspiration about promoting mushrooms.

They began doing research to closely define the mushroom user which became the foundation for all of their communication efforts. Once the ground work was laid, a successful promotions programme began to shape.

Immediate targets for consumer communication were food editors of newspapers and magazines, TV and radio personalities, chefs and cookbook writers. Mushroom recipes went out to hundreds of venues each year — thus increasing consumer awareness and demands for literature on mushrooms. In 1996 the Mushroom Council made the pages of more than ten national women's magazines including Family Circle, Women's Day and Good Housekeeping.

Today, the Mushroom Council plays a very important role in the national promotion of fresh mushrooms through consumer public relations, foodservice communications and retail communications.

Many different venues are used in promoting fresh mushrooms to consumers such as working with professional chefs in developing and promoting new recipes, working with produce department managers to maintain the highest quality mushroom product for customers and sending out thousands of brochures each year to consumers hungry for new mushroom ideas. Thanks to the Mushroom Council, mushrooms have their own month to be honored and eaten. September is National Mushroom Month.

Today mushrooms are commercially produced in virtually every state. Pennsylvania, however, still accounts for 61% of total U.S. production, which in 2006/07 reached 827 million pounds. From the caves of Paris to the dinner tables of millions of Americans, fresh mushrooms have come out of the dark and into a spotlight that's intensity is ever increasing.

MUSHROOM CULTIVATION

People have been eating mushrooms for a long time. They used to go the forests and other wild places and based on their personal knowledge of edible and poisonous mushrooms they used to collect the edible ones. Even now some people collect wild mushrooms from the forest and eat them. Sometimes they turn out to be poisonous and have harmful effects.

In India the 'Guchhi' mushroom was a delicacy known to the people prior to the 1950's. It came mostly from Kashmir. Around the early 1950's the government of Himachal Pradesh appointed Shri S.S.Jain as its first Asstt. Plant Pathologist and Mycologist for the state.

He worked in the Wild Flower Hall in Chharabra, Shimla. He was touring the interior areas of Himachal to help the apple orchardists and the farmers control the diseases of apples, other fruits and crops like potatoes and wheat. He noticed the poor hand to mouth condition of the poor farmers in the hilly state of HP. He wanted to help them.

While staying with some farmers in interior areas he noticed that there were rotting twigs and branches of apple and other fruit trees and wheat straw in the barn along with cow dung and in the environmental conditions there were a profusion of mushrooms growing in the dark barns. This led him to think of using the waste material with the farmers for growing edible mushrooms.

He searched the literature and found that edible mushrooms were being grown in France and Japan. He made a research proposal on growing of edible mushrooms and got the permission for the same from the state government and obtained the mushroom spawn from Japan and France and started a laboratory in Solan, Shimla Hills and started his research experiments on growing edible mushrooms of Agaricus and other species, in laboratory conditions simulating those found in Himachal Pradesh.

When he was able to grow the mushrooms successfully on substrate prepared from rotting apple tree twigs and branches, cow dung and wheat straw etc. he published the results through the magazine of the HP state Extension department. These results when publicized and brought to the notice of the farmers and the poor people people in the state led to dissemination of information and spawn to them and mushroom farming started in Himachal Pradesh. The laboratory established by Shri S.S.Jain, the pioneer of mushroom cultivation in India later became the only important centre for training in mushroom cultivation to farmers of Himachal Pradesh and other states as also the mycologists and plant pathologists from all over India. Mr. Seth and others actually worked with Shri Jain and later became important in the area of mushrooms. But it is a fact that Shri SS Jain in Solan successfully completed the first research project in India. Shri Jain left Solan in 1962-63 for Cuttack.

Shri S.S.Jain then became the OSD and set up the first campus and office of the HP Agricultural University in Solan and later joined Central Rice Research Institute, Cuttack Orissa under the ICAR as a Senior Scientist Plant Pathologist and retired from there in 1978 after having published over a hundred research papers and also having been the Chief Editor of the International Rice journal 'Oryza'.

Shri Jain had also done a monographical study of the Stem Rot disease of rice and also discovered the bacteria Xanthomonas oryzae, which caused the Bacterial Blight disease of rice, and Dr Devdath did his Ph.D on this bacteria and disease. Before Shri Jain expired after prolonged coma in Apollo Hospital Delhi and a small nursing home in Baraut, District Baghpat (Meerut), UP, he had been an award-winning President of the Rotary Club Baraut for his excellent social service work also winning International citation from Rotary.

Now the mushroom cultivation in India is something I could not have imagined from what I saw in the laboratory in Solan. I found a huge factory in Maharashtra near Talegaon, Lonavala, where there were huge godowns in a factory where tray upon tray of white beautiful button mushrooms created a sense of wonder and awe in me and I began thinking of the experiments of my father in the small room in Solan way back in the 50's when I was a student and used to walk to his office nearby and have lunch with him in his laboratory.

By chance the Mycologist in that factory turned out to be one who had undergone training in the laboratory established by my father in Solan. Mushroom cultivation has become a huge export oriented industry and large foreign exchange earning business and also profitable for small time growers. Many Universities and State departments of agriculture as also private people are giving training in growing mushrooms, which are mostly, exported and also used in many good hotels in a variety of culinary delights.

KINDS OF MUSHROOM CULTIVATION

ABOUT MUSHROOMS

There are three different groups of mushrooms. Selecting the right type of mushrooms to be cultivated must be based on climatic conditions and market demand. Mushrooms offer a wide range of proteins, vitamins and minerals necessary for the body and are becoming more popular and in demand.

Producing PDA Medium

How to well prepare spawn production is necessary for proper spawn multiplication. This part can be extended in further projects, in the case where a disabled person wishes to expand his knowledge and start spawn production. Only those trainees that are especially interested in this part will have specific activities and hands on training. In general, this part will be only theoretical.

Selecting Tissue Culture

A young, fresh and very healthy mushroom is used to prepare a tissue culture. This procedure is very delicate and requires extensive understanding and an extremely clean environment. It may not be suitable for beginners in mushroom cultivation.

Multiplying Spawn on Sorghum Seeds

This is also a highly specialized part of mushroom production and will attract only a few trainees due to its complexity. Therefore, only basic theory will be given, mostly in the classroom.

Trainees should, however, know how to select and buy good quality spawn from various suppliers. They should also know all steps involved in mushroom cultivation to allow future expansion of their mushroom farm.

Producing Substrate Bags

Extensive practice will be required by trainees to make sure that they can produce spawn bags by themselves or be able to verify the quality of bags of spawn bag producers. This is hands-on training and will be, with the subsequent steps, the focus of training.

Pasteurizing Bags

Pasteurization is necessary to completely sterilize substrate bags. If bags are not properly pasteurized due to insufficient residence time in the pasteurization chamber or because temperature is insufficient, bags will be contaminated resulting in poor growth of mushrooms or complete spoilage of bags.

Inoculating Bags with Sorghum Seeds

Inoculation must be done with extreme caution. It is an extremely delicate step that will ensure higher yield with disease free substrate bags. Work must be done near a flame from an alcohol lamp during inoculation.

Incubating Bags

During incubation, moisture, light, temperature and ventilation must be monitored constantly. Incubation time will differ according to the type of mushroom and climatic conditions.

Opening Bags

Following incubation, mushroom bags must be opened according to the type of mushrooms.

Maintaining and Monitoring

Maintenance of the mushroom house is crucial for higher yields. When kept clean, there are less insects and pest, less diseases. Bags must be checked individually and kept clean.

Cultivating Straw Mushrooms

Straw mushrooms are very popular in South East Asia and are cultivated using a straw bed. Because of their popularity and market demand, it is interesting to learn how to cultivate this type of mushroom.

Packaging

When selling on the fresh food market or from the farm directly very little packaging is required. Most people use plastic or paper bags.

Marketing

Marketing remains the key to a successful enterprise. Care must be taken to always review the competition and to offer clients reliability of supply and quality of mushrooms.

Processing

Processing of mushrooms is limited only by a person's imagination. There are already numerous methods and recipes, which can offer value, added products. Nevertheless, in rural areas, the market may be small because of financial limitations.

Waste Management and Recycling

Waste must be handled properly in each step of the mushroom cultivation process. Recycling and utilization of waste is not only a good way of preserving our environment but also of saving money.

Troubleshooting

It is necessary to know the most common problems found in mushroom production, their symptoms and their remedies.

Although this section will never replace the advice of an expert, it should help solve basic problems and help identify problems before they occur.

Preparing the Mushroom House

Mushroom houses can be built for as little as 500 Baht (US$ 12) made of readily available yet appropriate materials such as rice straw, grass, dried leaves, used rice bags and tree branches.

Starting the Business

As an entrepreneur in mushroom production, it is necessary to have basic knowledge in management and bookkeeping. This will allow tracking of profit and losses.

Keeping Records

Keeping records is very important since it allows monitoring of all expenses incurred in mushroom production.

It also allows to verify how much profit is generated in the business and identify how certain costs can be reduced in order to generate more profit.

THE WILD EDIBLE MUSHROOMS

In addition, not all members of the Basidiomycota are mushrooms with stalk, caps and gills. There are coral fungi, polypores, puffballs and boletes, just to name a few. Boletes are very similar to mushroom in appearance. The most obvious difference being that they have pores, as the polypores, instead of gills.

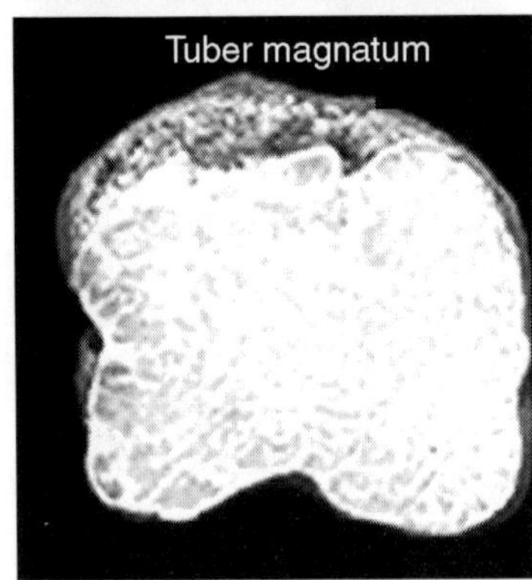

Fig. Examples of Ascomycota "Mushrooms". From Left to Right, *Sarcoscypha mesocyatha, Leotia lubrica, Tuber magnatum and Morchella esculenta.*

However, instead of having fruit bodies that are leathery to woody, boletes are fleshy like mushrooms and there are a number of highly desirable species, with respect to their edibility.

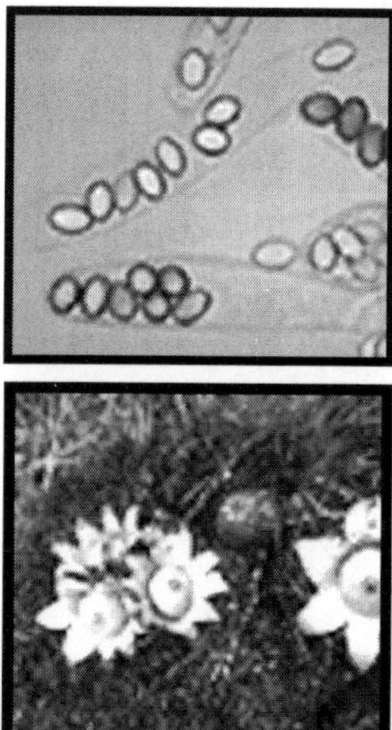

Fig. Asci and Ascospores and Basidia and Basidiospores, Respectively.

Obviously, there are species such as the *Pycnoporus sanguineus* and *Geastrum indica* that cannot be eaten because of the texture of their fruitbodies and the powdery masses of their spores, respectively, but they have traditionally been included in popular mushroom guide books since one of the goals of the authors of such books is also to show the reader the diversity that exists in mushrooms.

Although the topic of eating mushroom is inevitably tied to mushroom poisoning, we will cover this topic in a later lecture. This is a very fascinating topic because there are many people that are intrigued by eating wild mushrooms and will go out, daily, and forage for them in spite of the possibility that they may inadvertently eat a poisonous mushroom.

Despite this danger, the number of people, in this country, consuming wild mushrooms increases each year. However, while incidents of mushroom poisonings continue to occur each year, sometimes with fatal results, mushroom poisoning is still not a major problem in the United States. Even with an increase in the number of people going out to collect mushrooms, there is no evidence that the number of incidents of mushroom poisonings have increased in recent years.

The practice of eating mushroom probably began during the hunting and gathering period, in our prehistory. They were collected along with fruits and berries, as well as other plant material that could be consumed.

Also, like plants the gatherers learned which ones were edible and which were poisonous and if there were other uses for mushrooms, *i.e.*, medicinal or religious uses. However, unlike plants, mushrooms must have been have been shrouded in mysteries since unlike the plants, there was not an obvious way in which they could be reproduced. Even much later, during the dark ages, mushrooms became more firmly embedded in the mythology of the supernatural. Many myths arose because of their seemingly supernatural characteristics and strange habitat. Their growth was rapid and they seem to suddenly appear overnight as if from nowhere.

Fig. Fairy Ring" of *Chlorophyllum molybdites*. Middle Picture is Cluster of Mushrooms in its Habitat, Growing at base of Madrone Tree. Picture on Right is the Same Cluster of Mushrooms showing how the Gills can Glow at Night.

Fig. *Marasmius oreades,* "The Fairy Ring Mushroom".

Fig. *Tremella mesenterica,* "Witch's Butter".

Thus, their origin appeared to be magical. They sometimes formed circular patterns or "rings" as in *Chlorophyllum molybdites* where the grass is greener *inside* the ring. Some glow in the dark. Many have bizarre shapes, and are ephemeral. They became part of the lives of fairies, elves and witches. This concept is evident even today in common name of mushrooms, such as "The Fairy Ring Mushroom" for *Marasmius oreades* and "Witches Butter" or Fairy Butter for *Tremella mesenterica.*

Because so little was known about mushrooms, many misconceptions concerning the edibility of mushrooms have developed. Some of the more common ones are briefly discussed below:

- There is a fool-proof test for distinguishing edible from poisonous mushrooms. The most common ones that can be heard are that "a poisonous mushroom will turn silver black while it is being cooked", "if you can peel the cap of the mushroom it is safe to eat" and "observing which mushrooms foraging animals consume will tell you which species are safe to eat". While there are some generalizations that can be made within certain groups of mushrooms, there is no fool-proof test that can be used for all mushrooms. Those species of mushrooms that are edible are known to be edible because someone at one time had tried it and discovered it to be safe to eat.
- Most mushrooms are poisonous. Of the thousands of species known, perhaps 60 or so are poisonous, and of these only a handful will be fatal if consumed (these numbers will vary depending on your source). However, it does not require a lot of mushroom to poison a lot of people. In Europe, of those that die mushroom poisoning, probably 90% die as a result of mistaking *Amanita phalloides* (Death Cap) for *Amanita calytroderma* (Coccora). The remaining species, however, are not necessarily good to eat. I am using edible here to means non-poisonous and not necessarily good to eat. Thus, an edible mushroom may have a strong bitter, peppery or some other unpleasant taste, be bland or have no taste at all.
- There are a large number of people that die from mushroom poisoning each year. "Large" is somewhat ambiguous here. If we are talking about the number of people that go out collecting for mushrooms each year, in this country, then the number of people that die as a result of mushroom poisoning is few relative to that number.
- Poisonous mushrooms must taste bad. Many mushrooms that are non-poisonous may have a very bad taste. The opposite can also be true. *Amanita phalloides* is said to have a quite pleasant taste, but is one of the most deadly species of poisonous mushrooms.
- You can be poisoned by touching a poisonous mushroom. As deadly

as some toxins may be, touching the mushroom is harmless. The harmful toxins in mushrooms must be consumed in order to harm you.

- Collecting mushrooms for consumption is unsafe and even experts have died from picking the wrong mushrooms. This last misconception is the one that continues to be perpetuated by the news media every year. Probably every year, you can read a headline that goes something like "Expert Mushroom Hunter Dies From Eating Deadly Mushroom". However, upon closer examination of such a story it is often the case that the person that died is far from being an expert. Even those who are avid collectors that have been foraging for wild mushrooms, for only a short period of time, are unlikely to die from mushroom poisoning, if they have even had a minimum of training in the do's and don'ts of mushroom collecting and if common sense is used. There are a number of species that are very good to eat that cannot be mistaken for other species. If collectors stick with those species, mushroom poisoning is highly unlikely. New species can be tried through interaction with other collectors who have eaten other species.
- Species determined to be edible are always safe to eat. Whenever a new species is tried for the first time, even if it is one that is highly regarded and is said to be being very tasty, it is best to be cautious. Try only a few bites and wait 24 hours before consuming more. There are a vast number of compounds that occur in wild mushrooms that may cause adverse reactions, when consumed by a few individuals, but are safe for the general public. There is also the possibility of an allergic response to a particular species. Other precautions that should be taken:
  - When preparing mushrooms for a meal, always inspect the mushrooms to determine if it is firm and fresh. Bacterial and fungal decomposition may be taking place in old mushrooms.
  - Avoid eating raw mushrooms. Many edible species have toxins that are heat sensitive and will be rendered harmless by cooking the mushroom. Also, the cell wall of mushrooms is composed of chitin, which the human digestive system cannot break down. must also be degraded by heat so that we can absorb nutrients within cells. If the cell walls remain intact, the nutrients in the mushrooms will simply pass through our digestive system. Cooking will break down the cell wall and release its contents, which are digestible.
- Mushroom are of no nutritional value. Although mushrooms will never be one of the world s staples, it has been a food supplement in various cultures. Nutritionally speaking, mushrooms fall between

the best vegetables and animal protein source. Their protein content may vary anywhere between 15-40% of *dry* weight (keep in mind that mushrooms are more than 90% water). However, all essential amino acids are present in mushrooms, as well as water-soluble vitamins and all the minerals that our bodies require are present. A generous serving of mushrooms (0.5 lb) of fresh mushrooms provides approximately 70 kcal.

EAT MUSHROOMS FOR NUTRITIONAL VALUE

While some people may hype the nutritional value or even medicinal value, of mushrooms, as the reason for consumption, that does not appear to be the main reason for going out to collect wild mushrooms. Presently, there are a good number of species that have been cultivated.

Many of these have had research carried out indicating their high nutritional value as well as medicinal value. So, why not eat only cultivated mushrooms rather than taking the risk of possibly being ill eating an unsafe mushroom or perhaps even being fatally poisoned? As far as individual collectors are concerned this seems to be an impossible question to answer. Perhaps, it is the thrill of the hunt, or the idea of going back to nature and collecting non-cultivated food.

There are probably numerous reasons as to why an individual would participate in collecting and eating wild mushrooms. However, if we look at this question from a cultural perspective, according to R. Gordon Wasson, the father of ethnomycology (in its simplest definition it is the study of the relationship between people and fungi), how readily a person will collect and consume wild mushroom is dependent upon the culture in which they were raised.

Wasson believed that cultures could be divided into two categories, with respect to mushrooms: 1.) Those that are mycophilic may regard mushrooms as the epitome of gastronomy, and 2.) Those that are mycophobic may despise and regard them all as being poisonous and would surely cross the road just to stomp the life out of them.

With the exception of possibly a single species that has been cultivated (*Agaricus bisporus*), those cultures that belong to the latter category will usually have nothing to do with mushroom. While Wasson truly believed that there was this dramatic like or dislike of mushrooms, Benjamin (1995) has pointed out that there are cultures that neither like nor dislike mushrooms, with respect to their use as food. In a few cultures mushrooms have even been regarded as being magical and utilized in religious ceremonies.

The observation that different cultures may vary as to their attitudes concerning mushroom consumption was made in the late 1920s by R. Gordon Wasson and his wife Valentina, during their honeymoon in the Catskill Mountains, in New York State. A somewhat humorist recount of this observation was made by Wasson, in 1968, in his book, Soma, The Divine Mushroom of Immortality:

We had been married less than a year and we were off on our first holiday, at Big Indian in the Catskills. On that first day, as the sun was declining in the west, we set out on a stroll, the forest on our left and a clearing oil the right.

Though we had known each other for years we had never discussed mushrooms together. All of a sudden she darted from my side, with cries of ecstasy she flew to the forest glade, where she had discovered mushrooms of various kinds carpeting the ground. Since Russia she had seen nothing like it. Left planted on a mountain trail, I called to her to take care, to come back.

They were toadstools she was gathering, poisonous, putrid, disgusting. She only laughed the more: I can hear her now. She knelt in poses of adoration. She spoke to them with endearing Russian diminutives. She gathered the toadstools in a kind of pinafore that she was wearing, and brought them to our lodge. Some she strung on threads to hang up and dry for winter use. Others she served that night, either with the soup or the meat, according to their kind. I refused to touch them.

After this incident, the couple talked about the difference in their attitudes toward mushrooms. Upon further conversations with close friends, from various cultures, they discovered a relationship between their ethnic identity and their like or dislike concerning mushrooms. Their fascination with this topic would turn out to be a life-long interest and would lead to the origin of a new field of study, ethnomycology. Some of the attitudes of different cultures are briefly summarize, below, from Benjamin (1995), to demonstrate some of these differences.

Anglo-Saxon

Historically, the British and their colonies, *i.e.*, English-speaking cultures were widely recognized as being mycophobic or at least not very interested in consuming mushrooms.

It is also true that these cultures are for the most part reliant upon domesticated food rather than foraging for wild food. Those individuals in these countries that may have interest in collecting wild mushrooms as well as plants for consumptions are usually the descendents of Asian, and Slavic cultures of Eastern Europe and Russia. In the United States, such people are usually looked upon as being eccentric.

Mushrooms were often closely associated with toads, snails, snakes spiders and witches, in Western mythology. Although witches have never been a very popular figure in any country or cultures in which they have been recognized, it was only in some countries where a deep-seated fear of them existed. This aversion may be related to the association of witches with the devil. It was primarily in the Germanic, Celtic and Anglo-Saxon countries such as Germany, Switzerland, Scotland, England, and subsequently America that witches were actively and systematically persecuted.

The origin of this mycophobic attitude for any country is unknown. However, that it is a deep seated response can be seen by its expression in the English literature for centuries: They are all very cold and moist and therefore do approach unto a venomous and mothering faculty and ingender clammy and cold nutriment if they be eaten. – John Gerard, Herball or Generall Historie of Plantes (1597) But whatever dressing one gives to mushrooms, to whatever sauce our apiciuses put them, they are realy good but to be sent back to the dung heap where they were born. – Louis de Jacourt, Champignon (1753)

It is tempting to say that such writing may have shaped the attitudes of the English. However, this is unlikely since most people of that time had no access to such writings and few would have been able to read it if they had. It is speculated that the sexual connotations associated with some mushroom led to their rejection by a prudish Anglo-Saxon culture. Undoubtedly, the phallic aspects of many mushrooms did not go unnoticed. Certain species were also regarded as aphrodisiacs. While this may be a reasonable argument when applied to the period in history of Victorian England, it does not explain the mycophobic attitude of its earlier and later history nor does it explain this same attitude in America

One particular mushroom was even regarded as being obscene to the morals of Victorian England, *Phallus impudicus,* one of the many species of stinkhorns. However, it is obvious that it is not the particular species, but rather the resemblance of any species of stinkhorn to the male organ that upset Victorian England.

In our native woods there grows a kind of toadstool called in the vernacular The Stinkhorn (though in Latin it bears a grosser name). The name is justified for the fungus can be hunted by scent alone, and this was Aunt Ettys great invention. Armed with a basket and a pointed stick, and wearing a special hunting cloak and gloves, she would sniff her way through the wood, pausing here and there, her nostrils twitching when she caught a whiff of her prey.

Then with a deadly pounce she would fall upon her victim and poke his putrid carcass into her basket. At the end of the days sport the catch was brought back and burnt in the deepest secrecy on the drawing room fire with the door locked – because of the morals of the maids!! – Gwen Raverat, Period Piece (1952)

An example of myco-phobism can even be found in a children's story of Babar the Elephant, by Jean de Brunhoff. Babar the Elephant is a famous series of French children's stories that first came out in 1931. The first part of the story tells of how Babar was orphaned and then became king after his mother was killed by a hunter and his father died from mushroom poisoning:

Fig. *Phallus ravenellii,* One of the Many Species of Stinkhorns that Resembles the Male Organ and was the Reason for it being an Obscene Fungus in Victorian, England.

When Babar was young and lived in the jungle, his mother was killed by a hunter. The hunter was just about to capture Babar, when Babar quickly ran away into the forest and managed to escape. After a few days, he came across a town with many big buildings. There he met a kind old lady who adopted him. In this town, Babar bought clothes, was educated about the ways of humans and quite enjoyed himself.

The years passed by quickly and it wasn't long before 2 years had elapsed since Babar had run away from the forest. He began to miss the jungle and longed to play with his relatives and friends. One day, as he and the old lady were walking down the street, they saw 2 young elephants running along. They turned out to be Celeste and Arthur (Babar's cousins).

On seeing them, Babar ran and embraced them. He told his cousins of his life in the town and he decided to return to the forest with his cousins. Meanwhile, Arthur and Celeste's parents were very worried about their children's disappearance.

They organised a big search party. A little bird, who had seen the children in the town, reported back to them and told them where their children were located. Then Arthur and Celeste's cross mothers journeyed to the town to fetch them. Once there, they were very relieved to have found them, but scolded them for running away. Babar, Arthur, Celeste and the cousins' mothers decided they'd all travel back to the jungle together. After Babar and the old lady exchanged tearful goodbyes, he packed all his belongings and returned to the jungle.

Once Babar arrived, he was joyfully greeted by the elephants, but became quite shocked when hearing of an illness that had struck the King of the elephants. The king of the elephants had eaten a poisonous mushroom, become seriously ill and then died shortly before Babar had arrived. Cornelius (one of the older elephants) and some other elephant elders had been discussing who should become the new King before Babar had unexpectedly arrived. Cornelius suggested that Babar should become the king and the other elephants agreed. Babar gratefully accepted the honour and said he would marry his childhood sweetheart, Celeste.

While writings for adults may not shape the culture's attitudes towards mushrooms, they may be key element to how the children view the natural world as well as how they interpret the story they hear.

Russia and Eastern Europe

If the British are the consummate mycophobic society then Russia and Eastern Europe are at the opposite end of the spectrum. Culturally, the people in these area are Slavic, which is a branch of the Indo-European language family that includes Bulgarian, Belorussian, Czech, Macedonia, Polish, Russian, Serbo-Croatian, Slovak, Slovene, Ukrainian and Wendish. Mushrooms play a very important role in the Slavic culture

Here mushroom collecting and eating is a favorite past time. This passion for mushroom that was first demonstrated by R. Gordon Wassons wife, Valentina, shocked Wasson when he first observed her collecting mushrooms, but this was what began Wassons life-long quest into different cultures attitudes towards mushrooms.

Africa

Africa appears to be generally mycophilic. There are some some regions, such as Nigeria, where mushrooms are a part of everyday life as food, charms and remedies in traditional medicine. The most sought after species is the one belonging to the genus *Termitomyces*, a genus associated with termite nests.

There are also myths concerning mushrooms that are unique to this part of world. One is that if you feed a mushroom to a chicken, if it eats the mushroom, and nothing happens, it is thought to be edible, if it eats the mushrooms and vomits, it is edible with caution and if it rejects the mushroom, it is thought to be poisonous. Although there does not appear to be any logic to this myth, it should be kept in mind that this is also the case for those myths concerning mushrooms in Western cultures.

Neighboring Malawi is also a region of mushroom gourmands, whose women have knowledge of the edible and poisonous species, locally. Over 60 edible species are recognized in this area, predominantly belonging to the genera *Amanita, Cantharellus* and *Termitomyces*.

The responsibility of foraging and identifying the mushrooms fall upon the women. Mushrooms also sold commonly sold on roadsides as well as in town and village markets.

In rural Zambia and Zaire, mushrooms are widely consumed during "hunger" months from late November through early April. A survey in the 1950s demonstrated that they were second only to caterpillars, as a food source.

Although, there were a wide variety of edible species, the species selected for eating were restricted. *Termitomyces* was favored, but species of *Lactarius, Russula, Cantharellus* and *Amanita* are also eaten.

Thus, consumption of mushrooms appear to be out of necessity for food than as a preferred food item. So Africa is not entirely mycophilic. Some parts of Africa will not readily eat the variety of species just mentioned, but still may have other favorites. While such areas will consume few species, they will still more readily consume the species that they recognize, unlike in Anglo-Saxon cultures.

India

The Indian subcontinent appear to be mostly mycophobic or at least do not eat mushrooms to the extent of the Asian continent. Most consumption seems to be in mountainous area of Kasmir and the Himalayas. Mushroom consumption is also common in Bengal.

However, it generally appears that India lacks a culinary interest in mushrooms. One reason for this lack of interest may be that India was once a former British Colony, but it appears that this lack of interest predates British presence in India.

Despite the lack of gastronomic interest in mushrooms, in the district of Kerala, mushrooms are utilized in religious ceremonies. In this district, burial monuments, resembling mushrooms, built between 2000-1000 B.C., are worshiped by present day people who also consume some of the hallucinogenic mushrooms in this area. It is believed that these mushrooms enable the user to communicate with their gods and the dead.

Native North American Cultures

Despite the large number of species in North America, Native Americans appear to be mostly mycophobic. Most tribes have never used mushrooms as a significant source of food, and in some case are not used at all in their diets. However, Native Americans did use mushrooms for other purposes: medicinal, and spiritual, religious and ceremonial.

Puffballs were often used as a means to stop bleeding or to dry out wounds. This particular use is not unique and has been used for this purpose on all continents. Puffballs are also used for healing umbilical cord, in poultices, and a lotion to treat various skin conditions. Puffballs that grew in fairy rings were used for spiritual, religious and ceremonial purposes. They were used as incense to ward off evil spirits. No evidence that any hallucinogenic fungi were employed in any ceremonies as they were in Mesoamerica.

Europe

European cultures are generally fond of mushrooms, with the exception of Holland, which has an attitude similar to that of England, but to a lesser degree. Species favored by each country varies. The Italians prefer the porcini (*Boletus edulis*) and white truffle (*Tuber alba*); the Germans and Swiss, the chanterelle (*Cantharellus cibarius*) the Catalonians, the delicious milky cap (*Lactarius deliciosus*).

Switzerland has developed a very sophisticated level of collecting and marketing of wild mushrooms. During spring and fall seasons, there is a space reserved for sale of wild mushrooms in open-air markets. Markets are under supervision of an inspector, a local mycologist responsible to the state government.

Only truffles can be sold outside of these markets. All other mushrooms must pass the scrutiny of the inspector. The most important job of the inspector is to confirm the identities of the mushrooms that are being sold by the amateur collectors, and minors are not permitted to sell mushrooms. There is a list of approximately 54 species that are sanctioned for sale. Other duties include surveillance for occasional deceptive practices. For example, soaking mushrooms in water to increase weight. Boletes must be cut in half so that customers can see the quantity of "animal protein" inside.

In Finland, people were indifferent towards mushroom eating, except in the southeastern parts of the country closest to Russia and its Slavic influence. These areas had gathered mushrooms for centuries. However, during World War II, mushroom usage, as food, increased because of the scarcity of other food stuff.

Years later, the Finnish government, along with several other organizations, launched an education training programme. More than 1600 advisers, and 50,000 pickers were trained from 1969 to 1983. This effort was coordinated by 22 inspectors who provided the expertise in identification. Every citizen in Finland had the rights to pick mushrooms and berries on any land, provided no damage was done. By 1979, an estimated 72% of the population was picking mushrooms. Income from sale of mushroom, locally and abroad, is untaxed and the income generated during a good year can be substantial. Thus, the mycophilic attitude of the people was acquired shortly after WWII.

South America

For the most part, mushrooms are not a major food item for the majority of the people native to this continent. In studies carried out, few indigenous people have been identified who utilize fungi as part of their diet. Among those people who eat mushrooms, there is usually an elaborate taxonomic system for edible mushrooms and allows the distinction between species that look almost identical to the untrained eye. However, the inedible ones are just said to be "no good". This practice seems to be similar to other cultures whose mushroom knowledge is based on folk tradition.

Asia

Although the attitudes of different Asian cultures may vary, they are generally mycophilic. China has longest tradition in collecting mushrooms, not just for consumption as food, but also as an important role in traditional medicine.

However, unlike most other mycophilic societies, species of mushrooms that are used in China for food and medicine are generally cultivated since the localities where these species can be collected are a long way from the densely populated agricultural areas where most people live. Thus, the Chinese do not go out to collect mushrooms as other mycophilic cultures such as the Slavic and most Europeans, but instead have become very skillful in the cultivation of the various species that they utilize. Poisoning, for this reason, is not very frequent.

Japan is similar to China in having cultivation play a large role in supplying mushrooms for the diet and medicinal needs of its people. Once again, it is because of the population living in a limited space. However, the Japanese differ from the Chinese in that they have a great enthusiasm for mushroom collecting.

One species in particular, the Matsutake, *Tricholoma matsutake,* is a particular favorite. Unfortunately, in the last few decades, this species has come under pressure and is now in a serious decline due to nematode infestation in their pine forests. Taking advantage of this situation, Korea and the Pacific Northwest, from Oregon to British Columbia have developed a lucrative business supplying the Japanese market with a similar species of mushroom, *Tricholoma magnivelare* (=*Armillaria ponderosa*), which is found in those areas.

Fig. *Tricholoma magnivelare,* a Species Similar to *Tricholoma matsutake,* that Japan has been Importing as a Substitute for the Latter.

Medicinal value of mushrooms is also valued in China and Japan. *Ganoderma lucidum,* called the Ling Chi, in China and Reishi, in Japan is a highly regarded herb that was first documented in China approximately 2000 years ago. Today, it is cultivated in both countries. Another highly regarded group of fungi in Asia are the stinkhorns. Unlike in Anglo Saxon cultures, the phallic appearance here represents the power of enhancing potency and performance, and in China, *Dictyophora duplicata, D. indusiata* and *D. multicolour* are species of stinkhorns that are cultivated for this reason.

Australia

Australia, because they were originally settled by Anglo-Saxon settlers, brought with them their mycophobic attitude. Few mushrooms are used and picked by the white populations there. The aboriginal use of fungi is also limited to a few species and do not make up a significant part of their diet.

TYPES OF EDIBLE MUSHROOMS

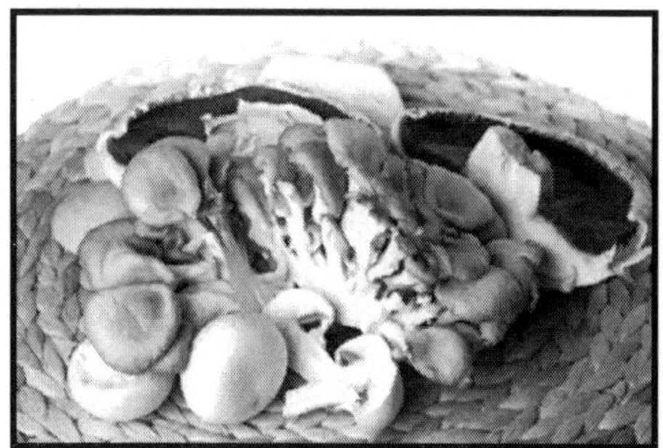

Mushrooms add something special to every meal and, when you are familiar with the different types of edible mushrooms, you can eat a different mushroom every night. Exotic mushrooms add a distinct flavour to your cooking, but unless you are a mushroom expert, known as a mycophagist, you are safer getting your mushrooms from the store. Some types of poisonous mushrooms look just like some types of edible mushrooms.

While wild mushrooms may look wild and taste wild, it is better to play it safe when choosing your mushrooms. There are three types of mushrooms available at most markets: common, exotic, and wild. The common mushroom, known as a button or champignon mushroom, is the most readily available.

CULTIVATED EXOTIC MUSHROOMS

Cultivated exotic mushrooms are grown in a controlled environment and are very safe to eat. They are sometimes more expensive than button mushrooms but, as an occasional treat, are worth the extra money and effort to find them.

Shiitake Mushrooms

Shiitake mushrooms are also known as Black Forest mushrooms or Golden Oak mushrooms. They are mostly cultivated in Japan, China, and South Korea, but are also available from Australia and North America.

When fresh, the mushrooms colour ranges from light golden brown to dark brown. They have a wide cap with a firm fleshy texture, but the stems are very tough and are either chopped very fine for sautéing or saved for making stock. These mushrooms are also available in a dried form. The dried shiitake can be stored for a long time and can be revived just by soaking in water. The water that the dried shiitakes have been reconstituted in can then be used to make a delicious mushroom sauce. As far as exotic mushrooms go, the dried shiitake is a good way to add great flavour to your recipes while saving money.

Oyster Mushroom

The oyster mushroom, also known as Pleurotte, gets its name from the way it looks and not its flavour. Oyster mushrooms are light tan or cream coloured with a large, fan-like cap and a short stem. These tender mushrooms have a delicate flavour, so they are best prepared simply so the flavour isn't overpowered.

Enoki Mushrooms

These mushrooms are also known as Enokitake or Enokidake. They have a tiny white cap on a long slender stem. They grow in bunches from a single base, so you will be selecting clusters rather than single mushrooms. You just trim off the base and give the Enoki a quick rinse to prepare them. Enoki have a crisp texture and a fruity, sweet flavour and are very good raw in a salad. If you are using them in a cooked dish, add them last to keep the texture and flavour.

Cremini Mushrooms

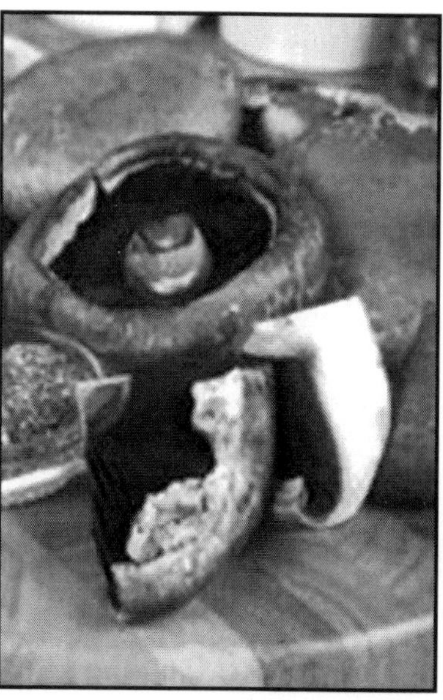

Cremini mushrooms are fun and tasty. Cremini are the slightly more mature variation of the common button mushroom. Use these wherever you would use button mushrooms but expect a deeper, richer flavour.

Portobello Mushrooms

The most mature version of the Cremini mushroom these mushrooms can grow up to 6-inches wide, are great for grilling or stuffing, and can be used as a substitute for meat in some recipes.

WILD MUSHROOMS

Wild mushrooms bring more flavour to every recipes, but only use wild mushrooms that you find at the market. Eating wild mushrooms that you find in the actual wild can be dangerous. These four wild mushrooms are available fresh as well as dried. You may want to consider the dried variation because they keep longer, have a more intense flavour, and the water that you use to restore them can be used to make a mushroom sauce.

Morel Mushrooms

Morels can be found in several varieties including black, golden, and white. Morels look like a conical sponge and are completely hollow inside. They are available fresh in the spring or dried all year long. Use them in butter or cream-based sauces.

Bolete Mushrooms

Also known as Cep, or Porchino, this brown capped mushroom has a light coloured bulbous stem and a cream coloured flesh. The smooth meaty texture of this mushroom has a rich earthy flavour and is best sautéed with butter and garlic. Bolete are usually available in late summer and early fall.

Chanterelle Mushrooms

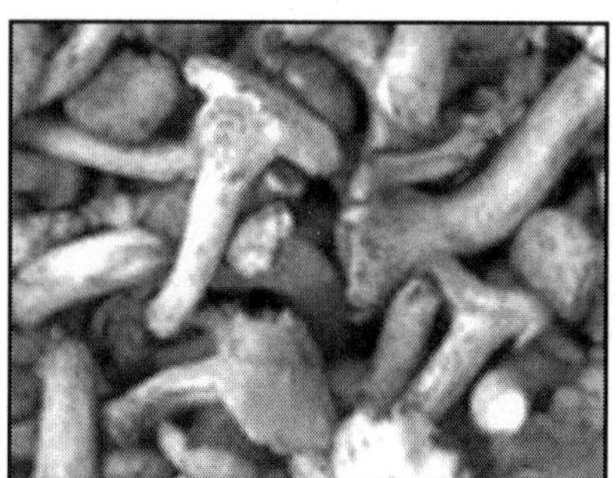

Chanterelle are also known as Girolle. They are yellow to orange in colour and look like an inverted umbrella. This mushroom has ridges rather than gills. Chanterelle have a rich woodsy flavour and aroma and are best when sautéed with butter and a little garlic. Chanterelle are available during the summer and fall.

Black Trumpet

These mushrooms are related to Chanterelles, but are black in colour with much thinner flesh.

TRUFFLES

Truffles are very rare and only found in southern France and Northern Italy. Black truffles can cost as much as $130 to $390 dollars per pound while white truffles can cost as much as $1350 to $2700 per pound. Black truffles grow only on the roots of oak trees while white truffles can be found growing on the roots of oak, hazel, poplar, and beech trees. Specially trained hogs and dogs are used to find these delightful fungi.

In general, truffles are shaved onto a meal just before serving. A more cost effective way of getting the rich, earthy flavour of these mushrooms into your food is to look for truffle oil, which is usually olive or vegetable oil infused with truffles.

EDIBLE MUSHROOMS: POPULAR AND READILY

Most of us are familiar with the most popular and readily available edible mushrooms because we purchase them from the super market. You may not go out foraging for mushrooms, but many people do collect, identify and eat wild mushrooms, an activity that can prove to be deadly. Therefore, only a person who is extremely knowledgeable and has been trained in the identification of mushrooms should pick and consume wild mushrooms—due to the number of poisonous species.

Toxins

The difference between edible and non-edible mushrooms is the toxins that are present in the non-edible or poisonous mushrooms. The fungi produce these toxins naturally, and the toxins that are present in a poisonous mushroom cannot be removed or made non-toxic by any process, including freezing, cooking, canning or any other process—these toxins are inherent to the mushroom.

Four Categories of Toxins

Mushroom toxins can be divided into four specific categories. Protoplasmic toxins/poisons destroy cells, and eventually lead to organ failure. Neurotoxins are compounds that cause various neurological symptoms like excessive sweating, convulsions, hallucinations, coma, depression and a spastic colon. The third category, gastrointestinal irritants, produce nausea, vomiting, diarrhea and abdominal cramps. Disulfiram-like toxins only produce symptoms if alcohol is consumed (within a 72-hour window after consuming the mushroom); the person will experience an acute toxic syndrome, which is short-lived.

Edible Species

People can have different reactions to the foods they eat, and this holds true when consuming mushrooms. What is "edible" for some may not be "edible" for everyone. There are approximately 250 North American edible species of mushrooms. These include Agaricus arvensis or horse mushroom, Agaricus campestris or field mushroom, Boletus badius or bay bolete, Boletus edulis or penny bun, Calocybe gambosum or St. George's mushroom, and Coprinus comatus or shaggy ink cap, to name a few.

Poisonous Species

Of the 10,000 North American species of mushrooms, 250 are edible and approximately 250 are poisonous, leaving an extremely large number of species that we know little about (edible or non-edible). Poisonous mushrooms, if ingested, can cause death within three to six days, which is why it is extremely important to seek treatment immediately. Symptoms are breathing problems, dizziness, vomiting, diarrhea and dehydration. Some poisonous species are Amanita phalloides or death cap mushroom, Amanita virosa or the destroying angel, Amanita muscaria or the fly Agaric, and Cortinarius rubellus.

How to Avoid Poisoning

To avoid poisoning you must be extremely knowledgeable in mushroom identification when collecting mushrooms, as there is no simple cut-and-dry method, or list of identifiable characteristics between an edible mushroom and a poisonous mushroom. If you do collect mushrooms, never mix the edible mushrooms with those that are non-edible, and only eat the edible mushrooms that are not damaged and are in good condition. Always refrigerate your edible mushrooms, and remember the number one rule: if you are in doubt about whether a mushroom is edible or non-edible, discard it.

4

Mushroom Hunting

INTRODUCTION

Mushroom hunting, mushrooming, mushroom picking, mushroom foraging, and similar terms describe the activity of gathering mushrooms in the wild, typically for eating.

This is popular in most of Europe, including the Nordic, Baltic, and Slaviccountries and the Mediterranean Basin, as well as in Australia,Japan, Korea, Canada, the Indian subcontinent, and the northwestern, northeastern,Midwestern and Appalachian United States.

IDENTIFYING MUSHROOMS

A large number of mushroom species are favored for eating by mushroom hunters. The king bolete is a popular delicacy. Sulphur shelf (also known as Chicken Mushroom or Chicken of the Woods) is often gathered because it occurs in bulk, recurs year after year, is easily identified, and has a wide variety of culinary uses.Pine mushrooms, chanterelles, morels, oyster mushrooms, puffballs and polyporesare among the most popular types of mushrooms to gather, most of these being fairly simple to properly identify by anyone with practice.

Much more care, education, and experience is typically required to make a positive identification of many species, however, and as such, few collect from more dangerous groups, such as Amanita, which include some of the most toxic mushrooms in existence.

Many field guides on mushrooms are available, but the ability to identify and prepare edible mushrooms is often passed down through generations, especially in the Slavic countries.

Identification is not the only element of mushroom hunting that takes practice; knowing where and when to search does as well. Most mushroom species require very specific conditions. Some only grow at the base of a certain type of tree, for example.

Finding a desired species that is known to grow in a certain region can be a challenge.

Safety issues

Fig. Clitocybe rivulosa is an example of a deadly mushroom species sometimes misidentified as an edible species.

There is an adage from Czech:"Všechny houby jsou jedlé, ale nekteré jenom jednou.", what is a warning. It tells literally:"Every mushroom is edible, but some just for once." Some mushrooms are deadly or extremely hazardous when consumed. Some that are not deadly can nevertheless cause permanent organ damage.

The literature strongly advises that you:

- Only eat mushrooms you have positively identified yourself.
- Identify mushrooms a second time during preparation and cook them properly, unless you know that the species can be eaten raw.
- Do not combine mushroom types.
- Retain a sample of any mushroom you are not well-experienced with for analysis in case of poisoning.
- Inform yourself about deadly mushrooms that are look-alikes of edible ones. "Deadly twins" differ regionally, so take into account regional variation.
- Do not gather mushrooms that are difficult to identify, unless you have expert knowledge. This applies especially to the mushrooms of the genusAmanita or Cortinarius and "little brown mushrooms".
- Consume only a small amount the first time you try a new species. People react differently to different mushrooms, and all mushroom species can cause an adverse reaction in a few individuals, even the common champignon.

"Little brown mushrooms"

"Little brown mushroom" (or LBM) refers to any of a large number of small, dull-coloured agaric species, with few macromorphological uniquely distinguishing characteristics. As a result, LBMs typically range from difficult to impossible for mushroom hunters to identify. Experienced mushroomers may discern more subtle identifying traits that help narrow the mushroom down to a particular genus or group of species, but exact identification of

LBMs often requires close examination of microscopic characteristics plus a certain degree of familiarity or specialization in that particular group.

Fig. Inocybe lacera is a typical little brown mushroom, and is easily identifiable only by distinctive microscopic features.

For mycologists, LBMs are the equivalent of LBJs ("little brown job") and DYCs ("damned yellow composite") that are the bane of ornithologists and botanists, respectively.

"Big white mushroom" (or BWM) is also sometimes used to describe groups of difficult to identify larger and paler agarics, many of which are in the genus Clitocybe.

Psychotropics

Fig. Psilocybe semilanceata is hunted for its psychotropic properties.

The Amanita muscaria's psychotropic properties have been traditionally used by shamans in Siberia in their rituals. However, its use for such purposes today is very rare, despite the mushroom's abundance.

Instead, the Psilocybe semilanceata, being the only psilocybin-containing mushroom common in Slavic countries, is sought after for its hallucinogenic properties, the latter being more desirable with fewer side effects than those of A. muscaria. The use of P. semilanceata is however significantly hindered by its small size, requiring larger quantities and being hard to spot. Other Psilocybe species are abundant in the American south and west, as well as Mexico, where they have been used by traditional shamans for centuries. In the west, one can often find mushroom pickers in cow pastures in a stereotypical stoop looking in the grass for Psilocybes. This can be quite dangerous, as many species grow in pastures and amateurs often misidentify Psilocybes.

AMANITA MUSCARIA

Amanita muscaria, commonly known as the fly agaric or fly amanita, is a poisonous and psychoactivebasidiomycete fungus, one of many in the genus Amanita. Native throughout the temperate and borealregions of the Northern Hemisphere, Amanita muscaria has been unintentionally introduced to many countries in the southern hemisphere, generally as a symbiont with pine plantations, and is now a truecosmopolitan species. It associates with various deciduous and coniferous trees.

The quintessential toadstool, it is a large white-gilled, white-spotted, usually red mushroom, one of the most recognisable and widely encountered in popular culture.

Several subspecies with differing cap colour have been recognised, including the brown regalis (considered a separate species), the yellow-orangeflavivolvata, guessowii, formosa, and the pinkish persicina. Genetic studies published in 2006 and 2008 show several sharply delineated clades that may represent separate species.

Although it is generally considered poisonous, there are few documented human deaths from its consumption, and after having been parboiled it is eaten as a food in parts of Europe, Asia, and North America. Amanita muscaria is noted for its hallucinogenic properties, with its main psychoactive constituent being the compound muscimol. The mushroom was used as an intoxicant and entheogen by thepeoples of Siberia, and has a religious significance in these cultures.

There has been much speculation on possible traditional use of this mushroom as an intoxicant in places other than Siberia, such as the Middle East, India, Eurasia, North America, and Scandinavia. The American banker and amateur ethnomycologistR. Gordon Wasson proposed that the fly agaric was the soma of the ancient Rig Veda texts of India; since its introduction in 1968, this theory has gained both followers and detractors in anthropological literature.The Dead Sea Scrolls scholar John Marco Allegro also proposed that early Christianity sprang from cultic use of the fly agaric in Second Temple Judaism, and that the mushroom itself was used by the Essenes as an allegory for none other than Jesus Christ.

TAXONOMY AND NAMING

The name of the mushroom in many European languages is thought to be derived from its use as aninsecticide when sprinkled in milk. This practice has been recorded from Germanic- and Slavic-speakingparts of Europe, as well as the Vosges region and pockets elsewhere in France, and Romania. Albertus Magnus was the first to record it in his work De vegetabilibus some time before 1256, commentingvocatur fungus muscarum, eo quod in lacte pulverizatus interficit muscas, "it is called the fly mushroom because it is powdered in milk to kill flies."

Fig. Buttons

The 16th-century Flemish botanist Carolus Clusius traced the practice of sprinkling it into milk to Frankfurtin Germany, while Carl Linnaeus, the "father of taxonomy", reported it from Småland in southern Sweden, where he had lived as a child.

He described it in volume two of his Species Plantarum in 1753, giving it the name Agaricus muscarius, the specific epithet deriving from Latin musca meaning "fly". It gained its current name in 1783, when placed in the genus Amanita by Jean-Baptiste Lamarck, a name sanctioned in 1821 by the "father of mycology", Swedish naturalist Elias Magnus Fries.

The starting date for all the mycota had been set by general agreement as January 1, 1821, the date of Fries's work, and so the full name was then

Amanita muscaria (L.:Fr.) Hook. The 1987 edition of the International Code of Botanical Nomenclature changed the rules on the starting date and primary work for names of fungi, and names can now be considered valid as far back as May 1, 1753, the date of publication of Linnaeus's work. Hence, Linnaeus and Lamarck are now taken as the namers of Amanita muscaria (L.) Lam..

The English mycologist John Ramsbottom reported that Amanita muscaria was used for getting rid of bugs in England and Sweden, and bug agaric was an old alternate name for the species. French mycologist Pierre Bulliard reported having tried without success to replicate its fly-killing properties in his work Histoire des plantes vénéneuses et suspectes de la France (1784), and proposed a new binomial name Agaricus pseudo-aurantiacus because of this.

One compound isolated from the fungus is 1,3-diolein, which attracts insects. It has been hypothesised that the flies intentionally seek out the fly agaric for its intoxicating properties. An alternative derivation proposes that the term fly- refers not to insects as such but rather the delirium resulting from consumption of the fungus.

This is based on the medieval belief that flies could enter a person's head and cause mental illness. Several regional names appear to be linked with this connotation, meaning the "mad" or "fool's" version of the highly regarded edible mushroomAmanita caesarea. Hence there is oriol foll "mad oriol" in Catalan, mujolo folo from Toulouse, concourlo fouolo from the Aveyron department in Southern France, ovolo matto from Trentino in Italy. A local dialect name in Fribourg in Switzerland is tsapi de diablhou, which translates as "Devil's hat".

Classification

Fig. Amanita muscaria var.formosa sensu Thiers, southernOregon Coast

Amanita muscaria is the type species of the genus. By extension, it is also the type species of Amanita subgenusAmanita, as well as section Amanita within this subgenus. Amanita subgenus Amanita includes all Amanita withinamyloid spores. Amanita section Amanita includes the species which have very patchy universal veil remnants, including a volva that is reduced to a series of concentric rings and the veil remnants on the cap to a series of patches or warts.

Most species in this group also have a bulbous base. Amanita section Amanita consists ofA. muscaria and its close relatives, including A. pantherina (the panther cap), A. gemmata, A. farinosa, andA. xanthocephala. Modern fungal taxonomists have classified Amanita muscaria and its allies this way based on gross morphology and spore inamyloidy. Two recent molecular phylogenetic studies have confirmed this classification as natural.

Amanita muscaria varies considerably in its morphology, and many authorities recognise several subspecies or varieties within the species. In The Agaricales in Modern Taxonomy, German mycologist Rolf Singer listed three subspecies, though without description: A. muscaria ssp. muscaria, A. muscaria ssp. americana, and A. muscariassp. flavivolvata.

Contemporary authorities recognise up to seven varieties:

- var. muscaria, the typical red-and-white spotted variety. Some authorities, such as Rodham Tulloss, only use this name for Eurasian and western Alaskan populations.
- var. flavivolvata is red, with yellow to yellowish-white warts. It is found from southern Alaska down through the Rocky Mountains, through Central America, all the way to Andean Colombia. Rodham Tulloss uses this name to describe all "typical" A. muscaria from indigenous New World populations.
- var. alba, an uncommon fungus, has a white to a silvery white cap that has white warts but is similar to the usual form of mushroom.
- var. formosa, has a yellow to orange-yellow cap with yellowish warts and stem (which may be tan). Some authorities (cf. Jenkins) use the name for allA. muscaria which fit this description worldwide, others (cf. Tulloss) restrict its use to Eurasian populations.

Fig. Amanita muscaria var. guessowii has a yellow to orange cap surface, with the centre of the cap more orange or perhaps even reddish orange.

- var. guessowii has a yellow to orange cap, with the centre more orange or perhaps even reddish orange. It is found most commonly in northeastern North America, from Newfoundland and Quebec south all the way to the state of Tennessee. Some authorities (cf. Jenkins) treat these populations as A. muscaria var.formosa, while others (cf. Tulloss) recognise them as a distinct variety.
- var. persicina is pinkish to orangish, sometimes called "melon"-coloured, with poorly formed, or at times absent remnants of universal veil on the stem and vassal bulb; it is known from the southeastern coastal areas of the United States, and was described in 1977. Recent DNA sequencing suggests this may be a separate species which may require naming.
- var. regalis, from Scandinavia and Alaska. is liver-brown and has yellow warts. It appears to be distinctive, and some authorities (cf. Tulloss) treat it as a separate species, while others (cf. Jenkins) treat it as a variety of the A. muscaria.

A 2006 molecular phylogenetic study of different regional populations of A. muscaria by mycologist József Geml and colleagues found three distinct clades within this species representing, roughly, Eurasian, Eurasian "subalpine", and North American populations.

Specimens belonging to all three clades have been found in Alaska; this has led to the hypothesis that this was the centre of diversification for this species.

The study also looked at four named varieties of the species: var. alba, var. flavivolvata, var. formosa(including var. guessowii), and var. regalis from both areas.

All four varieties were found within both the Eurasian and North American clades, evidence that these morphological forms are polymorphisms rather than distinct subspecies or varieties.

Further molecular study by Geml and colleagues published in 2008 show that these three genetic groups, plus a fourth associated with oak–hickory–pine forest in the southeastern United States and two more onSanta Cruz Island in California, are delineated from each other enough genetically to be considered separate species; thus A. muscaria as it stands currently is evidently a species complex.

The complex also includes at least three other closely related taxa that are currently regarded as species:A. breckonii is a buff-capped mushroom associated with conifers from the Pacific Northwest, and the brown-capped A. gioiosa and A. heterochromafrom the Mediterranean Basin and from Sardinia respectively. Both of these last two are found with Eucalyptus and Cistus trees, and it is unclear whether they are native or introduced from Australia.

Description

Fig. Cross section of fruiting body, showing pigment under skin and free gills

A large conspicuous mushroom, Amanita muscaria is generally common and numerous where it grows, and is often found in groups with basidiocarps in all stages of development. Fly agaric fruiting bodies emerge from the soil looking like white eggs.

After emerging from the ground, the cap is covered with numerous small white to yellow pyramid-shaped warts. These are remnants of the universal veil, a membrane that encloses the entire mushroom when it is still very young. Dissecting the mushroom at this stage will reveal a characteristic yellowish layer of skin under the veil; this is helpful in identification.

As the fungus grows, the red colour appears through the broken veil and the warts become less prominent; they do not change in size, but are reduced relative to the expanding skin area. The cap changes from globose to hemispherical, and finally to plate-like and flat in mature specimens. Fully grown, the bright red cap is usually around 8–20 cm (3–8 in) in diameter, although larger specimens have been found. The red colour may fade after rain and in older mushrooms.

The free gills are white, as is the spore print. The oval spores measure 9–13 by 6.5–9 μm; they do not turn blue with the application of iodine. The stipeis white, 5–20 cm high (2–8 in) by 1–2 cm (0.4–0.8 in) wide, and has the slightly brittle, fibrous texture typical of many large mushrooms. At the base is abulb that bears universal veil remnants in the form of two to four distinct rings or ruffs.

Between the basal universal veil remnants and gills are remnants of the partial veil (which covers the gills during development) in the form of a white ring. It can be quite wide and flaccid with age. There is generally no associated smell other than a mild earthiness.

Although very distinctive in appearance, the fly agaric has been mistaken for other yellow to red mushroom species in the Americas, such as Armillaria cf.mellea and the edible Amanita basii—a Mexican species similar to A. caesarea of Europe. Poison control centres in the U.S. and Canada have become aware that amarill (Spanish for 'yellow') is a common name for the A. caesarea-like species in Mexico. Amanita caesarea can be distinguished by its entirely orange to red cap which lacks the numerous white warty spots of the fly agaric. Furthermore the stem, gills and ring of A. caesarea are bright yellow, not white. The volva is a distinct white bag, not broken into scales. In Australia, the introduced fly agaric may be confused with the native vermilion grisette (Amanita xanthocephala), which grows in association with eucalypts. The latter species generally lacks the white warts of A. muscariaand bears no ring.

DISTRIBUTION AND HABITAT

Fig. A. muscaria in a Pinus radiataplantation, near Mount Field National Park,Tasmania

Amanita muscaria is a cosmopolitan mushroom, native to conifer and deciduous woodlands throughout thetemperate and boreal regions of the Northern Hemisphere, including higher elevations of warmer latitudes in regions such as Hindu Kush, the Mediterranean and also Central America. A recent molecular study proposes that it had an ancestral origin in the Siberian–Beringian region in the Tertiary period, before radiating outwards across Asia, Europe and North America.

The season for fruiting varies in different climates: fruiting occurs in summer and autumn across most of North America, but later in autumn and early winter on the Pacific coast. This species is often found in similar locations to Boletus edulis, and may appear in fairy rings. Conveyed with pine seedlings, it has been widely transported into the southern hemisphere, including Australia, New Zealand, South Africa and South America, where it can be found in the southern Brazilian state of Paraná.

Ectomycorrhizal, Amanita muscaria forms symbiotic relationships with many trees, including pine, spruce, fir,birch, and cedar. Commonly seen under introduced trees, A. muscaria is the fungal equivalent of a weedin New Zealand, Tasmania and Victoria, forming new associations with southern beech (Nothofagus).

The species is also invading a rainforest in Australia, where it may be displacing the native species. It appears to be spreading northwards, with recent reports placing it near Port Macquarie on the New South Wales north coast. It was recorded under silver birch (Betula pendula) in Manjimup,

Western Australia in 2010. Although it has apparently not spread to eucalypts in Australia, it has been recorded associating with them in Portugal.

TOXICITY

Fig. Mature. The white spots may wash off with heavy rainfall

Amanita muscaria poisoning has occurred in young children and in people who ingested the mushrooms for a hallucinogenic experience. Occasionally it has been ingested in error, because immature button forms resemble puffballs. The white spots sometimes wash away during heavy rain and the mushrooms then may appear to be the edible A. caesarea.

Amanita muscaria contains several biologically active agents, at least one of which, muscimol, is known to bepsychoactive. Ibotenic acid, a neurotoxin, serves as a prodrug to muscimol, with approximately 10–20% converting to muscimol after ingestion. A toxic dose in adults is approximately 6 mg muscimol or 30 to 60 mg ibotenic acid;this is typically about the amount found in one cap of Amanita muscaria. The amount and ratio of chemical compounds per mushroom varies widely from region to region and season to season, which can further confuse the issue. Spring and summer mushrooms have been reported to contain up to 10 times more ibotenic acid and muscimol than autumn fruitings.

A fatal dose has been calculated as 15 caps. Deaths from this fungus A. muscaria have been reported in historical journal articles and newspaper reports, but with modern medical treatment, fatal poisoning from ingesting this mushroom is extremely rare.

Many older books list Amanita muscaria as "deadly", but this is an error that implies the mushroom is more toxic than it is. The North American Mycological Association has stated there were no reliably documented fatalities from eating this mushroom during the 20th century. The vast majority (90% or more) of mushroom poisoning deaths are from eating the greenish to yellowish "death cap", (A. phalloides) or perhaps even one of the several whiteAmanita species which are known as destroying angels.

The active constituents of this species are water soluble, and boiling and then discarding the cooking water at least partly detoxifies A. muscaria.Drying may increase potency, as the process facilitates the conversion of ibotenic acid to the more potent muscimol. According to some sources, once detoxified, the mushroom becomes edible.

Pharmacology

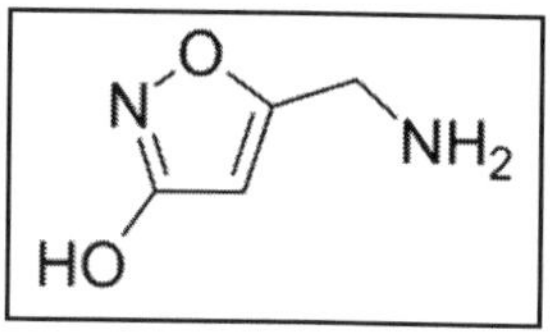

Fig. Muscimol, the principal psychoactive constituent of A. muscaria.

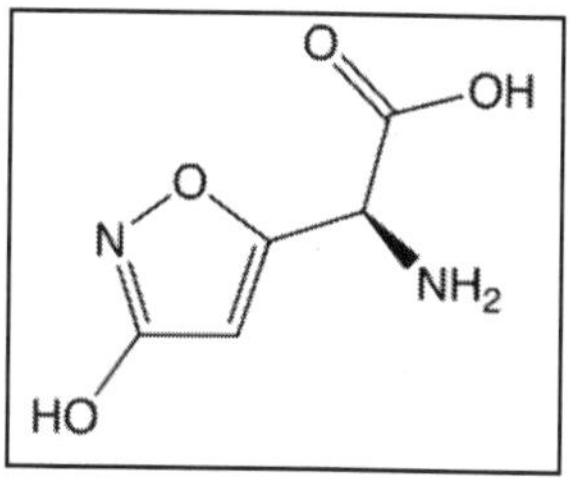

Fig. Ibotenic acid, a prodrug to muscimol found in A. muscaria.

Muscarine, discovered in 1869, was long thought to be the active hallucinogenic agent in A. muscaria. Muscarine binds with muscarinic acetylcholine receptors leading to the excitation of neurons bearing these receptors. The levels of muscarine in Amanita muscaria are minute when compared with other poisonous fungi such as Inocybe erubescens, the small white Clitocybe species C. dealbata and C. rivulosa. The level of muscarine in A. muscaria is too low to play a role in the symptoms of poisoning.

The major toxins involved in A. muscaria poisoning are muscimol (3-hydroxy-5-aminomethyl-1-isoxazole, anunsaturated cyclic hydroxamic acid) and the related amino acid ibotenic acid. Muscimol is the product of thedecarboxylation (usually by drying) of ibotenic acid. Muscimol and ibotenic acid were discovered in the mid-20th century. Researchers in England, Japan, and Switzerland showed that the effects produced were due mainly to ibotenic acid and muscimol, not muscarine.

These toxins are not distributed uniformly in the mushroom. Most are detected in the cap of the fruit, rather than in the base, with the smallest amount in the stalk (Lampe, 1978; Tsunoda et al., 1993). Quite rapidly, between 20 and 90 minutes after ingestion, a substantial fraction of ibotenic acid is excreted unmetabolised in the urine of the consumer. Almost no muscimol is excreted when pure ibotenic acid is eaten, but muscimol is detectable in the urine after eating A. muscaria, which contains both ibotenic acid and muscimol.

Ibotenic acid and muscimol are structurally related to each other and to two major neurotransmitters of the central nervous system: glutamic acid and GABA respectively. Ibotenic acid and muscimol act like these neurotransmitters, muscimol being a potent GABAA agonist, while ibotenic acid is an agonist of NMDA glutamate receptors and certain metabotropic glutamate receptors which are involved in the control of neuronal activity. It is these interactions which are thought to cause the psychoactive effects found in intoxication. Muscimol is the agent responsible for the majority of the psychoactivity.

Muscazone is another compound that has more recently been isolated from European specimens of the fly agaric. It is a product of the breakdown of ibotenic acid by ultra-violet radiation. Muscazone is of minor pharmacological activity compared with the other agents. Amanita muscaria and related species are known as effective bioaccumulators of vanadium; some species concentrate vanadium to levels of up to 400 times those typically found in plants. Vanadium is present in fruit-bodies as an organometallic compound called amavadine. The biological importance of the accumulation process is unknown.

Symptoms

Fly agarics are known for the unpredictability of their effects. Depending on habitat and the amount ingested per body weight, effects can range fromnausea and twitching to drowsiness, cholinergic crisis-like effects (low blood pressure, sweating and salivation), auditory and visual distortions, mood changes, euphoria, relaxation, ataxia, and loss of equilibrium.

In cases of serious poisoning the mushroom causes delirium, somewhat similar in effect to anticholinergic poisoning (such as that caused by Datura stramonium), characterised by bouts of marked agitation with confusion, hallucinations, and irritability followed by periods of central nervous systemdepression. Seizures and coma may also occur in severe poisonings. Symptoms typically appear after around 30 to 90 minutes and peak within three hours, but certain effects can last for several days. In the majority of cases recovery is complete within 12 to 24 hours. The effect is highly variable between individuals, with similar doses potentially causing quite different reactions. Some people suffering intoxication have exhibited headaches up to ten hours afterwards. Retrograde amnesia and somnolence can result following recovery.

Treatment

Medical attention should be sought in cases of suspected poisoning. If the delay between ingestion and treatment is less than four hours, activated charcoal is given. Gastric lavage can be considered if the patient presents within one hour of ingestion. Inducing vomiting with syrup of ipecac is no longer recommended in any poisoning situations.

There is no antidote, and supportive care is the mainstay of further treatment for intoxication. Though sometimes referred to as a deliriant and whilemuscarine was first isolated from A. muscaria and as such is its namesake, muscimol does not have action, either as an agonist or antagonist, at themuscarinic acetylcholine receptor site, and therefore atropine or physostigmine as an antidote is not recommended. If a patient is delirious or agitated, this can usually be treated by reassurance and, if necessary, physical restraints.

A benzodiazepine such as diazepam or lorazepam can be used to control combativeness, agitation, muscular overactivity, and seizures. Only small doses should be used, as they may worsen the respiratory depressant effects of muscimol.

Recurrent vomiting is rare, but if present may lead to fluid and electrolyte imbalances; intravenous rehydration or electrolyte replacement may be required. Serious cases may develop loss of consciousness or coma, and may need intubation and artificial ventilation. Hemodialysiscan remove the toxins, although this intervention is generally considered unnecessary. With modern medical treatment the prognosis is typically good following supportive treatment.

PSYCHOACTIVE USE

Unlike psilocybin mushrooms, the effects of A. muscaria have generally been considered undesirable for recreational use. The effects of intoxication can be variously described as depressant, sedative-hypnotic, dissociative, and deliriant; paradoxical effects may occur.

Perceptual phenomena such asmacropsia and micropsia may occur, which may have been the inspiration for the effect of mushroom-consumption in Lewis Carroll's Alice's Adventures in Wonderland. Additionally, A. muscaria cannot be commercially cultivated, due to its mycorrhizal relationship with the roots of pine trees. However, following the outlawing of psilocybin mushrooms in the United Kingdom in 2006, the sale of the still legal A. muscaria began increasing.

Professor Marija Gimbutas, a renowned Lithuanian historian, reported to R. Gordon Wasson on the use of this mushroom in Lithuania. In remote areas ofLithuania Amanita muscaria has been consumed at wedding feasts, in which mushrooms were mixed with vodka. The professor also reported that the Lithuanians used to export A. muscaria to the Lapps in the Far North for use in shamanic rituals. The Lithuanian festivities are the only report that Wasson received of ingestion of fly agaric for religious use in Eastern Europe.

Siberia

Amanita muscaria was widely used as an entheogen by many of the indigenous peoples of Siberia. Its use was known among almost all of the Uralic-speaking peoples of western Siberia and the Paleosiberian-speaking peoples of the Russian Far East.

There are only isolated reports of A. muscaria use among the Tungusic and Turkic peoples of central Siberia and it is believed that entheogenic use of A. muscaria was largely not practised by these peoples. In western Siberia, the use of A. muscaria was restricted to shamans, who used it as an alternative method of achieving a trance state. (Normally, Siberian shamans achieve trance by prolonged drumming and dancing.)

In eastern Siberia, A. muscaria was used by both shamans and laypeople alike, and was used recreationally as well as religiously. In eastern Siberia, the shaman would take the mushrooms, and others would drink his urine. This urine, still containing psychoactive elements, may be more potent than the A. muscaria mushrooms with fewer negative effects such as sweating and twitching, suggesting that the initial user may act as a screening filter for other components in the mushroom.

The Koryak of eastern Siberia have a story about the fly agaric (wapaq) which enabled Big Raven to carry a whale to its home. In the story, the deityVahiyinin ("Existence") spat onto earth, and his spittle became the wapaq, and his saliva becomes the warts. After experiencing the power of the wapaq, Raven was so exhilarated that he told it to grow forever on earth so his children, the people, could learn from it. Among the Koryaks, one report said that the poor would consume the urine of the wealthy, who could afford to buy the mushrooms.

Other reports of entheogenic use

The Finnish historian T. I. Itkonen mentions that A. muscaria was once used among the Sami people: sorcerers in Inari would consume fly agarics with seven spots. In 1979, Said Gholam Mochtar and Hartmut Geerken published an article in which they claim to have discovered a tradition of medicinal and recreational use of this mushroom among a Parachi-speaking group in Afghanistan. There are also unconfirmed reports of religious use ofA. muscaria among two Subarctic Native American tribes. Ojibwa ethnobotanist Keewaydinoquay Peschel reported its use among her people, where it was known as the miskwedo. This information was enthusiastically received by Wasson, although evidence from other sources was lacking.There is also one account of a Euro-American who claims to have been initiated into traditional Tlicho use of Amanita muscaria.

Soma

In 1968, R. Gordon Wasson proposed that A. muscaria was the Soma talked about in the Rig Veda of India, a claim which received widespread publicity and popular support at the time. He noted that descriptions of Soma omitted any description of roots, stems or seeds, which suggested a mushroom, and used the adjective hári "dazzling" or "flaming" which the author interprets as meaning red.

One line described men urinatingSoma; this recalled the practice of recycling urine in Siberia. Soma is mentioned as coming "from the mountains", which Wasson interpreted as the mushroom having being brought in with the Aryan invaders from the north. Indian scholars Santosh Kumar Dash and Sachinanda Padhy pointed out that both eating of mushrooms and drinking of urine were proscribed, using as a source the Manusm?ti.

In 1971, Vedic scholar John Brough from Cambridge University rejected Wasson's theory and noted that the language was too vague to determine a description of Soma. In his 1976 survey,Hallucinogens and Culture, anthropologist Peter T. Furst evaluated the evidence for and against the identification of the fly agaric mushroom as the Vedic Soma, concluding cautiously in its favour.

Vikings

The notion that Vikings used A. muscaria to produce their berserker rages was first suggested by the Swedish professor Samuel Ödmann in 1784.Ödmann based his theories on reports about the use of fly agaric among Siberian shamans. The notion has become widespread since the 19th century, but no contemporary sources mention this use or anything similar in their description of berserkers. Muscimol is generally a mild relaxant, but it can create a range of different reactions within a group of people. It is possible that it could make a person angry, or cause them to be "very jolly or sad, jump about, dance, sing or give way to great fright".

Christianity

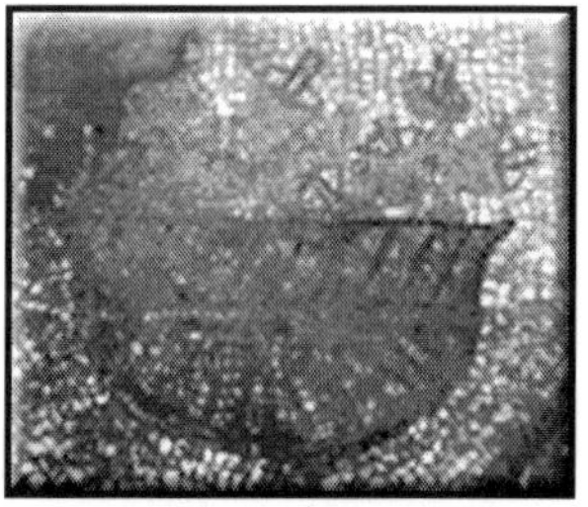

Fig. Mosaic of red mushrooms, found in the Christian Basilicaof Aquileia in northern Italy, dating to before 330 AD.

Philologist, archeologist, and Dead Sea Scrolls scholar John Marco Allegro postulated that early Christian theology was derived from a fertility cult revolving around the entheogenic consumption of A. muscaria in his 1970 book The Sacred Mushroom and the Cross, but his theory has found little support by scholars outside the field of ethnomycology. The book was roundly discredited by academics and theologians, including Sir Godfrey Driver, Emeritus Professor of Semitic Philology at Oxford University, and Henry Chadwick, the Dean of Christ Church, Oxford.

Christian author John C. King wrote a detailed rebuttal of Allegro's theory in the 1970 book A Christian View of the Mushroom Myth; he notes that neither fly agarics nor their host trees are found in the Middle East, even though cedars and pines are found there, and highlights the tenuous nature of the links between biblical and Sumerian names coined by Allegro. He concludes that if the theory was true, the use of the mushroom must have been "the best kept secret in the world" as it was so well concealed for two thousand years.

In Magic Mushrooms in Religion and Alchemy (formerly called Strange Fruit), Clark Heinrich suggests A. muscariausage by Adam and Eve, Moses, Elijah and Elisha, Isaiah, Ezekiel, Jonah, Jesus and his disciples, and John of Patmos. In the book Apples of Apollo, the mushroom is identified in a wide range of mythological tales such as those involving Perseus, Prometheus,Heracles, Jason and the Argonauts, Jesus and the Holy Grail.

CULINARY USE

The toxins in A. muscaria are water soluble. When sliced thinly, or finely diced and boiled in plentiful water until thoroughly cooked, it seems to be detoxified. Although its consumption as a food has never been widespread, the consumption of detoxified A. muscaria has been practised in some parts of Europe (notably by Russian settlers in Siberia) since at least the 19th century, and likely earlier.

The German physician and naturalist Georg Heinrich von Langsdorff wrote the earliest published account on how to detoxify this mushroom in 1823. In the late 19th century, the French physician Félix Archimède Pouchet was a populariser and advocate of A. muscaria consumption, comparing it to manioc, an important food source in tropical South America that must be detoxified before consumption.

Use of this mushroom as a food source also seems to have existed in North America. A classic description of this use of A. muscaria by an African-American mushroom seller in Washington, D.C., in the late 19th century is described by American botanist Frederick Vernon Coville. In this case, the mushroom, after parboiling, and soaking in vinegar, is made into a mushroom sauce for steak. It is also consumed as a food in parts of Japan. The most well-known current use as an edible mushroom is in Nagano Prefecture, Japan. There, it is primarily salted and pickled.

A 2008 paper by food historian William Rubel and mycologist David Arora gives a history of consumption of A. muscaria as a food and describes detoxification methods. They advocate that Amanita muscaria be described in field guides as an edible mushroom, though accompanied by a description on how to detoxify it. The authors state that the widespread descriptions in field guides of this mushroom as poisonous is a reflection of cultural bias, as several other popular edible species, notably morels, are toxic unless properly cooked.

CULTURAL DEPICTIONS

Fig. Moritz von Schwind's 1851 painting of Rübezahl features fly agarics.

Fig. A ticket booth in an amusement park in Montevideo, Uruguay

The red-and-white spotted toadstool is a common image in many aspects of popular culture. Garden ornaments and children's picture books depictinggnomes and fairies, such as the Smurfs, often show fly agarics used as seats, or homes. Fly agarics have been featured in paintings since theRenaissance, albeit in a subtle manner. In the Victorian era they became more visible, becoming the main topic of some fairy paintings. Two of the most famous uses of the mushroom are in the video game series Super Mario Bros. (specifically two of the power-up items and the platforms in several stages), and the dancing mushroom sequence in the 1940 Disney filmFantasia.

Literature

An account of the journeys of Philip von Strahlenberg to Siberia and his descriptions of the use of the mukhomor there was published in English in 1736. The drinking of urine of those who had consumed the mushroom was commented on by Anglo-Irish writer Oliver Goldsmith in his widely read 1762 novel,Citizen of the World. The mushroom had been identified as the fly agaric by this time.

Other authors recorded the distortions of the size of perceived objects while intoxicated by the fungus, including naturalistMordecai Cubitt Cooke in his books The Seven Sisters of Sleep and A Plain and Easy Account of British Fungi. This observation is thought to have formed the basis of the effects of eating the mushroom in the 1865 popular story Alice's Adventures in Wonderland.

A hallucinogenic "scarlet toadstool" from Lappland is featured as a plot element in Charles Kingsley's 1866 novel Hereward the Wake based on themedieval figure of the same name. Thomas Pynchon's 1973 novel Gravity's Rainbow describes the fungus as a "relative of the poisonous Destroying Angel" and presents a detailed description of a character preparing a cookie bake mixture from harvested Amanita muscaria. Fly agaric shamanism is also explored in the 2003 novel Thursbitch by Alan Garner.

Christmas decorations and Santa Claus

Fly agarics appear on Christmas cards and New Year cards from around the world as a symbol of goodluck. The ethnobotanist Jonathan Ott has suggested that the idea of Santa Claus and tradition of hanging stockings over the fireplace is based centrally upon the fly agaric mushroom. He argues that Santa Claus' suit, with its red and white colour scheme, is related to the mushroom.

However, Civil War cartoonist Thomas Nast first changed the color of Santa Claus' coat from tan to red, and it was popularized by early Coca-ColaChristmas ads. Jonathan Ott also draws parallels with flying reindeer: reindeer had been reported to consume the mushroom and prance around in an intoxicated manner afterwards.

American ethnopharmacologist Scott Hajicek-Dobberstein, researching possible links between religious myths and the red mushroom, notes, "If Santa Claus had but one eye [like Odin], or if magic urine had been a part of his legend, his connection to the Amanita muscaria would be much easier to believe." The connection was reported to a wider audience with an article in the magazine of The Sunday Times in 1980, and New Scientist in 1986.Historian Ronald Hutton has since disputed the connection; he noted reindeer spirits did not appear in Siberian mythology, shamans did not travel by sleigh, nor did they wear red and white, or climb out of smoke holes in yurt roofs.

It IS common in shamanic cosmology, however, for shamans to travel to the Upper World (one of three worlds in shamanism, Upper, Middle and Lower) by means of ascending through a tree, the smoke hole of a yurt or tent, by means of a rainbow, and other similar avenues.

PSILOCYBE SEMILANCEATA

Psilocybe semilanceata, commonly known as the liberty cap, is a psychedelic (or "magic") mushroom that contains the psychoactive compounds psilocybin and baeocystin. Of the world's psilocybin mushrooms, it is the most common in nature, and one of the most potent. The mushrooms have a distinctive conical to bell-shaped cap, up to 2.5 cm (1.0 in) in diameter, with a small nipple-like protrusion on the top.

They are yellow to brown in color, covered with radial grooves when moist, and fade to a lighter color as they mature. Their stems tend to be slender and long, and the same color or slightly lighter than the cap. The gill attachment to the stem is adnexed (narrowly attached), and they are initially cream-colored before tinting purple as the spores mature. The spores are dark purplish-brown in mass, ellipsoid in shape, and measure 10.5–15 by 6.5–8.5 micrometers.

The mushroom grows in fields, grassy meadows, and similar habitats, particularly in wet, north-facing fields (south-facing for southern hemisphere) that are well-fertilized by sheep and cattle feces. But unlikeP. cubensis and P.

coprophila, the fungus does not grow directly on dung; rather, it is a saprobic species that feeds off decaying grass roots. It is widely distributed in the cool temperate and subarctic regions of the Northern Hemisphere, particularly in Europe.

However, it has also been reported occasionally from warmer locations such as India, South America, and Australasia. The earliest reliable history ofP. semilanceata intoxication dates back to 1799 in London, and in the 1960s the mushroom was the first European species confirmed to contain psilocybin. Further investigations into the chemical makeup of the fungus revealed the presence of the substances phenylethylamine and the psychotropic baeocystin.

TAXONOMY AND NAMING

The species was first described by Elias Magnus Fries as Agaricus semilanceatus in his 1838 Epicrisis Systematis Mycologici. Paul Kummer transferred it to Psilocybe in 1871 when he raised many of Fries's sub-groupings of Agaricus to the level of genus.

Panaeolus semilanceatus, named by Jakob Emanuel Lange in both 1936 and 1939 publications, is a synonym. According to the taxonomical databaseMycoBank, several taxa once considered varieties of P. semilanceata are synonymous with the species now known as Psilocybe strictipes: the caerulescens variety described by Pier Andrea Saccardo in 1887 (originally named Agaricus semilanceatus var. coerulescens by Mordecai Cubitt Cooke in 1881),the microspora variety described by Rolf Singer in 1969, and the obtusata variety described by Marcel Bon in 1985.

Fig. The mushroom gets its common name from its resemblance to thePhrygian cap.

Several molecular studies published in the 2000s (decade) demonstrated that Psilocybe, as it was defined then, waspolyphyletic. The studies supported the idea of dividing the genus into two clades, one consisting of the bluing, hallucinogenicspecies, and the other the non-bluing, non-hallucinogenic species.

However, the generally accepted lectotype (a specimen later selected when the original author of a taxon name did not designate a type) of the genus as a whole was Psilocybe montana, which is a non-bluing, non-hallucinogenic species. If the non-bluing, non-hallucinogenic species in the study were to be segregated, it would have left the hallucinogenic clade without a valid name.

To resolve this dilemma, several mycologists proposed in a 2005 publication to conserve the name Psilocybe, withP. semilanceata as the type. As they explained, conserving the name Psilocybe in this way would preventnomenclatural changes to a well-known group of fungi, many species of which are "linked to archaeology, anthropology, religion, alternate life styles, forensic science, law enforcement, laws and regulation".Further, the name P. semilanceata had historically been accepted as the lectotype by many authors in the period 1938–68.

The proposal to conserve the name Psilocybe, with P. semilanceata as the type was accepted unanimously by the Nomenclature Committee for Fungi in 2009.

The mushroom takes its common name from the Phrygian cap, also known as the "liberty cap", which it resembles; P. semilanceata shares its common name with P. pelliculosa, a species from which it is more or less indistinguishable in appearance. The Latin word for Phrygian cap is pileus, nowadays the technical name for what is commonly known as the "cap" of a fungal fruit body. In the 18th century Phrygian caps were placed on Liberty poles, which resemble the stem of the mushroom. The generic name is derived from the Ancient Greek psilos (?????) ("smooth" or "bare") and the Byzantine Greek kubê (??ß?) ("head"). The specific epithet comes from the Latin semi ("half") and lanceata, from lanceolatus, meaning "spear-shaped".

DESCRIPTION

Fig. A collection from The Netherlands

The cap of P. semilanceata is 5–25 mm (0.2–1.0 in) in diameter and 6–22 mm (0.24–0.87 in) tall. It varies in shape from sharply conical to bell-shaped, often with a prominent papilla (a nipple-shaped structure), and does not change shape considerably as it ages. The cap margin is initially rolled inward but unrolls to become straight or even curled upwards in maturity. The cap is hygrophanous, meaning it assumes different colors depending on its state of hydration.

When it is moist, the cap is ochraceous to pale brown to darkchestnut brown, but darker in the center, often with a greenish-blue tinge. When moist, radial grooves (striations) can be seen on the cap that correspond to the positions of the gills underneath. When the cap is dry, it becomes much paler, a light yellow-brown color. Moist mushrooms have sticky surfaces that result from a thin gelatinous film called a pellicle. This film becomes apparent if a piece of the cap is broken by bending it back and peeling away the piece. When the cap dries from exposure to the sun, the film turns whitish and is no longer peelable.

On the underside of the mushroom's cap, there are between 15 and 27 individual narrow gills that are moderately crowded together, and they have a narrowly adnexed to almost free attachment to the stem. Their color is initially pale brown, but becomes dark gray to purple-brown with a lighter edge as the spores mature.

The slender yellowish-brown stem is 45–140 mm (1.8–5.5 in) long by 1–3.5 mm (0.04–0.14 in) thick, and usually slightly thicker towards the base. The mushroom has a thin cobweb-like partial veil that does not last long before disappearing; sometimes, the partial veil leaves an annular zone on the stem that may be darkened by spores.

The flesh is thin and membrane-like, and roughly the same color as the surface tissue. It has a farinaceous (similar to freshly ground flour) odor and taste. All parts of the mushroom will stain a bluish color if handled or bruised, and it may naturally turn blue with age.

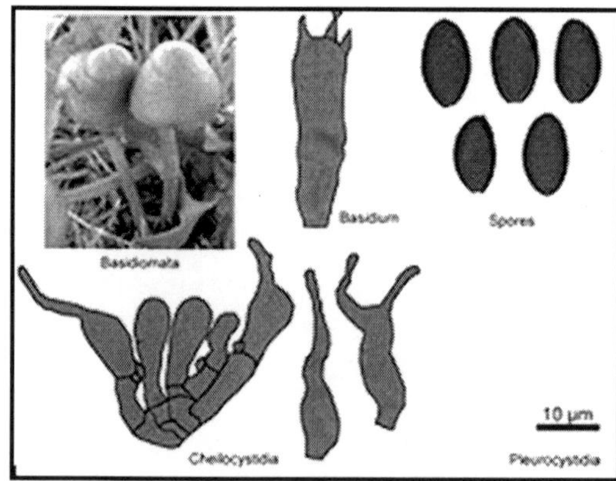

Fig. Microscopic characteristics

Other forms

The anamorphic form of P. semilanceata is an asexual stage in the fungus's life cycle involved in the development of mitotic diaspores (conidia). In culture, grown in a petri dish, the fungus forms a white to pale orange cottony or felt-like mat of mycelia. The conidia formed are straight to curved, measuring 2.0–8.0 by 1.1–2.0 μm, and may contain one to several small intracellular droplets. Although little is known of the anamorphic stage of P. semilanceata beyond the confines of laboratory culture, in general, the morphology of the asexual structures may be used as classical characters in phylogenetic analyses to help understand the evolutionary relationships between related groups of fungi.

Scottish mycologist Roy Watling described sequestrate (truffle-like) or secotioid versions ofP. semilanceata he found growing in association with regular fruit bodies. These versions had elongated caps, 20–22 cm (7.9–8.7 in) long and 0.8–1 cm (0.3–0.4 in) wide at the base, with the inward curved margins closely hugging the stem from the development of membranous flanges.

Their gills were narrow, closely crowded together, and anastomosed (fused together in a vein-like network). The color of the gills was sepia with a brownish vinaceous (red wine-colored) cast, and a white margin. The stems of the fruit bodies were 5–6 cm (2.0–2.4 in) long by 0.1–0.3 cm (0.04–0.12 in) thick, with about 2 cm (0.8 in) of stem length covered by the extended cap.

The thick-walled ellipsoid spores were 12.5–13.5 by 6.5–7 μm. Despite the significant differences in morphology, molecular analysis showed the secotioid version to be the same species as the typical morphotype.

SIMILAR SPECIES

Fig. Lookalikes include P. mexicana (left), P. pelliculosa (center), and P. strictipes (right).

There are several other Psilocybe species that may be confused with P. semilanceata due to similarities in physical appearance. P. strictipes is a slender grassland species that is differentiated macroscopically fromP. semilanceata by the lack of a prominent papilla.P. mexicana, commonly known as the "Mexican liberty cap", is also similar in appearance, but is found in manure-rich soil in subtropical grasslands in Mexico.

It has somewhat smaller spores than P. semilanceata, typically 8–9.9 by 5.5–7.7 μm. Another lookalike species isP. samuiensis, found in Thailand, where it grows in well-manured clay-like soils or among rice paddies. This mushroom can be distinguished from P. semilanceata by its smaller cap, up to 1.5 cm (0.6 in) in diameter, and its rhomboid-shaped spores. P. pelliculosa is physically similar to such a degree that it may be indistinguishable in the field. It differs from P. semilanceata by virtue of its smaller spores, measuring 9–13 by 5–7 μm.

The toxic species Cortinarius rubellus (formerly known as C. orellanoides) has been confused with P. semilanceata by novice collectors looking to consume the mushrooms for hallucinogenic effects, sometimes with drastic consequences.

The expanded and bluntly umbonate cap of C. rubellus is orange-brown with a larger diameter than P. semilanceata, typically ranging from 2–6 cm (0.8–2.4 in).

The gills are adnate to sinuate in attachment to the stem, and cinnamon-brown in color (rather than dark gray to purple-brown). Its stem is roughly the same color as the cap, 5–8 cm (2.0–3.1 in) long and much thicker than P. semilanceata—usually 0.6–1 cm (0.2–0.4 in), and sometimes bears lemon-yellow bands.

It is a mycorrhizal species that grows onacidic soil among mosses, usually in wet coniferous forests. P. semilanceata has also been confused with the toxic muscarine-containing speciesInocybe geophylla, a whitish mushroom with a silky cap, yellowish-brown to pale grayish gills, and a dull yellowish-brown spore print.

ECOLOGY AND HABITAT

Fig. Psilocybe semilanceata is a saprobic grassland species.

Psilocybe semilanceata is a saprobic fungus, meaning it obtains nutrients by breaking down organic matter. The mushroom grows solitarily or in groups on the ground, typically in fields and pastures. It is often found in fields that have been fertilized with sheep or cow dung, although it does not typically grow directly on the dung. The mushroom is also associated with sedges in moist areas of fields, and it is thought to live on the decaying root remains. Like some other grassland species such as P. mexicana, P. tampanensis and Conocybe cyanopus, P. semilanceatamay form sclerotia, a dormant form of the fungus, which affords it some protection from wildfires and other natural disasters.

Laboratory tests have shown P. semilanceata to suppress the growth of the soil-borne water mold Phytophthora cinnamomi, a virulent plant pathogen that causes the disease root rot. When grown in dual culture with other saprobic fungi isolated from the rhizosphere of grasses from its habitat, P. semilanceata significantly suppresses their growth.

This antifungal activity, which can be traced at least partly to two phenolic compounds it secretes, helps it compete successfully with other fungal species in the intense competition for nutrients provided by decaying plant matter. Using standard antimicrobial susceptibility tests, Psilocybe semilanceata was shown to strongly inhibit the growth of the human pathogen methicillin-resistant Staphylococcus aureus (MRSA). The source of the antimicrobial activity is unknown.

DISTRIBUTION

Psilocybe semilanceata is considered the most common psilocybin-containing mushroom. In Europe, P. semilanceata has a widespread distribution, and is found in Austria, Belgium, Bulgaria, the Channel Islands, Czech republic, Denmark, Estonia, the Faroe Islands, Finland, France, Germany, Georgia, Hungary, Iceland, Ireland, Italy, Latvia, Lithuania, Netherlands, Norway, Poland, Romania, Russia, Slovakia, Spain, Sweden, Switzerland and the United Kingdom. It is generally agreed that the species is native to Europe; Watling has demonstrated that there exists little difference between specimens collected from Spain and Scotland, at both the morphological and genetic level.

The mushroom also has a widespread distribution in North America. In Canada it has been collected from British Columbia, New Brunswick,Newfoundland, Nova Scotia, Prince Edward Island and Quebec. In the United States, it is most common in the Pacific Northwest, west of the Cascade Mountains, where it fruits abundantly in autumn and early winter; fruiting has also been reported to occur infrequently during spring months.

Charles Horton Peck reported the mushroom to occur in New York in the early 20th century, and consequently, much literature published since then has reported the species to be present in the eastern United States. Gaston Guzman later examined Peck's herbarium specimen, and in his comprehensive 1983monograph on Psilocybe, concluded that Peck had misidentified it with the species now known as Panaeolina foenisecii.

P. semilanceata is much less common in South America, where it has been recorded from southern Brazil, Argentina, Uruguay and Chile. It is also known in Australia (where it may be an introduced species) and New Zealand, where it grows in high-altitude grasslands. In 2000, it was reported from Golaghat, in the Indianstate of Assam.

PSYCHOACTIVE USE

The first reliably documented report of Psilocybe semilanceata intoxication involved a British family in 1799, who prepared a meal with mushrooms they had picked in London's Green Park. According to the chemistAugustus Everard Brande, the father and his four children experienced typical symptoms associated with ingestion, including pupil dilation, spontaneous laughter and delirium. The identification of the species responsible was made possible by James Sowerby's 1803 book Coloured Figures of English Fungi or Mushrooms, which included a description of the fungus, then known as Agaricus glutinosus (originally described by Moses Ashley Curtis in 1780). According to German mycologist Jochen Gartz, the description of the species is "fully compatible with current knowledge about Psilocybe semilanceata."

In the early 1960s, the Swiss scientist Albert Hofmann—known for the synthesis of the psychedelic drug LSD—chemically analyzed P. semilanceata fruit bodies collected in Switzerland and France by the botanistRoger Heim. Using the technique of paper chromatography, Hofmann confirmed the presence of 0.25% (by weight) psilocybin in dried samples. Their 1963 publication was the first report of psilocybin in a European mushroom species; previously, it had been known only in Psilocybe species native to Mexico, Asia and North America.

This finding was confirmed in the late 1960s with specimens from Scotland and England,Czechoslovakia (1973), Germany (1977), Norway (1978), and Belgium and Finland (1984).In 1965, forensic characterization of psilocybin-containing mushrooms seized from college students in British Columbia identified P. semilanceata—the first recorded case of intentional recreational use of the mushroom in Canada. The presence of the psilocybin analog baeocystin was confirmed in 1977.Several studies published since then support the idea that the variability of psilocybin content inP. semilanceata is low, regardless of country of origin.

Microscopic characteristics

In deposit, the spores are a deep reddish purple-brown color. The use of a light microscope can reveal further details: the spores are oblong when seen in side view, and oblong to oval in frontal view, with dimensions of 10.5–15 by 6.5–8.5 μm. The basidia (spore bearing cells of the hymenium), are 20–31 by 5–9 μm, four-spored, and have clamps at their bases; there are no basidia found on the sterile gill edge.

The cheilocystidia (cystidia on the gill edge) measure 15–30 by 4–7 μm, and are flask-shaped with long thin necks that are 1–3.5 μm wide. P. semilanceata does not have pleurocystidia (cystidia on the gill face). The cap cuticle is up to 90 μm thick, and is made of a tissue layer called an ixocutis—a gelatinized layer of hyphae lying parallel to the cap surface. The hyphae comprising the ixocutis are cylindrical, hyaline, and 1–3.5 μm wide. Immediately under the cap cuticle is the subpellis, made of hyphae that are 4–12 μm wide with yellowish-brown encrusted walls. There are clamp connections present in the hyphae of all tissues.

Properties

Several studies have quantified the amounts of hallucinogenic compounds found in the fruit bodies of Psilocybe semilanceata. In 1993, Gartz reported an average of 1% psilocybin (expressed as a percentage of the dry weight of the fruit bodies), ranging from a minimum of 0.2% to a maximum of 2.37%, which is the highest psilocybin concentration reported for a mushroom. In an earlier analysis, Tjakko Stijve and Thom Kuyper (1985) found a high concentration in a single specimen (1.7%) in addition to a relatively high concentration of baeocystin (0.36%).

Smaller specimens tend to have the highest percent concentrations of psilocybin, but the absolute amount is highest in larger mushrooms. A Finnish study assayed psilocybin concentrations in old herbarium specimens, and concluded that although psilocybin concentration decreased linearly over time, it was relatively stable. They were able to detect the chemical in specimens that were 115 years old.

Michael Beug and Jeremy Bigwood, analyzing specimens from the Pacific Northwest region of the United States, reported psilocybin concentrations ranging from 0.62% to 1.28%, averaging 1.0 ±0.2%. They concluded that the species was one of the most potent, as well as the most constant in psilocybin levels.

In a 1996 publication, Paul Stamets defined a "potency rating scale" based on the total content of psychoactive compounds (including psilocybin, psilocin, and baeocystin) in 12 species of Psilocybe mushrooms. Although there are certain caveats with this technique—such as the unconfirmed assumption that these compounds contribute equally to psychoactive properties—it serves as a rough comparison of potency between species.

Despite its small size, Psilocybe semilanceata is considered a "moderately active to extremely potent" hallucinogenic mushroom (meaning the combined percentage of psychoactive compounds is typically between 0.25% to greater than 2%), and of the 12 mushrooms compared, only 3 were more potent: P. azurescens, P. baeocystis, and P. bohemica.

According to Gartz (1995), P. semilanceata is Europe's most popular psychoactive species, and Psilocybe authority Gastón Guzmán, in his 1983 monograph on psilocybin mushrooms, claimed it is the world's most common psychoactive mushroom.

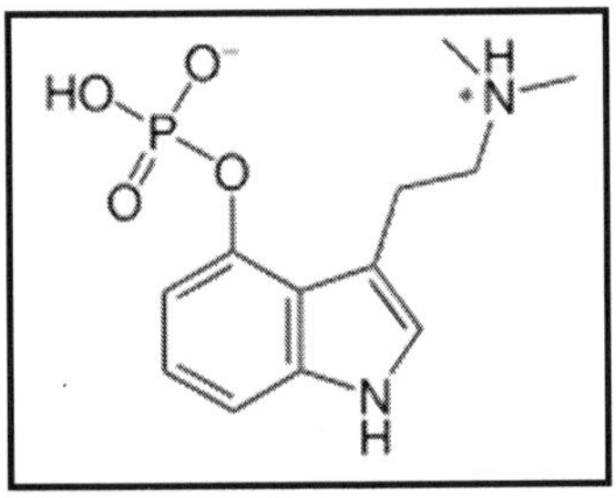

Fig. Psilocybin

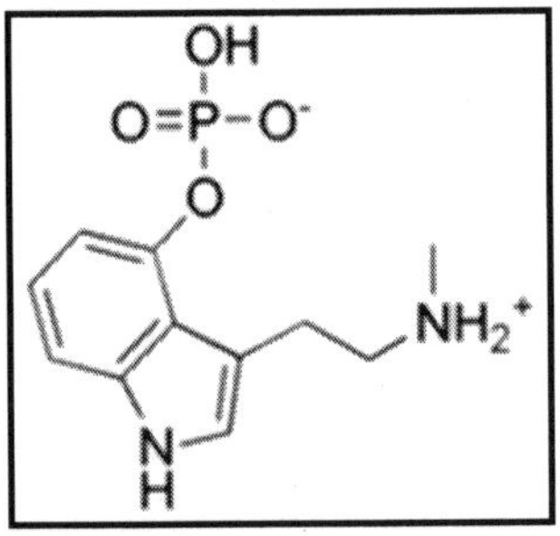

Fig. Baeocystin

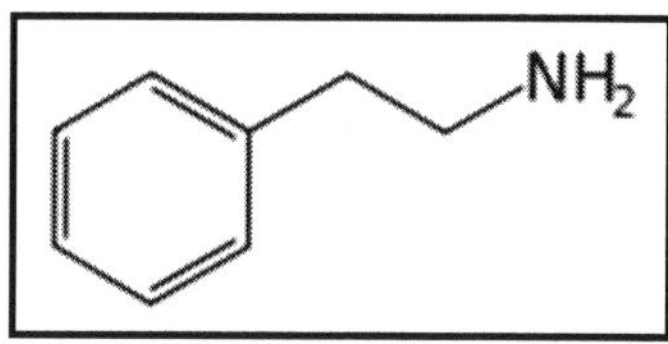

Fig. Phenylethylamine

Several reports have been published in the literature documenting the effects of consumption of P. semilanceata. Typical symptoms include visual distortions of color, depth and form, progressing to visual hallucinations. The effects are similar to the experience following consumption of LSD, although milder.

Common side effects of mushroom ingestion includepupil dilation, increased heart rate, unpleasant mood, and overresponsive reflexes. As is typical of the symptoms associated with psilocybin mushroom ingestion, "the effect on mood in particular is dependent on the subject's pre-exposure personality traits", and "identical doses of psilocybin may have widely differing effects in different individuals."

Although most cases of intoxication resolve without incident, there have been isolated cases with severe consequences, especially after higher dosages or persistent use. In one case reported in Poland in 1998, an 18-year-old man developed Wolff-Parkinson-White syndrome, arrhythmia, and suffered myocardial infarction after ingestingP. semilanceata frequently over the period of a month.

The cardiac damage and myocardial infarction was suggested to be a result of either coronary vasoconstriction, or because of platelet hyperaggregation and occlusion of small coronary arteries.

In 1998, a study reported the presence of the pharmacologically active drug phenylethylamine from samples collected in Sweden. The concentration of the compound was highly variable in the samples tested, but in one case was as high as 146 micrograms per gram of mushroom (wet weight).

This compound, a decarboxylated product of the amino acidphenylalanine, has received considerable interest in psychiatric research, as it may be a neuromodulator of aminergic synapses (neurons that use monoamines as a neurotransmitter) and it has been suggested to enhance energy, elevatemood, and promote aggression. The authors propose that there may be an interaction between phenylethylamine and psilocin (the metabolic breakdown product of psilocybin) through competitive inhibition of monoamine oxidaseenzymes.

One danger of attempting to consume hallucinogenic or other wild mushrooms, especially for novice mushroom hunters, is the possibility of misidentification with toxic species. In one noted case, an otherwise healthy young Austrian man mistook the poisonous Cortinarius rubellus for P. semilanceata.

As a result, he suffered end-stage renal failure, and required a kidney transplant. In another instance, a young man developed cardiac abnormalities similar to those seen in Takotsubo cardiomyopathy, characterized by a sudden temporary weakening of the myocardium. A polymerase chain reaction-based test to specifically identity P. semilanceata was reported by Polish scientists in 2007.

Legal status

The legal status of psilocybin mushrooms varies worldwide. Psilocybin and psilocin are listed as Class A (United Kingdom) or Schedule I (US) drugs under the United Nations 1971 Convention on Psychotropic Substances. The possession and use of psilocybin mushrooms, including P. semilanceata, is therefore prohibited by extension. Although many European countries remained open to the use and possession of hallucinogenic mushrooms after the US ban, starting in the 2000s (decade) there has been a tightening of laws and enforcements.

In The Netherlands, where the drug was once routinely sold in licensed cannabis coffee shops and smart shops, laws were instituted in October 2008 to prohibit the possession or sale of psychedelic mushrooms—the final European country to do so.

REGIONAL IMPORTANCE

Fig. Locals are selling mushrooms and berries collected in the Dainava Forest,Lithuania

- In the United States mushroom picking is popular in the Appalachian area and on the west coast from San Francisco Bay northward, in northern California, Oregon and Washington, and in many other regions.
- British enthusiasts today enjoy an extended average picking season of 75 days compared to just 33 in the 1950s.
- In Slavic countries and Baltic countries, mushroom picking is a common family activity. After a heavy rain during the mushroom

season whole families often venture into the nearest forest, picking bucketfuls of mushrooms, which are cooked and eaten for dinner upon return (mostly like omelette with eggs or fried on butter) or alternatively dried or marinated for later consumption.

FESTIVALS

The popularity of mushroom picking in some parts of the world has led to mushroom festivals. The festivals are usually between September and October, depending on the mushrooms available in a particular region.

Festivals in North America include:

- Aerie Resort on Vancouver Island—Great Fall Mushroom Hunt
- Bamfield, Vancouver Island—Bamfield Mushroom festival
- Boyne City, Michigan—Annual National Morel Mushroom Festival
- Buena Vista, Colorado—Buena Vista Heritage's Mushroom Festival
- Washington's Long Beach Peninsula—Wild Mushroom Celebration
- Lake Quinault Lodge in Washington's Olympic National Forest—Quinault Rain Forest Mushroom Festival
- Mendocino County (North of San Francisco)--Mushroom Festival
- Madisonville, Texas—Mushroom Festival
- Telluride, Colorado—Fungifest
- Kennett Square, Pennsylvania—Mushroom Festival
- Girdwood, Alaska—Fungus Fair
- Muscoda, Wisconsin—Morel Mushroom Festival
- Eugene, Oregon—Mushroom Festival
- Richmond, Missouri—Mushroom Festival

Radiation

Nuclear fallout from the Chernobyl disaster is an important issue concerning mushroom picking in Europe. Due to the wide spread of their mycelium, mushrooms tend to accumulate more radioactive caesium-137 than surrounding soil and other organisms.

State agencies (e.g. Bellesrad in Belarus) monitor and analyze the degree of radionuclide accumulation in various wild species of plants and animals. In particular, Bellesrad claims that Svinushka (Paxillus ssp.), Maslenok (Suillus ssp.), Mokhovik (Xerocomus ssp.), and Horkushka (Lactarius rufus) are the worst ones in this respect. The safest one is Opyonok Osyenniy (Armillaria mellea). This is an issue not only in Poland, Belarus, Ukraine and Russia: the fallout also reached western Europe, and until recently the German government discouraged people gathering certain mushrooms.

GUIDELINES FOR MUSHROOM PICKING

Poisonous mushrooms commonly confused with edible ones

Good mushroom guidebooks call attention to similarities between species, especially if an edible species is similar to or commonly confused with one that is potentially harmful.

Examples:

1. False chanterelles (Hygrophoropsis aurantiaca) can look like real chanterelles (Cantharellus cibarius) to the inexperienced eye. The latter do not have sharp gills, but rather blunt veins on the underside. A mistake here would, however, not be very serious, since false chanterelles are considered edible, just not tasty. Mild symptoms have reported from consuming them. The Jack O'Lantern Mushroom, on the other hand, is often mistaken for a chanterelle, and it is potently toxic.
2. True morels are distinguished from false morels (Gyromitra spp. and Verpa spp.). The impostors have caps attached at the top of the stalk, while true morels have a honeycombed cap and a single, continuous hollow chamber within.
3. Immature Chlorophyllum molybdites can be confused with edible Agaricus mushrooms.
4. Immature puffballs are generally edible, but care must be taken to avoid species such as Scleroderma citrinum and immature Amanitas. These can be identified by cutting a puffball in half and looking for a dark reticulated gleba or the articulated, nonhomogenous structures of a gilled mushroom, respectively.
5. Conocybe filaris, and some Galerina species can look like, and grow next to, Psilocybe. Psilocybe is not deadly but contains the alkaloids psilocybin and psilocin, hence it is often sought for use as a recreational psychedelic drug. Galerina and Conocybe Filaris on the other hand are highly poisonous.

Eating poisonous species

There are treatments to reduce or eliminate the toxicity of certain (but not all) poisonous species to the point where they may be edible. For instance,false morels are deadly poisonous when eaten raw or incorrectly prepared, but their toxins can be reduced by a proper method of parboiling Prepared in this way, this mushroom is widely used and considered a delicacy in the Scandinavian countries, although recent research suggests that there may still be long-term health consequences from eating it.

COMMONLY GATHERED MUSHROOMS

Commonly gathered species, grouped by their order taxa, are as follows

Mushroom species mentioned in each group are listed at the end of the paragraph using the following convention: Latin name (common English names, if any).

Agaricaceae

The Macrolepiota genus, usually the Macrolepiota procera, and, to a lesser extent, the M. rhacodes are highly regarded, especially in Europe, being very palatable and very large, with specimens of M. procera as high as 1 metre being reported.

- Agaricus bisporus also known as the table or button mushroom. Sales of this mushroom in 1996 reached $209 million in Canada. Another well known mushroom known as the portobello is a large brown strain of this fungus.
- Coprinus comatus (Shaggy Ink Cap) decomposes into ink, and hence must be prepared soon after picking and only young specimens should be collected. While being a general mushroom hunting guideline, the avoidance of specimens growing in areas with high pollution is especially important with this family, as it is a very effective pollutant absorber.
- Macrolepiota procera (The Parasol Mushroom)

Amanitaceae

While the family of Amanitas should be approached with extreme caution, as it contains the lethal Amanita phalloides and Amanita virosa, those confident in their skills often pick the Amanita rubescens, which is highly prized in Europe and to a much lesser extent in Russia, accounted by some not to superior taste, but to its relation to the Amanita caesarea, which is not found in Russia, but was considered a delicacy worthy of the emperor in Ancient Rome.

- Amanita rubescens (European blusher)
- Amanita caesarea (Caesar's Mushroom)

Boletaceae

Fig. A collection of Boletus edulis

This order is often viewed as the order of "noble" mushrooms, containing few poisonous species, identifiable with relative ease, and having superior palatability. The most notable species is the Boletus edulis, the "mushroom king", a beautiful, almost legendary, relatively rare mushroom, edible in almost any (even raw) form, and commonly considered the best-tasting mushroom. (Note: Do not confuse the Russian name, literally "white mushroom", with Champignons, often known in English as "white mushrooms".)

- Boletus edulis (Hrib Smrkový, Borowik szlachetny, Porcino, King Bolete, Cep, Steinpilz)

The Leccinum family includes two well-known mushroom species named after the trees they can usually be found next to. The Leccinum aurantiacum (as well as the Leccinum versipelle), found under aspen trees, and the Leccinum scabrum (as well as the L. holopus), found under birch trees. The secondary mentioned species, are significantly different in cap colour only. Both types are very sought after, being highly palatable and beautiful, while more common than the B. edulis.

- Leccinum aurantiacum (Red-capped scaber stalk)
- Leccinum scabrum (Birch bolete)

The Suillus family, characterised by its slimy cap, is another prized mushroom, the Suillus luteus and Suillus granulatus being its most common varieties, and while abundant in some parts of Eurasia, is a rare occurrence in others. It is easy to identify and very palatable.

- Suillus (Klouzek, The Slippery Jack, Butter Mushroom)

The Xerocomus genus is generally considered a less desirable (though mostly edible) mushroom group, due to common abundant mould growth on their caps, which can make them poisonous. The Xerocomus badius, however is an exception, being moderately sought after, especially in Europe. Note that some scientific classifications now consider species in the Xerocomus genus as members of Boletus.

- Xerocomus (Mossiness Mushroom)
- Xerocomus badius (Hrib Hnedý)

Cantharellaceae

Fig. Chanterelles

The Cantharellus cibarius, a common and popular mushroom, especially in Europe, is a choice edible and unique mushroom. It is very rarely infested by worms or larvae, has a unique appearance, and when rotting, the decomposed parts are easily distinguishable and separable from those that are edible.

- Cantharellus cibarius (Chanterelle, Yellow Chanterelle, Pfifferling)

Helvellaceae

The Gyromitra esculenta is considered poisonous, but can be consumed if dried and stored for over a year, according to Slavic literature, and can be used to supplement or replace morel mushrooms, while Western literature claims that even the fumes of the mushroom are dangerous. It is similar to morels both in appearance and palatability.

- Gyromitra esculenta (False Morel, Beefsteak morel, Lorchel)

Morchellaceae

Fig. A basket of morels

The Morel, Morchella esculenta is highly prized in Western Europe, India and North America. It is significantly less prized in Slavic countries where, like the Gyromitra esculenta, is considered marginally edible with mediocre palatability. Boiling the mushroom and discarding the water is often recommended.

- Morchella esculenta (Morel, Yellow morel)

Lactarius

Members of the genus Lactarius, as the name suggests, lactate a milky liquid when wounded and are often scoffed upon by Western literature. The Lactarius deliciosus is however regarded as one of the most palatable mushrooms in Slavic culture, comparable to the Boletus edulis. Also considered as similarly palatable are the species Lactarius necator and particularly Lactarius resimus. Thermal treatment may however be necessary in some cases. Slightly less appealing due to its bitter taste is the Lactarius pubescens.

- Lactarius deliciosus (Saffron Milk-Cap)
- Lactarius resimus (Pepper Cap)
- Lactarius necator (Black Pepper Cap)
- Lactarius pubescens (Wooly Milk-Cap)

Russulaceae

The Russula family includes over 750 species and is one of the most common and abundant mushrooms in Eurasia. Their cap colours include red, brown, yellow, blue and green and can be easily spotted. The Russula vesca species, one of the many red-capped varieties, is one of the most common, is reasonably palatable and can be eaten raw. The edible Russulas have a mild taste, compared to many inedible/poisonous species that have a strong hot or bitter taste.

The Russula emetica (The Sickener) is known to cause gastrointestinal upset and has a very hot taste when a small bit is placed on the tongue. Due to their abundance they are however often regarded as an inferior mushroom for hunting. Note that mushrooms should not be eaten raw without proper cleaning and removal of all insects and decay.

- Russula vesca (Russula)

Tricholomataceae

- Armillaria (The Honey Mushroom, Shoestring Rot). The genus Armillaria, with the popular species A. gallica and A. mellea, being so similar that they are rarely differentiated, are palatable, highly abundant mushrooms. Generally found on decaying tree stumps, they grow in very large quantities and are easy to spot and identify, arguably reducing the fun and challenge in mushroom hunting.
- Pleurotus ostreatus (The Oyster Mushroom). It is the most commonly picked tree-dwelling mushroom and is often also artificially cultivated for sale in grocery stores. This sturdy mushroom can be quite palatable when young. Growing these mushrooms at home can be a profitable enterprise and some Russians engage in the activity.
- Tricholoma matsutake - = syn. T. nauseosum, the rare red pine mushroom that has a very fine aroma. Its undeniable fragrance is both sweet and spicy. They grow under trees and are usually concealed under fallen leaves and/or the duff layer. It forms a symbiotic relationship with the roots of a limited number of tree

species. In Japan it is most commonly associated with Japanese Red Pine. However in the Pacific Northwest it is found in coniferous forests of Douglas fir, Noble fir, sugar pine, and Ponderosa pine. Farther south, it is also associated with hardwoods, namely Tanoak and Madrone forests. The Pacific Northwest and other similar temperate regions along the Pacific Rim also hold great habitat producing these and other quality wild mushrooms. In 1999, N. Bergius and E. Danell reported that Swedish (Tricholoma nauseosum) and Japanese matsutake (T. matsutake) are the same species. The report aroused the import from Northern Europe to Japan because of the comparable flavor and taste. Matsutake are difficult to find and are therefore very expensive. Moreover, domestic productions of Matsutake in Japan have been sharply reduced over the last fifty years due to a pine nematodeBursaphelenchus xylophilus, and it has influenced the price a great deal. The annual harvest of Matsutake in Japan has since further decreased. The price for Matsutake in the Japanese market is highly dependent on quality, availability and origin. The Japanese Matsutake at the beginning of the season, which is the highest grade, can go up to $2000 per kilogram, while the average value for imported Matsutake from China, Europe, and the United States is only about $90 per kilogram.

- The Tricholoma magnivelare is a prized mushroom in North America. British Columbia exports large quantities of this mushroom overseas to Asia where it is in high demand.

AGARICACEAE

The Agaricaceae are a family of basidiomycete fungi and includes the genus Agaricus, as well as basidiomycetes previously classified in the families Tulostomataceae, Lepiotaceae, and Lycoperdaceae.

TAXONOMY

The family Agaricaceae was published by French botanist François Fulgis Chevallier in 1826. It is named after the type genus Agaricus, originally circumscribed by Carl Linnaeus in his 1753 work Species Plantarum. In his authoritative 1986 classification of the Agaricales, Rolf Singer divided the Agaricaceae into four tribesdistinguished largely by spore color: Leucocoprineae, Agariceae, Lepiotear, and Cystodermateae.Species once separately classified into the families Tulostomataceae, Battarreaceae, Lycoperdaceae, and Mycenastraceae have since been folded back into the Agaricaceae. According to a standard reference text, the Agaricaceae contains 85 genera and 1340 species.

DESCRIPTION

Agaricaceae species use a wide variety of fruit body morphology. Although the pileate form (i.e., with a capand stipe) is predominant, gasteroid and secotioid forms are known. In pileate species, the gills are typically thin, and free from attachment to the stipe. Caps are scurfy to smooth, and range from roughly flat toumbonate. They typically have a centrally attached stipe and a membrane-like partial veil.

The spore print color of Agaricaceae species ranges from greenish to ochraceous to pink or sepia; rusty-brown or cinnamon brown colours are absent. Microscopically, the spore surface ranges from smooth to ornamented, and the presence of a germ pore is variable. Amyloidity (i.e. sensitivity to staining in Melzer's reagent) is also variable. The basidia (spore-bearing cells) are usually small, four-spored, and may have interspersed cystidia.

GENERA

The extinct genus Coprinites is one of four known Agaricaceae genera in the fossil record. Others include Aureofungus, Protomycena, andArchaeomarasmius. Archaeomarasmius leggeti, from Atlantic Coastal Plain amber, is 90–94 Ma); the other fossil genera are from Dominican amberand date to 15–20 Ma.

The family currently includes the following genera:

- Agaricus
- Allopsalliota
- Barcheria
- Bovista
- Calvatia
- Chamaemyces
- Chlorophyllum
- Clarkeinda
- Coniolepiota
- †Coprinites
- Coprinus
- Cystoagaricus

- Cystolepiota
- Disciseda
- Endoptychum
- Eriocybe
- Gyrophragmium
- Heinemannomyces
- Hymenagaricus
- Lepiota
- Leucoagaricus
- Leucocoprinus
- Lycoperdon
- Macrolepiota
- Melanophyllum
- Micropsalliota
- Montagnea
- Podaxis
- Ripartitella
- Rugosospora
- Sericeomyces
- Smithiomyces
- Tulostoma
- Verrucospora

AMANITACEAE

The Amanitaceae are a family of fungi or mushrooms. The family, also commonly called the amanita family, is in order Agaricales, gilled mushrooms. The family consists primarily of the genus Amanita, but also includes the genera Catatrama and Limacella.

Mycological works show great divergence in their definitions of families and the up-to-date and authoritative Index fungorum classifies these fungi as part of Pluteaceae. For a long time, they were placed in Agaricaceae.

The species are usually found in woodlands. They emerge from an egg-like structure formed by theuniversal veil.

This family contains several species valued for edibility and flavor, and other deadly poisonous ones. More than half the cases of mushroom poisoning stem from members of this family. The most toxic members of this group have names that warn of the poisonous nature, but others, of varying degrees of toxicity, do not.

SOME NOTABLE SPECIES IN AMANITACEAE

- Amanita caesarea, Caesar's mushroom
- Amanita muscaria, fly agaric
- Amanita rubescens, blusher
- Amanita pantherina, panther cap
- Amanita phalloides, death cap.
- Amanita velosa, orange spring amanita.
- Amanita virosa, destroying angel
- Limacella solidipes, ringed limacella

BOLETACEAE

Boletaceae are a family of mushrooms, primarily characterized by developing their spores in small pores on the underside of the mushroom, instead of gills, as are found in agarics. Nearly as widely distributed as agarics, they include the Cep or King Bolete (Boletus edulis), much sought after by mushroom hunters. As a whole, the typical members of the family are commonly known as boletes.

Boletes are a relatively safe group of mushrooms for human consumption, as none are known to be deadly to adults, and they are the most sought after fungi for mushroom hunting. They are especially suitable for novice mushroom hunters, since there is little danger of confusing them with deadly mushrooms, like various Amanita agarics, which are the most poisonous mushrooms in the world. They are easily distinguished from agarics, and easily recognized for colour, pores and thick stems and caps.

DESCRIPTION

Most species in Boletaceae produce large fleshy mushrooms with a central stipe. The spore print colours are commonly olivaceous (yellowish-green), yellowish, brownish, or vinaceous (red-wine coloured). In many species, flesh that is bruised or cut will turn blue, a result of the oxidation of pulvinic acid derivatives, like variegatic, xerocomic, and atrotomentinic acid. The mushrooms usually have tubular hymenophores, although some species (like those in the genus Phylloporus) are lamellate.

TAXONOMY

Boletaceae were first described by the French botanist François Fulgis Chevallier in 1826 as a family distinct from Agaricaceae. Five genera were included in Chevallier's circumscription: Boletus,Cladosporus (now synonymous with Laetiporus), Physisporus (now Perenniporia), Polyporus, andFistulina.

GENERA

Fig. Devil's bolete (Boletus satanas)

Rolf Singer, in the 4th edition (1986) of his Agaricales in Modern Taxonomy, included 26 genera and 415 species in the Boletaceae. Molecular phylogenetic studies of the 2000s have revised our concept of the family; in a highly cited 2006 publication, Manfred Binder and David Hibbett included 38 genera.

Even after recent changes in classification that have moved many members out of the Boletaceae, it remains a large family with many genera.

According to the Dictionary of the Fungi (10th edition, 2008), 35 genera are recognized in Boletaceae, which collectively contain 787 species. Several new genera have since been described.

Genus	Authority	Year	# of species	Distribution
Afroboletus	Pegler & T.W.K.Young	1981	7	tropical Africa
Aureoboletus	Pouzar	1957	5	widespread
Australopilus	Halling & Fechner	2012	1	Australia
Austroboletus	Wolfe	1980	~30	America; Australasia
Boletellus	Murrill	1909	~50	widespread
Boletochaete	Singer	1944	3	Africa; Southeast Asia
Boletus	Fr.	1821	~300	widespread
Borofutus	Hosen & Zhu L.Yang	2012	1	Bangladesh
Bothia	Halling, T.J.Baroni, & Binder	2007	1	North America
Buchwal-doboletus	Pilát	1962	3	Europe; Australia
Chalciporus	Bataille	1908	25	widespread
Chamonixia	Rolland	1899	8	widespread
Corneroboletus	N.K.Zeng & Zhu L.Yang	2012	1	Singapore; Malaysia; tropical China
Fistulinella	Henn.	1901	15	pantropical
Gastroboletus	Lohwag	1962	13	widespread
Gastroleccinum	Thiers	1989	1	North America
Harrya	Halling, Nuhn & Osmundson	2012	2	Asia; North America; Central America
Heimioporus	E.Horak	2004	~15	widespread
Heliogaster	(Kobayasi) Orihara & Iwase	2010	1	Japan
Hemileccinum	Šutara	2008	2	
Leccinellum	Bresinsky & Manfr. Binder	2003	10	widespread
Leccinum	Gray	1821	~75	widespread
Mycoama-ranthus	Castellano, Trappe & Malajczuk	1992	3	Australasia; Africa, Southeast Asia
Notholepiota	E.Horak	1971	1, possibly 2	Europe, New Zealand
Octaviania	Vittad.	1831	15	widespread
Paxillogaster	E.Horak	1966	1	South America

Phylloboletellus	Singer	1952	1	Central and South America
Phyllobolites	Singer	1942	1	South America
Phylloporus	Quel.	1888	~50	cosmopolitan
Pseudoboletus	Šutara	1991	2	north temperate regions
Pulveroboletus	Murrill	1909	25	cosmopolitan
Retiboletus	Manfr. Binder & Bresinksy	2002	5	north temperate regions
Rhodactina	Pegler & T.W.K.Young	1989	1	India
Rossbeevera	T.Lebel & Orihara	2011	9	Asia, Australia
Royoungia	Castellano, Trappe & Malajczuk	1992	1	Australia
Setogyroporus	Heinem. & Rammeloo	1999	1	tropical Africa
Singeromyces	M.M.Moser	1966	1	Argentina
Sinoboletus	M.Zang	1992	10	China
Solioccasus	Trappe, Osmundson, Manfr.Binder, Castellano & Halling	2013	1	Australasia
Spongiforma	Desjardin, Manf. Binder, Roekring & Flegel	2009	2	Thailand; Malaysia
Strobilomyces	Berk.	1851	~20	cosmopolitan
Sutorius	Halling, Nuhn & Fechner	2012	3	North America, Costa Rica, Africa, S.E. Asia and Australia
Tubosaeta	E.Horak	1967	5	Africa; Asia
Tylopilus	P.Karst	1881	~75	widespread
Velopor-phyrellus	L.D.Gómez & Singer	1984	1	Central America
Wakefieldia	Corner & Hawker	1952	2	Asia; Europe
Xanthoconium	Singer	1944	7	cosmopolitan
Xerocomellus	Šutara	2008	12	North and South America, Europe
Xerocomus	Quel	1887	>20	widespread
Zangia	Yan C.Li & Zhu L.Yang	2011	6	China

Many other genera formerly part of this family have been moved into other, smaller families as work with molecular phylogeny shows that they are more distantly related, even if physically similar. Representative of this adjustment is the move of the slimy-capped genus Suillus to Suillaceae.

DISTRIBUTION

Boletes are found worldwide, on every continent except Antarctica. Well-known and well-described in the temperate latitudes in the northern hemisphere, newer research has shown significant diversity in tropical and southern hemisphere regions as well. E. J. H. Corner found evidence of at least 60 species on the island of Singapore alone. In 1972 he described 140 species from the Malay Peninsula and Borneo and estimated there were an equal number again to be found.

Similar statements about the biodiverse richness of Australian Boletaceae have also been made.

Fig. Phylloporus sp. Wielangta Forest,Tasmania

EDIBILITY

Many of the boletes are considered to be true culinary delicacies, especially the king bolete (Boletus edulis); the Scandinavian cuisine praises boletes. In Finnish cuisine, the king bolete is universally considered to be the tastiest culinary mushroom. A large number of boletes are delicious or at least edible. Poisonous or otherwise inedible species do exist, however, such as the unpalatable bitter species Boletus calopus and the aptly named bitter bolete (Tylopilus felleus) with a taste compared to gall bladder juice, and some orange-capped species of Leccinum.

As the bitter bolete resembles somewhat the king bolete, it can produce literally a bitter disappointment to the mushroom hunter! The rule of thumb is that the bitter bolete has pink pores, and a brownish stipe with a dark brown (sometimes approaching black) reticulum, while the cep has whitish pale grey, occasionally cream colored to cream colored with faint green tones, pore surface, a light colored (white and/or similar in color to the rest of the stipe) reticulum and white hyphae tufts at the base of the stipe. If there is any confusion, the most simple solution is to taste a small amount of cap context. If the taster detects a strong, foul bitter taste immediately or near immediately, it is Tylopilus felleus, unless, of course, the taster lacks the necessary genes to detect the chemical responsible for the bitter taste. They also grow in different habitats. The bitter bolete lacks the stuffed or plugged pore appearance (caused by a hyphal mat of cheilocystidia) that is common in the cep and allies. The peppery bolete (Chalciporus piperatus) has extremely strong taste, and has been used in place of pepper.

Finnish cuisine uses boletes for various soups, sauces, casseroles and hotpots. They are sometimes also used as pizza filling, not unlike champignons,shiitake or portobellos.

Two of the best common edible boletes however are the bay bolete (Boletus badius), whose pores bruise blue-green, and the orange birch bolete, which is a Leccinum with an orange cap and which bruises a bluish grey.

Several guidebooks recommend avoiding all red-pored boletes, however both B. erythropus and B. luridus are edible when well-cooked. However, there has been one recorded instance of death from Boletus pulcherrimus in 1994; a couple developed gastrointestinal symptoms after eating this fungus with the husband succumbing. Autopsy revealed infarction of the midgut. Boletus satanas has also long considered to be poisonous, though it has not been responsible for any deaths. The symptoms are predominantly gastrointestinal in nature. A glycoprotein, bolesatine, has been isolated. A similar compoundbolevenine has been isolated from the poisonous Boletus venenatus of Japan.

CANTHARELLACEAE

The Cantharellaceae are a family of fungi in the order Cantharellales. The family contains the chanterelles and related species, a group of fungi that superficially resemble agarics (gilled mushrooms) but have smooth, wrinkled, or gill-like hymenophores (spore-bearing undersurfaces). Species in the family areectomycorrhizal, forming a mutually beneficial relationship with the roots of trees and other plants. Many of the Cantharellaceae, including the chanterelle (Cantharellus cibarius), the Pacific golden chanterelle (Cantharellus formosus), the horn of plenty (Craterellus cornucopioides), and the trumpet chanterelle (Craterellus tubaeformis), are not only edible, but are collected and marketed internationally on a commercial scale.

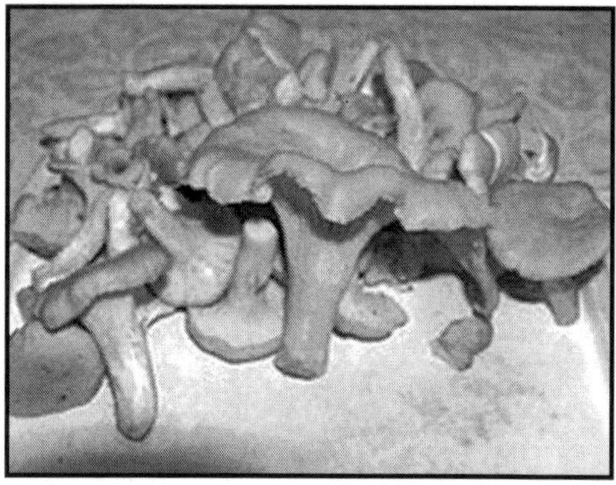

TAXONOMY

History

The family was originally described in 1888 by German mycologist Joseph

Schröter to accommodate the chanterelles, which at that time were thought to be an evolutionary link between "primitive" Thelephoraspecies with smooth hymenophores (spore-bearing surfaces) and more "advanced" Agaricus species with gilled hymenophores.

In 1903, French mycologist René Maire proposed a new classification system that emphasized the possession of "stichic" basidia (basidia with nuclear spindles arranged longitudinally), a characteristic of the Cantharellaceae that linked the family to the Hydnaceae andClavulinaceae. This led Ernst Albert Gäumann to include the genus Hydnum (the hedgehog fungi) within the Cantharellaceae.

In his 1964 survey of fungal families, Dutch mycologist Marinus Anton Donk limited the Cantharellaceae to Cantharellus and Craterellus species, together with some close tropical associates, and this disposition was widely accepted.

Current status

Molecular research, based on cladistic analysis of DNA sequences, has confirmed Donk's circumscription of the Cantharellaceae, though the smaller genera have not yet been sequenced. According to a standard 2008 reference work, the family contains 5 genera and over 90 species worldwide.

DESCRIPTION

Fruit bodies of most species in the family are mushroom-like or trumpet-like, with spore-bearing surfaces that are smooth, wrinkled, veined, or gill-like and that are typically decurrent (running down the upper stem). The consistency is fleshy, the hyphal system being monomitic (consisting of generative hyphae only).

Thebasidia are comparatively large and often have more than the standard 4 sterigmata. Spores are smooth and white to yellowish or pinkish in deposit.

HABITAT AND DISTRIBUTION

All species within the Cantharellaceae are believed to be ectomycorrhizal, forming a mutually beneficial relationships with the roots of living trees and other plants. Basidiocarps typically occur on the ground or in leaf litter in woodland. The family has a cosmopolitan distribution, though the majority of species are tropical.

ECONOMIC IMPORTANCE

Many species of Cantharellus, Craterellus, and Goossensia are edible and several are collected and marketed on a commercial scale. In Europe, the commercial species are Cantharellus cibarius, Craterellus cornucopioides, and Craterellus tubaeformis which are sold fresh, dried, or canned and are either sourced in Europe or imported, mainly from China. Various African Cantharellus species (often collected in miombo woodlands) are also imported into Europe and marketed as "chanterelles". In North America, Cantharellus formosus is an additional, widely marketed species. The global trade in species of the Cantharellaceae has been estimated (2005) to be worth over £1bn (US$1.5bn) per year.

HELVELLACEAE

The Helvellaceae are a family of ascomycete fungi, the best known members of which are the elfin saddles of the genus Helvella. Originally erected by Elias Magnus Fries in 1823 as Elvellacei, it contained many genera. Several of these, such as Gyromitra and Discina, have been found to be more distantly related in a molecular study of ribosomal DNA by mycologist Kerry O'Donnell in 1997, leaving a much smaller core clade now redefined as Helvellaceae.

Instead, this narrowly defined group is most closely related to the true truffles of theTuberaceae. According to the Dictionary of the Fungi, the family contains six genera and 63 species.

MORCHELLACEAE

The Morchellaceae are a family of ascomycete fungi. According to a standard reference work, the family has contained at least 49 species distributed among 4 genera, but in 2012, 5 genera producing the sequestrateand hypogeous ascoma were added.

The best-known members are the highly regarded and commercially picked true morels of the genus Morchella, the thimble morels of the genus Verpa, and a genus of cup-shaped fungi Disciotis. The remaining four genera produce the sequestrate fruit bodies.

Analysis of the ribosomal DNA of many of the Pezizales showed the three genera Verpa, Morchella, andDisciotis to be closely related. Thus they are now included in the family Morchellaceae.

GENERAL DESCRIPTION

Other than the anamorph genus Costantinella, the three remaining genera of Morchellaceae are distinguished by ascocarp morphology. Morchella species have an ascocarp with a sponge-like pileus, with a hollow stipeand pileus. Verpa species have a cup-like or thimble-shaped, smooth or wrinkled pileus above a hollow stipe.Disciotis has a cup-like pileus with vein-like hymenial folds and a small or nonexistent stipe. Theascospores are ellipsoid, smooth, and usually hyaline.

LACTARIUS

Lactarius is a genus of mushroom-producing fungi. The genus, collectively known commonly as milk-caps, are characterized by the fact that they exude a milky fluid ('latex') if cut or damaged. Like the genusRussula, with which they are grouped in the family Russulaceae, their flesh has a distinctive brittle consistency.

Often the gills are decurrent (starting to run down the stem) and the cap is depressed or even funnel-shaped when older. The stem and cap sometimes show 'strobicules' (or 'strobiculi'), which are flat-based shallow oval pits.

To identify to which of the roughly 400 Lactarius species a given specimen belongs, note whether the cap is bald/greasy or velvety or hairy/shaggy at the rim, particularly in young individuals. Also the initial colour of the milk (white, cream, orange, violet...) and the final colour on drying are determining characteristics.

The genus was described by Christian Hendrik Persoon in 1797. Lactarius is derived from the Latin lac'milk'.

ECOLOGY

Lactarius is one of the most prominent genera of ectomycorrhizal fungi. With more than 400 species described worldwide, Lactarius taxa play a significant role as late-stage colonizers of trees and shrubs in a vast range of ecosystems, from boreal coniferous forests to temperate Mediterranean-type maquis. An interesting case is that of the strict association of selected Lactarius species - such as L. tesquorum andL. cistophilus - with Cistus spp., a group of about 20 woody, evergreen or semideciduous shrub species found in wide semi-arid areas from the Canary Islands throughout the Mediterranean region to the Caucasus. Cistus species are obligate seeding, early colonizers that follow disturbance, particularly fire, in low maquis-type Mediterranean ecosystems, rendering their ectomycorrhizal ecology particularly intriguing.

A SELECTION OF WELL-KNOWN EUROPEAN SPECIES

Fig. Lactarius

- Lactarius turpis - ugly milk-cap
- Lactarius torminosus - woolly milk-cap
- Lactarius piperatus - peppery milk-cap
- Lactarius uvidus

Section Deliciosi

- Lactarius deliciosus
- Lactarius deterrimus
- Lactarius salmonicolor

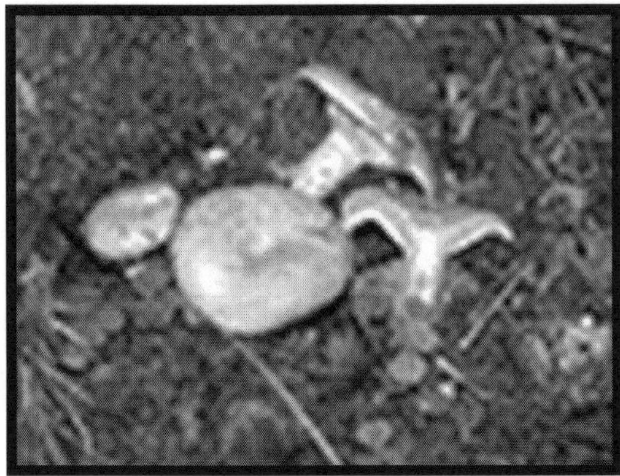

Fig. Lactarius salmonicolor

This group of mushrooms has orange or red milk and carrot-orange coloration, in many cases becoming flecked with green or blue-green with age. They are all generally considered to be edible and tasty, the appetizingly named Lactarius deliciosusreputedly being much better than the others. They grow in coniferous woods.

L. deliciosus is the only one with an English name: 'saffron milk-cap'. It is found under pine or spruce. L. deterrimus was formerly considered to be a variety of L. deliciosus and is distinguished by the milk turning wine-red on drying - but only after up to 30 minutes. L. salmonicolor is associated with spruce and remains a pure orange, unlike the other two which discolour green.

Lactarius chrysorrheus

The milk of this mushroom emerges white but immediately changes to a deep yellow colour.

The top of the cap is a pinkish red with concentric zoning on a background showing yellow tints. It is common under broad-leaved trees, especially oak. There are conflicting reports as to its edibility.

Lactarius decipiens

This flesh-coloured Lactarius is closely related to L. chrysorrheus, and again the milk is initially white and turns yellow, but only after several seconds. To allow the milk to contact the air this is best tested on a paper tissue (a cloth handkerchief is liable to be permanently stained).

Lactarius quietus

L. quietus, which is commonly found under oak trees, is often thought to be a non-descript mushroom, and in fact that is the significance of its Latin epithet quietus. It has a distinctive smell said to be of bedbugs or of wet laundry. The milk goes a little cream but does not change further.

TRICHOLOMATACEAE

The Tricholomataceae are a large family of mushrooms within the Agaricales. A classic "wastebasket taxon", the family is inclusive of any white-, yellow-, or pink-spored genera in the Agaricales not already classified as belonging to the Amanitaceae, Lepiotaceae, Hygrophoraceae, Pluteaceae, orEntolomataceae.

The name derives from the Greek trichos (τριχοζ) meaning hair and loma (λωμα) meaning fringe or border, although not all members display this feature.

Arnolds (1986) and Bas (1990) also place the genera of the Hygrophoraceae within this family, but this classification is not accepted by the majority of fungal taxonomists.

Molecular phylogenetic analysis has greatly aided in the demarcation of clear monophyletic groups among the Tricholomataceae. So far, most of these groups have been defined cladistically rather than being defined as formal Linnean taxa, though there have been several cases in which older proposed segregates from the Tricholomataceae have been validated by evidence coming from molecularphylogenetics. As of 2006, validly published families segregated from the Tricholomataceae include theHydnangiaceae, Lyophyllaceae, Marasmiaceae, Mycenaceae, Omphalotaceae, Physalacriaceae, andPleurotaceae.

The name "Tricholomataceae" is nevertheless seen as having validity in describing Tricholoma and its close relatives, and whatever other genera can at some future point be described as part of a monophyletic family including Tricholoma. To that end, the International Botanical Congress has voted on two occasions (1988 and 2006) to conserve the name "Tricholomataceae" against competing names.This decision does not invalidate the use of segregate families from the Tricholomataceae, but simply validates the continued use of Tricholomataceae.

The extinct genus Archaeomarasmius, described from Turonian-age New Jersey amber, is one of four known genera of Agaricales in the fossil record.

5

Fungiculture

Fungiculture is the process of producing food, medicine, and other products by the cultivation of mushrooms and other fungi.

The word is also commonly used to refer to the practice of cultivating fungi by leafcutter ants, termites, ambrosia beetles, and marsh periwinkles.

INTRODUCTION

Mushrooms are not plants, and require different conditions for optimal growth. Plants develop through photosynthesis, a process that converts atmosphericcarbon dioxide into carbohydrates, especially cellulose. While sunlight provides an energy source for plants, mushrooms derive all of their energy and growth materials from their growth medium, through biochemical decomposition processes. This does not mean that light is an irrelevant requirement, since some fungi use light as a signal for fruiting. However, all the materials for growth must already be present in the growth medium. Mushrooms grow well at relative humidity levels of around 95-100%, and substrate moisture levels of 50 to 75%.

Instead of seeds, mushrooms reproduce asexually through spores. Spores can be contaminated with airborne microorganisms, which will interfere with mushroom growth and prevent a healthy crop.

Mycelium, or actively growing mushroom culture, is placed on a substrate—usually sterilized grains such as rye or millet—and induced to grow into those grains. This is called inoculation. Inoculated grains are referred to as spawn. Spores are another inoculation option, but are less developed than established mycelium. Since they are also contaminated easily, they are only manipulated in laboratory conditions with a laminar flow cabinet.

TECHNIQUES

All mushroom growing techniques require the correct combination of humidity, temperature, substrate (growth medium) and inoculum (spawn or starter culture). Wild harvests, outdoor log inoculation and indoor trays all provide these elements.

Wild harvesting

Due to its climate, the Pacific Northwest of the USA produces commercially valuable mushrooms. Valued species include:

- American matsutake or pine mushroom (Tricholoma magnivelare)
- Chanterelles (Cantharellus formosus, Cantharellus subalbidus, and Cantharellus cibarius)
- Horn of plenty (Craterellus cornucopioides)
- Boletes (Boletus edulis and others)
- Truffles (Tuber gibbosum and Leucangium carthusiana)
- Hedgehogs/ "spreading-hedgehog mushroom" (Hydnum repandum)
- Edible morel (Morchella esculenta)
- Coral tooth mushroom (Hericium abietis)
- Shaggy parasol (Lepiota rhacodes)
- Black picoa (Picoa carthusiana)
- Cauliflower mushroom (Sparassis crispa)

Mushroom gatherers have few requirements to begin business. Gatherers only need to supply funds for possible park fees, knowledge for identifying mushrooms and gathering time.

There are significant disadvantages to relying on natural mushroom production. These sales may be unregulated, placing buyers at risk for buying toxic or inedible mushrooms. By honest error, harvests may include toxic or inedible species. No controls exist to regulate the quality or frequency of harvests, since gatherers rely on favorable natural conditions and weather to produce fruiting. Conflicts may arise between competing gatherers trying to harvest from the same location.

State parks in the Pacific Northwest or elsewhere may charge fees for mushroom gathering permits. Appalachia also produces edible wild mushrooms, including chanterelles and morels. Pickers may sell directly to distributors, restaurants, or sell their harvest through roadside stands wherever a natural supply of mushrooms is plentiful.

While there may be concern that harvesting wild mushrooms may exploit or damage a natural environment, harvesting wild mushrooms is different from harvesting wild plants, fishing or hunting animals. In these last three cases, removing individuals decreases the ability of a wild population to reproduce, since fewer adults remain. Removing adults leaves fewer individuals capable of reproducing and reduces genetic diversity.

Harvesting wild mushrooms removes only fruiting bodies and their attached spores. However, the fruiting bodies (mushrooms) have likely dropped spores before harvest time, or will likely drop them en route to the harvester's destination, further expanding the fungi's habitat. Arguably, the practice of mushroom harvesting may actually help the species being harvested. While truffles also represent the fruiting body of a larger underground network, they are an exception, since they rely on animal spore dispersion.

Additionally, reproduction and propagation can still occur by propagation of the parent mycelium. Harvesting removes none of the parent mycelium, which remains intact underground.

Outdoor logs

Mushrooms can be grown on logs placed outdoors in stacks or piles, as has been done for hundreds of years. Sterilization is not performed in this method. Since production may be unpredictable and seasonal, less than 5% of commercially sold mushrooms are produced this way. Here, tree logs are inoculated with spawn, then allowed to grow as they would in wild conditions. Fruiting, or pinning, is triggered by seasonal changes, or by briefly soaking the logs in cool water. Shiitake and oyster mushrooms have traditionally been produced using the outdoor log technique, although controlled techniques such as indoor tray growing or artificial logs made of compressed substrate have been substituted.

Indoor trays

Indoor growing provides the ability to tightly regulate light, temperature and humidity while excluding contaminants and pests. This allows consistent production, regulated by spawning cycles. This is typically accomplished in windowless, purpose-built buildings, for large scale commercial production.

Indoor tray growing is the most common commercial technique,and talented followed by containerized growing. The tray technique provides the advantages of scalability and easier harvesting. Unlike wild harvests, indoor techniques provide tight control over growing substrate composition and growing conditions. Indoor harvests are much more predictable.

According to Daniel Royse and Robert Beelman, "[Indoor] Mushroom farming consists of six steps, and although the divisions are somewhat arbitrary, these steps identify what is needed to form a production system. The six steps are phase I composting, phase II fertilizing, spawning, casing, pinning, and cropping."

SUBSTRATES

Mushroom production converts the raw natural ingredients into mushroom tissue, most notably the carbohydrate chitin.

An ideal substrate will contain enough nitrogen and carbohydrate for rapid mushroom growth. Common bulk substrates include:

- Wood chips or sawdust
- Mulched straw (usually wheat, but also rice and other straws)
- Strawbedded horse or poultry manure

- Corncobs
- Waste or recycled paper
- coffee pulp or grounds
- Nut and seed hulls
- Cottonseed hulls
- Cocoa bean hulls
- Cottonseed meal
- Soybean meal
- Brewer's grain
- Ammonium nitrate
- Urea

Mushrooms metabolize complex carbohydrates in their substrate into glucose, which is then transported through the mycelium as needed for growth and energy. While it is used as a main energy source, its concentration in the growth medium should not exceed 2%. For ideal fruiting, closer to 1% is ideal.

PESTS AND DISEASES

Parasitic insects, bacteria and other fungi all pose risks to indoor production. The sciarid fly or phorid fly may lay eggs in the growth medium, which hatch into worms and damage developing mushrooms during all growth stages.

Bacterial blotch caused by Pseudomonas bacteria or patches of Trichodermagreen mold also pose a risks during the fruiting stage. Pesticides and sanitizing agents are available to use against these infestations. Biological controls for insect sciarid and phorid flies have also been proposed.

A recent epidemic of Trichoderma green mold has significantly affected mushroom production: "From 1994-96, crop losses in Pennsylvania ranged from 30 to 100%".

COMMERCIALLY CULTIVATED FUNGI

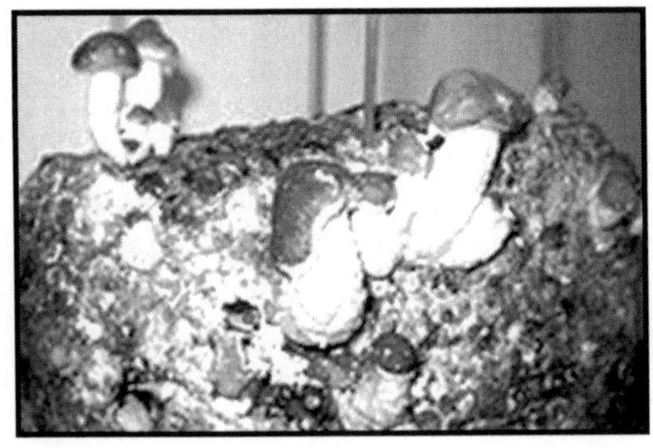

Fig. Home cultivated shiitake developing over approximately 24 hours.

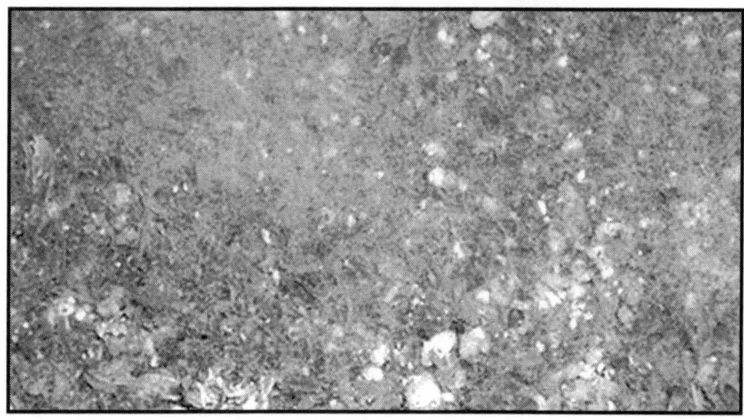

Fig. 9-day old Pleurotus ostreatus mycelium. The structure is a network of millions of interweived threads called hyphae. One can also discern individual spores.

- Agaricus bisporus, also known as champignon and the button mushroom. This species also includes the portobello and crimini mushrooms.
- Auricularia polytricha or Auricularia auricula-judae (Tree ear fungus), two closely related species of jelly fungi that are commonly used in Chinese cuisine.
- Flammulina velutipes, the "winter mushroom", also known as enokitake in Japan
- Hypsizygus tessulatus (also Hypsizygus marmoreus), called shimeji in Japanese, it is a common variety of mushroom available in most markets in Japan. Known as "Beech mushroom" in Europe.
- Lentinus edodes, also known as shiitake, oak mushroom. Lentinus edodes is largely produced in Japan,China and South Korea. Lentinus edodes accounts for 10% of world production of cultivated mushrooms. Common in Japan, China, Australia and North America.
- Pleurotus species are the second most important mushrooms in production in the world, accounting for 25% of total world production. Pleurotus mushrooms are cultivated worldwide; China is the major producer. Several species can be grown on carbonaceous

matter such as straw or newspaper. In the wild they are usually found growing on wood.

- Pleurotus cornucopiae
- Pleurotus eryngii (king trumpet mushroom)
- Pleurotus ostreatus (oyster mushroom)

Fig. Details of the gill structure of the edible oyster mushroom Pleurotus ostreatus.

- Rhizopus oligosporus - the fungal starter culture used in the production of tempeh. In tempeh the mycelia of R. oligosporus are consumed.
- Sparassis crispa - recent developments have led to this being cultivated in California.
- Tremella fuciformis (Snow fungus), another type of jelly fungus that is commonly used in Chinese cuisine.
- Tuber species, (the truffle), Truffles belong to the ascomycete grouping of fungi. The truffle fruitbodies develop underground in mycorrhizalassociation with certain trees e.g. oak, poplar, beech, and hazel. Being difficult to find, trained pigs or dogs are often used to sniff them out for easy harvesting.
- Tuber aestivum (Summer or St. Jean truffle)
- Tuber magnatum (Piemont white truffle)
- Tuber melanosporum (Périgord truffle)
- T.melanosporum x T.magnatum (Khanaqa truffle)
- Terfezia sp. (Desert truffle)
- Ustilago maydis (Corn smut), a fungal pathogen of the maize plants. Also called the Mexican truffle, although not a true truffle.
- Volvariella volvacea (the "Paddy straw mushroom.") Volvariella mushrooms account for 16% of total production of cultivated mushrooms in the world.

PRODUCTION REGIONS IN THE UNITED STATES

Pennsylvania is the top-producing mushroom state in the United States, and celebrates September as "Mushroom Month".

The borough of Kennett Square is a historical and present leader in mushroom production. It currently leads production of Agaricus-type mushrooms, followed by California, Florida and Michigan.

Other mushroom-producing states:

- *East:* Connecticut, Delaware, Florida, Maryland, New York, Pennsylvania, Tennessee, and Vermont
- *Central:* Illinois, Oklahoma, Texas, and Wisconsin
- *West:* California, Colorado, Montana, Oregon, Utah and Washington

Vancouver, British Columbia, also has a significant number of producers — about 60 as of 1998 — mostly located in the lower Fraser Valley.

AGARICUS BISPORUS

Agaricus bisporus—known variously when white as common mushroom, button mushroom, white mushroom, cultivated mushroom, table mushroom, champignon mushroom, when brown as Swiss brown mushroom, Roman brown mushroom, Italian brown, Italian mushroom, cremini/crimini mushroom, brown cap mushrooms, chestnut mushroom, and when mature as Portobello mushroom—is an edible basidiomycete mushroom native to grasslands in Europe and North America.Agaricus bisporus is cultivated in more than 70 countries and is one of the most commonly and widely consumed mushrooms in the world.

TAXONOMY AND NAMING

The common mushroom has a complicated taxonomic history. It was first described by English botanistMordecai Cubitt Cooke in his 1871 Handbook of British Fungi, as a variety (var. hortensis) of Agaricus campestris. Danish mycologist Jakob Emanuel Lange later reviewed a cultivar specimen, and dubbed it Psalliota hortensis var. bispora in 1926. In 1938, it was promoted to species status and renamedPsalliota bispora.

Emil Imbach imparted the species' current scientific name, Agaricus bisporus, after the genus Psalliota was renamed to Agaricus in 1946. The specific epithet bispora distinguishes the two-spored basidia from four-spored varieties.

Among English speakers, Agaricus bisporus is known by many names. A young specimen with a closed cap and either pale white or light brown flesh is known as a button mushroom or white mushroom. In strains with darker flesh, the immature mushroom is variously marketed as a cremini mushroom, baby portobello, baby bella, mini bella, portabellini, Roman mushroom, Italian mushroom, or brown mushroom. At this stage of maturation, the cap may also begin to open slightly. In maturity, it is called aportobello. The French name is champignon de Paris ("Paris mushroom").

The spellings "portobello", "portabella", and "portabello" are all used, but the first of these spellings is the most common.

DESCRIPTION

Agaricus bisporus, white raw	
Nutritional value per 100 g (3.5 oz)	
Energy	93 kJ (22 kcal)
Carbohydrates	3.26 g
- Sugars	1.98 g
- Dietary fiber	1 g
Fat	0.34 g
Protein	3.09 g
Water	92.45 g
Thiamine (vit. B_1)	0.081 μg (7%)
Riboflavin (vit. B_2)	0.402 μg (34%)
Niacin (vit. B_3)	3.607 μg (24%)
Pantothenic acid (B$_5$)	1.497 μg (30%)
Vitamin B_6	0.104 μg (8%)
Folate (vit. B_9)	17 μg (4%)
Vitamin B_{12}	0.04 μg (2%)
Vitamin C	2.1 μg (3%)
Vitamin D	0.2 μg (1%)
Iron	0.5 μg (4%)
Magnesium	9 μg (3%)
Phosphorus	86 μg (12%)
Potassium	318 μg (7%)
Sodium	3 μg (0%)
Zinc	0.52 μg (5%)

The pileus or cap of the original wild species is a pale grey-brown in color, with broad, flat scales on a paler background and fading toward the margins. It is first hemispherical in shape before flattening out with maturity, and 5–10 cm (2–4 in) in diameter. The narrow, crowded gills are free and initially pink, then red-brown and finally a dark brown with a whitish edge from the cheilocystidia. The cylindrical stipe is up to 6 cm (2? in) tall by 1–2 cm wide and bears a thick and narrow ring, which may be streaked on the upperside.

The firm flesh is white though stains a pale pinkish-red on bruising. The spore print is dark brown. The spores are oval to round and measure around 4.5–5.5 x 5–7.5 μm, and the basidia usually two-spored, although two tetrasporic varieties have been described from the Mojave desert and theMediterranean with predominantly heterothallic and homothallic lifestyles, respectively

Commonly found in fields and grassy areas after rain from late spring through to autumn worldwide, especially in association with manure. It is widely collected and eaten, even by those who would not normally experiment with mushroom hunting.

Similar species

The common mushroom could be confused with young specimens of the deadly poisonous destroying angel (Amanita sp.), but the latter can be distinguished by their volva or cup at the base of the mushroom and pure white gills (as opposed to pinkish or brown of Agaricus bisporus). Thus it is important to always clear away debris and examine the base of a mushroom, as well as cutting open young specimens to check the gills. Furthermore, the destroying angel grows in mossy woods and lives symbiotically withspruce.

A more common and less dangerous mistake is to confuse Agaricus bisporus with Agaricus xanthodermus, an inedible mushroom found worldwide in grassy areas. Agaricus xanthodermus has an odor reminiscent of phenol; its flesh turns yellow when bruised. This fungus causes nausea and vomiting in some people.

The poisonous European species Entoloma sinuatum has a passing resemblance but has yellowish gills turning pink and lacks a ring.

CULTIVATION

Fig. Agaricus bisporus being cultivated.

The earliest description of the commercial cultivation of Agaricus bisporus was made by French botanistJoseph Pitton de Tournefort in 1707. French agriculturist Olivier de Serres noted that transplanting mushroom mycelia would lead to more mushrooms. Originally, cultivation was unreliable as mushroom growers would watch for good flushes of mushrooms in fields before digging up the mycelium and replanting in beds of composted manure or inoculating 'bricks' of compressed litter, loam and manure. Spawn collected this way contained pathogens and crops would be commonly infected or not grow at all. In 1893, sterilized, or pure culture, spawn was discovered and produced by the Pasteur Institute in Paris, for cultivation on composted horse manure. Today's commercial variety of the common mushroom was originally a light brown color.

In 1926, a Pennsylvania mushroom farmer found a clump of common mushrooms with white caps in his mushroom bed. Like white bread it was seen as a more attractive food item and was very popular. As was done with the navel orange and Red Delicious apple, cultures were grown from the mutant individuals, and most of the cream-colored store mushrooms we see today are products of this chance natural mutation.

Agaricus bisporus is now cultivated in at least 70 countries around the world. Global production in the early 1990s was reported to be more than 1.5 million tons, worth more than US$ 2 billion.

VITAMIN D

While Agaricus bisporus only contains 16 IU of vitamin D as ergocalciferol (vitamin D2), since they also contain high amounts of ergosterol, by temporary exposure to UV light, the ergocalciferol contents increase.

POTENTIAL MEDICINAL VALUE

Agaricus bisporus also contains sodium, potassium, and phosphorus, conjugated linoleic acid and antioxidants. Protocatechuic acid andpyrocatechol are found in A. bisporus. A 2009 case control study of 2,018 women correlated a large decrease of breast cancer incidence in women who consumed mushrooms. Women in the study who consumed fresh mushrooms daily were 64% less likely to develop breast cancer, while those that combined a mushroom diet with regular green tea consumption reduced their risk of breast cancer by nearly 90%.

A phytochemical (2-aminophenoxazine-3-one) in white button mushrooms was shown to have aromatase inhibitor properties in vitro.

The table mushroom has also been shown to possess possible immune system enhancing properties. An in vitro study demonstrated the mushroom enhanced dendritic cell function.

PHYTOCHEMICAL RESEARCH

Some studies have revealed that compounds in raw A. bisporus - along with some other edible mushrooms - contain hydrazine derivatives includingagaritine and gyromitrin that have been evaluated for carcinogenic activity. In preliminary research, administration of uncooked mushrooms to mice induced a significant increase in the number of bone, stomach and lung tumours. However, research has also noted that when cooked, these compounds were reduced significantly and may, in fact, provide anti-carcinogenic activity by stimulating apoptosis.

According to a more recent scientific publication, the available evidence to date suggests that agaritine (a hydrazine) from consumption of cultivated A. bisporus mushrooms poses no known toxicological risk to healthy humans.

AURICULARIA AURICULA-JUDAE

Auricularia auricula-judae, known as the Jew's ear, wood ear, jelly ear or by a number of othercommon names, is a species of edible Auriculariales fungus found worldwide.

The fruiting body is distinguished by its noticeably ear-like shape and brown colouration; it grows upon wood, especially elder. Its specific epithet is derived from the belief that Judas Iscariot hanged himself from an elder tree; the common name "Judas's ear" eventually became "Jew's ear", while today "jelly ear" and other names are sometimes used. The fungus can be found throughout the year in temperate regions worldwide, where it grows upon both dead and living wood.

In the West, A. auricula-judae was used in folk medicine as recently as the 19th century for complaints including sore throats, sore eyes and jaundice, and as an astringent. Although it is not widely consumed in the West, it has long been popular in China, to the extent that Australia exported large volumes to China in the early twentieth century. Today, the fungus is a popular ingredient in many Chinese dishes, such as hot and sour soup, and also used in Chinese medicine. It is also used in Ghana, as a blood tonic. Modern research into possible medical applications have variously concluded that A. auricula-judae hasantitumour, hypoglycemic, anticoagulant and cholesterol-lowering properties.

TAXONOMY AND NAMING

The species was first mentioned in the scientific literature asTremella auricula by Carl Linnaeus in his 1753 Species Plantarum, and later (1789) described by Jean Baptiste François Pierre Bulliard as Tremella auricula-judae.However, the genus Tremella is now reserved for fungal species that live as parasites on other fungi. Tremella auricula-judae is now considered a basionym. In 1791, Bulliard transferred the species to the genus Peziza. In 1822,Elias Magnus Fries transferred the species to Exidia, and, in so doing, sanctioned the name. In 1860, Miles Joseph Berkeley described the species as a member ofHirneola, a genus described by Fries in 1848, now considered synonymous with Auricularia.

The species was given the name Auricularia auricula-judae in 1888 by Joseph Schröter. The specific name of A. auricula-judae comprises auricula, the Latin word meaning ear, and Judae, meaning of Judas.Under binomial nomenclature, a species name can comprise only two words; but the taxonomists responsible for this naming hyphenated the specific name to "bend the rules" and keep the name "within the letter of the law".

The name was criticised by mycologist Curtis Gates Lloyd, who said "Auricularia auricula-Judae is cumbersome and in addition is a slander on the Jews". Though critical of Lucien Marcus Underwood, saying he "would probably not have known the Jew's ear from the calves' liver", he followed him in using Auricularia auricula, which was in turn used by Bernard Lowy in an article on the entire genus.Despite this, Auricularia auricula-judae is the currently recognised name for the species by many sources, though Auricularia auricula is still occasionally used.

As well as the obligate synonyms from Bulliard, Fries and Berkeley, there are numerous other synonymous names. Mycologist George Willard Martin, writing in 1943, noted that the species was known by at least 12binomials, of which none appeared to be valid, and noted that "the citations given for the various names are extremely erratic". Mycologist Mary F. Barrett attributes "such multiplication of names" to "the wide distribution of the Judas' ear, its ability to grow upon many different kinds of decaying wood, and to its great variation in size, colour and shape".

The fungus is associated with Judas Iscariot because of the belief that he hanged himself on an elder tree after his betrayal of Jesus Christ. Folklore suggests that the ears are Judas's returned spirit, and are all that are left to remind us of his suicide.

The common name of the fungus was originally Judas's ear, but this was later shortened to Judas ear and, in the late 19th century, shortened again to Jew's ear. Common names for the fungus which refer to Judas can be traced back to at least the end of the 16th century; for instance, in the 17th century, Thomas Browne wrote of the species:

In Jews' ears something is conceived extraordinary from the name, which is in propriety but fungus sambucinus, or an excrescence about the roots of elder, and concerneth not the nation of the Jews, but Judas Iscariot, upon a conceit he hanged on this tree; and is become a famous medicine in quinsies sore throats, and strangulations, ever since.

While the term Jew's meat was a deprecatory term used for all fungi in the Middle Ages, the term is unrelated to the name Jew's ear. A further change of name to jelly ear was recommended in the List of Recommended Names for Fungi. The idea was rejected by mycologist Patrick Harding who considered it "to be the result of political correctness where it is not necessary", and who "will continue to call [the species] Jew's ear", explaining that, while anti-Semitism was commonplace in Britain, the name Jew's ear is in reference to Judas, who was a Jew. However, the name has been adopted in some recent field guides.

Unrelated common names include the ear fungus, common ear fungus, the Chinese Fungus, the pig's ear, the wood ear, the black wood ear, the tree ear and Kikurage. The species was known as "fungus sambuca" among herbalists, in reference to Sambuca, the generic name for elder.

DESCRIPTION

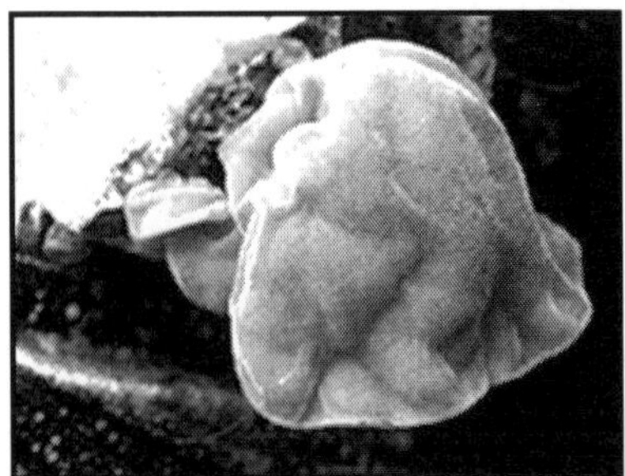

Fig. The surface of the fruit bodies are often covered in tiny, downy hairs, as well as folds and wrinkles

Fig. As the fruit bodies age, they become darker in colour.

The fruit body of A. auricula-judae is normally 3 to 8 centimetres (1.2 to 3.1 in) across, but can be as much as 12 centimetres (4.7 in). It is distinctively shaped, typically being reminiscent of a floppy ear, though the fruit bodies can also be cup-shaped. It is normally attached to the substrate laterally and sometimes by a very short stalk. The species has a tough, gelatinous, elastic texture when fresh, but it dries hard and brittle. The outer surface is a bright reddish-tan-brown with a purplish hint, often covered in tiny, downy hairs of a grey colour. It can be smooth, as is typical of younger specimens, or undulating with folds and wrinkles. The colour becomes darker with age. The inner surface is a lighter grey-brown in colour and smooth. It is sometimes wrinkled, again with folds and wrinkles, and may have "veins", making it appear even more ear-like.

Microscopic features

The spores of A. auricula-judae are long and sausage shaped, ranging in size from 16 to 18 micrometres (μm) long by 6 to 8 μm thick. The spores themselves are white, cream or yellowish, and are hyaline. The spores can sometimes be seen in a whitish mass on the underside of the fruit body. The species has elongated cylindrical basidia with three transverse septa (internal cross-walls dividing the hyphae). Basidia 60-72x 4-7.5μm; sterigmata lateral, well developed, 3-4.5μm long. Spores smooth, hyaline, reniform to allantoid, 14-18 ? 6-8μm, guttulate. Hairs on the fruit body are from 85 to 100 μm in length, and 5 to 6 μm in diameter. They are hyaline, lack a central strand and have rounded tips. They do not grow in dense tufts.

Similar species

Auricularia auricula-judae is similar to A. fuscosuccinea in colour and texture, and "may be confused with it if only external features are considered". The spore and basidia sizes of the two species are slightly different, but this is not a reliable way to tell them apart. A. cornea is another similar species in the same genus, but has distinct internal differences, is normally more pilose (more covered in soft hair) and tends to fruit in larger numbers.

HABITAT, ECOLOGY AND DISTRIBUTION

Fig. Auricularia auricula-judae fruit bodies can be found in large numbers on old wood.

Auricularia auricula-judae grows upon the wood of deciduous trees and shrubs, favouring elder. In up to 90% of cases, the mushroom is found on elder, but it is often incorrectly assumed to grow exclusively on elder. It has also been recorded on Acer pseudoplatanus (known in the United Kingdom as sycamore),beech, ash, spindle, and in one particular case, the sycamore draining board of an old sink in Hatton Garden. Recently, A. auricula-judae has been recorded from semi-evergreen to evergreen and wet evergreen shola forests in the Western Ghats, India.

This species occurs scattered and in clusters on dead or dying branches of trees, on main trunk, decaying logs, etc. This species occurs during the monsoon period in large imbricate clusters and under high humid conditions produces exceptionally large sized basidiomes. A. auricula-judae growing in wetevergreen and shola forests shows remarkable variation in size, shape and colour. In Australia, it is found in Eucalyptus woodland and rainforests; in the rainforests, it can grow in very large colonies on fallen logs. It favours older branches, where it feeds as a saprophyte(on dead wood) or a weak parasite (on living wood), and it causes white rot.

Commonly growing solitarily, it can also be gregarious (in a group) or caespitose (in a tuft). Spores are ejected from the underside of the fruit bodies with as many as several hundred thousand an hour, and the high rate continues when the bodies have been significantly dried. Even when they have lost some 90% of their weight through dehydration, the bodies continue to release a small number of spores.

It is found all year, but is most common in autumn. It is widespread throughout temperate and sub-tropical zones worldwide, and can be found across Europe, North America, Asia, Australia, South America and Africa. There has been some debate about the appearance of the species in the tropics; while it has been frequently reported there, Bernard Lowy, in an article on Auricularia, said that "of the specimens I have examined, none could be assigned here".

USES

Food

Auricularia auricula-judae has a soft, jelly-like texture. Though edible, it was not held in high culinary regard in the west for many years. It has been likened to "eating an Indian rubber with bones in it", while in 19th century Britain, it was said that "it has never been regarded here as an edible fungus". It has a mild flavour, and is useful for mixed mushroom recipes, but is still considered bland in the west.

It can be dried and rehydrated, sometimes swelling to a very large size. Young specimens are best, but the species is not edible when raw, needing to be cooked thoroughly. The whole fruit body can be eaten, but should be thoroughly washed before cooking. Cooking can sometimes take a comparatively long time. The nutritional content of 100 g (3.5 oz) of dried fungus includes 370 kcal, 10.6 g of protein, 0.2 g of fat, 65 g of carbohydrate, 5.8 g ash, and 0.03% mg of carotene. Fresh mushrooms contain about 90% moisture. Dried specimens may be ground up into a powder and used to absorb excess liquid in soups and stews, as it rehydrates into tiny fragments.

Both A. auricula-judae and the similar A. polytricha are popular in China, where the medicinal use of food is common; a soup containing the species is used medicinally for dealing with colds and fevers by reducing the heat of the body.

There is evidence that the species were being cultivated in China as early as the Tang dynasty (618–907). Li Shih-chen, in his Pen Tsao Kang Mu, quotes Tang Ying-chuan from that period as saying "... put the steamed bran on logs, cover with straw, Wood Ear will grow". In the early 20th century, large volumes of A. auricula-judae were exported from Australia to China, and it is today still sold in Asian food shops for culinary use.

It is also popular in Vietnam, although the climate is there more suited to A. polytricha. A report on small-scale fungi cultivation concluded that A. auricula-judaewould be suitable for cultivation only in cooler climates. According to a 2010 publication, the annual production of Auricularia species worldwide is the fourth highest among all industrially cultivated culinary and medicinal mushrooms, and in China, the estimated output was roughly 1.655 million tonnes (based on 2003 data), most of which are A. polytricha however (which has by and large replaced A. auricula-judae in international trade).

Auricularia auricula-judae is also in cultivation elsewhere in the world, for instance, in Ghana. In the Brong-Ahafo and Ashanti regions, it is grown with what is referred to as the "plastic bag method". Sawdust is packed into polypropylene bags and then sterilised by steam for several hours. Once the sawdust has cooled, Sorghum grain spawn is added, and the bags are kept in moderately dark conditions. Once the sawdust is exposed to a humid environment,A. auricula-judae fruit bodies begin to grow. Elsewhere in the world, a study on the use of mushrooms by the Bini people inhabiting a remote village in southern Nigeria found that the local inhabitants collected and ate A. auricula-judae, but that it was not one of the mushrooms they used medicinally.

Collection of the mushroom for culinary use has also been documented in Nepal. However, the Nepalese do not consider it a choice mushroom for eating; of the three grades given to edible mushrooms, it was given the worst. Again, unlike other mushrooms, no medicinal use was reported. The mushroom has also been the only non-morel species exported from Nepal for culinary use. Other places where A. auricula-judae has been recorded as commonly consumed include Poland, Mozambique and Indonesia, while, in Bolivia,Goeldi's monkeys have been recorded as commonly eating the sporocarps.

Folk medicine

Auricularia auricula-judae has been used as a medicinal mushroom by many herbalists. It was used as apoultice to treat inflammations of the eye, as well as a palliative for throat problems. The 16th-century herbalist John Gerard, writing in 1597, recommended A. auricula-judae for a very specific use; other fungi were used more generally. He recommends the preparation of a liquid extract by boiling the fruit bodies in milk, or else leaving them steeped in beer, which would then be sipped slowly in order to cure a sore throat.

The resultant broth was probably not dissimilar to the Chinese soups that use A. polytricha.Carolus Clusius, writing in 1601, also said that the species could be gargled to cure a sore throat, andJohn Parkinson, writing in 1640, reported that boiling in milk or steeping in vinegar was "the onely use the are put unto that I know".

Writing in 1694, herbalist John Pechey described A. auricula-judae by saying "It grows to the Trunk of the Elder-Tree. Being dried it will keep a good year.

Boyl'd in Milk, or infus'd in Vinegarm 'tis good to gargle the Mouth or Throat in Quinsies, and other inflammations of the Mouth and Throat. And being infus'd in some proper Water, it is good in Diseases of the Eyes." The species also saw use as an astringent due to its ability to absorb water. There are recorded medicinal usages from Scotland, where it was again used as a gargle for sore throats, and from Ireland, where, in an attempt to cure jaundice, it was boiled in milk. The medicinal use of A. auricula-judae continued until at least 1860, when it was still sold at Covent Garden; at the time, it was not considered edible in the United Kingdom.

Medicinal use in Indonesia was also recorded in the 1930s, and was more recently reported in modern-day Ghana. A report for the 2005 Commonwealth Forestry Conference examining the possible effects of deforestation in southern Ghana on medicinal and edible fungi found thatA. auricula-judae was in use as a blood tonic.

Pharmacology

Auricularia auricula-judae has been the subject of research into possible medicinal applications. Experiments in the 1980s concluded that two glucansisolated from the species showed potent antitumour properties when used on mice artificially implanted with Sarcoma 180 tumours. This was despite the conclusion of earlier research indicating that, while aqueous extracts from several other fungal species had antitumour effects, extracts fromA. auricula-judae did not. Further, research on genetically diabetic mice showed that a polysaccharide extracted from A. auricula-judae had ahypoglycemic effect; mice fed with food including the polysaccharide showed reduced plasma glucose, insulin, urinary glucose and food intake.

Another chemical extracted from the species was an acidic polysaccharide (made up of mostly mannose, glucose, glucuronic acid and xylose) which showed anticoagulant properties. The article concluded that "the polysaccharides from these mushrooms may constitute a new source of compounds with action on coagulation, platelet aggregation and, perhaps, on thrombosis".

Another study reported that the species may be effective in stopping plateletbinding in vitro, with possible uses regarding hypercholesterolemia. Research has shown that A. auricula-judae can be used to lower cholesterol levels generally, and, in particular, is one of two fungi shown to reduce the level of bad cholesterol.

CULTURAL DEPICTIONS

The species is referred to in Christopher Marlowe's play The Jew of Malta. Iathamore proclaims: "The hat he wears, Judas left under the elder when he hanged himself". Later, the species was probably partially the inspiration for Emily Dickinson's poem beginning "The Mushroom is the Elf of Plants", which depicts a mushroom as the "ultimate betrayer". Dickinson had both a religious and naturalistic background, and so it is more than likely that she knew of the common name of A. auricula-judae, and of the folklore surrounding Judas's suicide.

ENOKITAKE

Enokitake, also Enokidake or Enoki is a long, thin white mushroom used in East Asian cuisine (such as that of China, Japan andKorea). These mushrooms are cultivars of Flammulina velutipes, also known by the name, golden needle mushroom or lily mushroom. Wild forms differing in color, texture, and sliminess are calledwinter mushrooms, velvet foot or velvet stem, amongst other names.

This mushroom is available fresh or canned, with experts recommending fresh enoki specimens with firm, white, shiny caps, rather than those with slimy or brownish stalks that are best avoided. It is traditionally used for soups, but can also be used for salads and other dishes. The mushroom has a crisp texture and can be refrigerated for approximately one week.

FEATURES

The mushroom naturally grows on the stumps of the Chinese Hackberry tree ("enoki" in Japanese), but also on other trees, such as mulberry and persimmon trees. There is a significant difference in appearance between the wild and cultivated types of the mushroom. Cultivated mushrooms have not been exposed to light, resulting in a white color, whereas wild mushrooms usually display a dark brown color. Cultivated mushrooms are grown in a carbon dioxide (CO2)-rich environment to nurture the development of long thin stems, whereas wild mushrooms produce a much shorter and thicker stem.

NAMES

The names, enokitake, enokidake and enoki are derived from the Japanese language.

HEALTH PROPERTIES

Enokitake mushrooms contain antioxidants, like ergothioneine. Animal testing has indicated possible applications in the development of vaccines and cancer immunotherapy.

Research at the National University of Singapore, first published in 2005, stated that the stalk of the golden needle mushroom contains a large quantity of a protein, named "Five" by the researchers, that helps in the regulation of the immune system.

The mushroom also contains flammutoxin, a cytolytic and cardiotoxicprotein that has proven to be non-toxic when absorbed orally.

SHIMEJI

Fig. Japanese popular mushrooms, clockwise from left, enokitake, buna-shimeji, bunapi-shimeji, king oyster mushroom and shiitake(front).

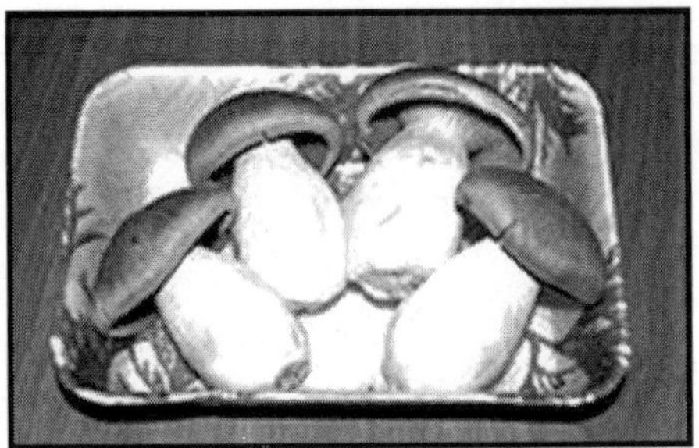

Fig. Lyophyllum shimeji

Fig. Bunapi (Hokto Corp. develops)

Shimeji is a group of edible mushrooms native to East Asia, but also found in northern Europe.

Hon-shimeji (Lyophyllum shimeji) is a mycorrhizal fungus and difficult to cultivate. Other species are saprotrophs, and buna-shimeji is now widely cultivated. Shimeji is rich inumami tasting compounds such as guanylic acid, glutamic acid, and aspartic acid.

SPECIES

There are several species sold as shimeji mushrooms. All are saprotroph except Lyophyllum shimeji.

Mycorrhiza

- Hon-shimeji, Lyophyllum shimeji

The cultivation methods have been patented by several groups, such as Takara Bio and Yamasa,and the cultivated hon-shimeji is available from several manufacturers in Japan.

Saprotroph

- Buna-shimeji, Hypsizygus tessellatus, also known in English as the Brown Beech or Brown Clamshell Mushroom

Hypsizygus marmoreus is a synonym of Hypsizigus tessellatus. Cultivation of Buna-shimeji was first patented by Takara Shuzo Co.,Ltd. in 1972 as hon-shimeji and the production started in 1973 in Japan. Now, several breeds are widely cultivated and sold fresh in markets.

- Bunapi-shimeji, known in English as the White Beech or White Clamshell Mushroom

Bunapi was selected from UV-irradiated buna-shimeji and the breed was registered as 'hokuto shiro #1' by Hokto Corporation.

- Hatake-shimeji, Lyophyllum decastes
- Shirotamogidake, Hypsizigus ulmarius

These two species had been also sold as hon-shimeji.

COOKING

Shimeji should always be cooked: it is not a good mushroom to serve raw due to a somewhat bitter taste, but the bitterness disappears completely upon cooking. The cooked mushroom has a pleasant, firm, slightly crunchy texture and a slightly nutty flavor. Cooking also makes this mushroom easier to digest. In stir-fried foods, as well as with wild game or seafood it is a good mushroom. Also it can be used in soups, stews and in sauces. When cooked alone, Shimeji mushrooms can be sautéed as a whole, including the stem or stalk (only the very end cut off), using a higher temperature or they can be slow roasted on a low temperature with a small amount of butter or cooking oil. Shimeji is used in soups, nabe and takikomi gohan.

SHIITAKE

The Shiitake (Lentinula edodes) is an edible mushroom native to East Asia, which is cultivated and consumed in many Asian countries. It is also considered a medicinal mushroom in some forms of traditional medicine.

TAXONOMY AND NAMING

The name shiitake originates from its Japanese name. Shii is the Japanese name of the tree Castanopsis cuspidata that provides the dead logs on which it is typically cultivated, and take means "mushroom". Other common names by which the mushroom is known in English include "Sawtooth oak mushroom", "black forest mushroom", "black mushroom", "golden oak mushroom", or "oakwood mushroom".

The species was formerly known as Lentinus edodes and Agaricus edodes. The latter name was first applied by the English botanist Miles Joseph Berkeley in 1878.

Fig. Wild Shiitake, Hokkaido Japan

CULTIVATION HISTORY

Shiitake are native to Japan, China and Korea and have been grown in all three countries since prehistoric times. The oldest record regarding the shiitake mushroom dates back to AD 199 at the time of Emperor Chuai in Japan.

They have been cultivated for over 1,000 years. The first written record of shiitake cultivation can be traced to Wu Sang Kwuang in China, born during the Song Dynasty (AD 960–1127).

During the Ming Dynasty (AD 1368–1644), physician Wu Juei wrote that the mushroom could be used not only as a food but as a medicinal mushroom, taken as a remedy for upper respiratory diseases, poor blood circulation, liver trouble, exhaustion and weakness, and to boost qi, or life energy. It was also believed to prevent premature aging.

The Japanese cultivated the mushroom by cutting shii trees with axes and placing the logs by trees that were already growing shiitake or contained shiitake spores.

Before 1982, the Japanese variety of these mushrooms could only be grown in traditional locations using ancient methods. In 1982, Gary F. Leatham published an academic paper based on his research on the budding and growth of the Japan Islands variety; the work helped make commercial cultivation possible in the United States.

In 1974, total production was estimated at about 143 000 tonnes, with Japan representing 94.5% of the total, China 4.2%, Taiwan 1.1%, and South Korea 0.2%. in 1997 China's shiitake production had risen from 4.2% to 85.1%.

CULINARY USE

Fig. Japanese Ekiben "Shiitake-meshi"

Fresh and dried shiitake have many uses in the cuisines of East Asia. In Japan, they are served in miso soup, used as the basis for a kind of vegetarian dashi, and also as an ingredient in many steamed and simmered dishes. In Chinese cuisine, they are often sauteed in vegetarian dishes such as Buddha's delight. In Thailand, they may be served either fried or steamed.

Shiitake are also dried and sold as preserved food. These are rehydrated by soaking in water before using. Many people prefer dried shiitake to fresh, considering that the sun-drying process draws out theumami flavour from the dried mushrooms. The stems of shiitake are rarely used in Japanese and othercuisines, primarily because the stems are harder and take longer to cook than the soft fleshy caps.

One type of high grade shiitake is called donko in Japanese and donggu in Chinese, literally "winter mushroom". Another high grade of mushroom is called huagu in Chinese, literally "flower mushroom", which has a flower-like cracking pattern on the mushroom's upper surface. Both of these are produced at lower temperatures. Today, shiitake mushrooms have become popular in other countries as well. Russia produces and also consumes large amounts of them, mostly sold pickled; and the shiitake is slowly making its way into western cuisine as well. There is a global industry in shiitake production, with local farms in most western countries in addition to large scale importation from China, Japan, Korea and elsewhere.

Like all mushrooms, shiitakes produce vitamin D2 upon exposure of the ergosterol to the UVB rays of sunlight or broadband UVB fluorescent tubes.

While all mushrooms have ergosterol in and the potential to produce vitamin D2 in such a manner, the transparent white of the shiitake gills permits greater contact of the UVB with ergosterol and very high D2 values can be achieved with exposure to broadband UVB fluorescent tubes.

Mushrooms, shiitake, dried	
Nutritional value per 100 g (3.5 oz)	
Energy	1,238 kJ (296 kcal)
Carbohydrates	75.37 g
- Sugars	2.21 g
- Dietary fiber	11.5 g
Fat	0.99 g
Protein	9.58 g
Thiamine (vit. B_1)	0.3 μg (26%)
Riboflavin (vit. B_2)	1.27 μg (106%)
Niacin (vit. B_3)	14.1 μg (94%)
Pantothenic acid (B_5)	21.879 μg (438%)
Vitamin B_6	0.965 μg (74%)
Folate (vit. B_9)	163 μg (41%)
Vitamin C	3.5 μg (4%)
Vitamin D	3.9 μg (26%)
Calcium	11 μg (1%)
Iron	1.72 μg (13%)
Magnesium	132 μg (37%)
Manganese	1.176 μg (56%)
Phosphorus	294 μg (42%)
Potassium	1534 μg (33%)
Sodium	13 μg (1%)
Zinc	7.66 μg (81%)

PRELIMINARY RESEARCH

Has evaluated whether consumption of shiitake mushrooms may affect the immune system, possess antibacterial properties, reduce platelet aggregation, or possess antiviral properties, possibly through proteinase inhibitors.

Active Hexose Correlated Compound (AHCC) is an a-glucan-rich compound isolated from shiitake. In Japan, AHCC is the second most popular complementary and alternative medicine used by cancer patients and is metabolized via the CYP450 2D6 pathway. Eritadenine, an isolate of the mushroom, is an inhibitor of S-adenosyl-L-homocysteine hydrolase (SAHH) and has hypocholesterolemic activity.

Other basic research tested if AHCC may increase the body's resistance to pathogens as shown in experiments with the influenza virus, West Nile virus, or bacterial infection. Animal research and limited clinical trials indicate that AHCC may enhance immune function. Other basic research has shown that AHCC may affect hepatocellular carcinoma and prostate cancer. Rarely, consumption of raw or slightly cooked shiitake mushrooms may evoke signs of allergy, including "anerythematous, micro-papular, streaky, extremely pruriginous rash" that occurs all over the body including face and scalp, appearing about 48 hours after consumption and disappearing after several days. This effect, presumably caused by the polysaccharide lentinan, is known in Asia, but is unfamiliar to Europeans. Although it may occur in roughly 2% of the population, thorough cooking may eliminateallergenicity.

PLEUROTUS

Pleurotus is a genus of gilled mushrooms which includes one of the most widely eaten mushrooms, P. ostreatus. Species of Pleurotus may be called oyster, abalone, or tree mushrooms, and are some of the most commonly cultivated edible mushrooms in the world. Pleurotus fungi have been used inmycoremediation of pollutants such as petroleum and polycyclic aromatic hydrocarbons.

DESCRIPTION

The caps may be laterally attached (with no stem). If there is a stem, it is normally eccentric and the gills aredecurrent along it. The term pleurotoid is used for mushrooms having this general shape.

The spores are smooth and elongated (described as "cylindrical"). Where hyphae meet, they are joined byclamp connections. Pleurotus is not considered to be a bracket fungus, and most of the species aremonomitic (with a soft consistency). However, remarkably, Pleurotus dryinus can sometimes be dimitic, meaning that it has additional skeletal hyphae, which give it a tougher consistency like bracket fungi.

ECOLOGY

Pleurotus fungi are found in both tropical and temperate climates throughout the world. Most species ofPleurotus are white-rot fungi on hardwood trees, although some also decay conifer wood. P. eryngii is unusual in its association with herbaceous plants, and P. tuber-regium produces underground sclerotia.In addition to being saprotrophic, all species of Pleurotus are also nematophagous, catching nematodesby paralyzing them with a toxin.

CUISINE

Oyster mushrooms are popular for cooking, torn up instead of sliced, especially in stir fry or sauté, because they are consistently thin, and so will cook more evenly than uncut mushrooms of other types.

TAXONOMY

Fig. P. pulmonarius, Sweden

The classification of species within the genus Pleurotus is difficult due to high phenotypic variability across wide geographic ranges, geographic overlap of species, and ongoing evolution and speciation. Earlytaxonomic efforts placed the oyster mushrooms within Agaricus (Agaricus ostreatus Jacq. 1774). Paul Kummer defined the genus Pleurotus in 1871; since then, the genus has been narrowed with species moving to other genera such as Favolaschia, Hohenbuehelia, Lentinus, Marasmiellus, Omphalotus, Panellus,Pleurocybella, and Resupinatus.

PHYLOGENY

More recently, molecular phylogenetics has been utilized to determine genetic and evolutionary relationships between groups within the genus, delineating discrete clades. Pleurotus, along with the closely related genus Hohenbuehelia, has been shown to be monophyletic. Tests of cross-breeding viability between groups have been used to further define which groups are deserving of species rank, as opposed tosubspecies, variety, or synonymy. If two groups of morphologically distinct Pleurotus fungi are able to cross-breed and produce fertile offspring, they meet one definition of species. These reproductively discrete groups, referred to as intersterility groups, have begun to be defined in Pleurotus. Many binomial names used in literature are now being grouped together as species complexes using this technique, and may change.

Phylogenetic species

The following species list is organized according to 1. phylogenetic clade, 2. intersterility group (group number in Roman numerals) or sub-clade, and then 3. any older binomial names that have been found to be closely related, reproductively compatible, or synonymous, although they may no longer be taxonomically valid. This list is likely to be incomplete.

Fig. P. populinus, Pennsylvania, USA

Fig. Pleurotus mushrooms production at the Agricultural Science and Technology School Science City of Muñoz#SchoolsPhilippines Science City of Muñoz.

- P. ostreatus clade
- I. P. ostreatus (oyster or pearl oyster mushroom) – North America and northern Eurasia
- P. florida
- II. P. pulmonarius (phoenix or Indian oyster mushroom) – North America, Eurasia, and Australasia
- P. columbinus
- P. sapidus

- III. P. populinus – North America
- VI. P. eryngii (king oyster mushroom) – Europe and the Middle East
- P. ferulae
- P. fossulatus – Afghanistan
- P. nebrodensis
- XII. P. abieticola – Asia
- XIII. P. albidus – Caribbean, Central America, South America
- P. djamor-cornucopiae clade

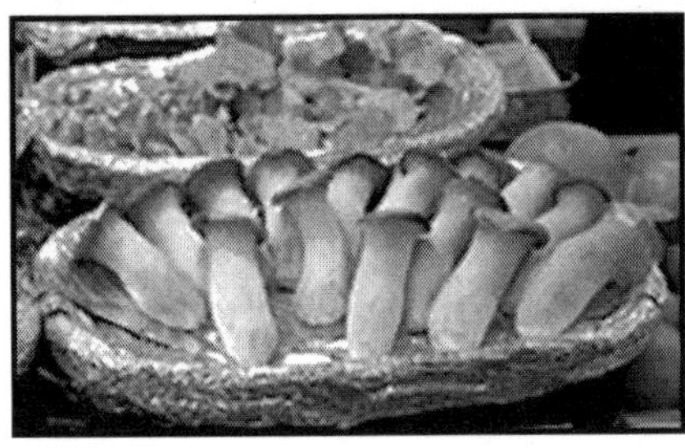

Fig. P. eryngii, Spain

- IV. P. cornucopiae (branched oyster mushroom) – Europe
- P. citrinopileatus (golden oyster mushroom) – eastern Asia
- P. euosmus (tarragon oyster mushroom)
- V. P. djamor (The pink oyster mushroom) – pantropical
- P. flabellatus
- P. salmoneo-stramineus
- P. salmonicolor
- XI. P. opuntiae – North America, New Zealand
- XVI. P. calyptratus
- P. cystidiosus clade

Fig. P. citrinopileatus

- VII. P. cystidiosus (abalone mushroom) – Global
- P. abalonus – Taiwan

- P. fuscosquamulosus – Africa, Europe
- P. smithii – Mexico
- IX. P. dryinus – North America, Europe, and New Zealand
- VIII. P. levis – subtropical to tropical
- X. P. tuber-regium (king tuber mushroom) – Africa, Asia, Australasia
- XIV. P. australis (brown oyster mushroom) – Australia and New Zealand
- XV. P. purpureo-olivaceus – Australia and New Zealand
- P. rattenburyi

Species of unclear relationship

- P. gardneri
- P. parsonsii
- P. velatus

Former species

- P. sajor-caju was moved to the genus Lentinus.
- P. nidiformis was moved to the genus Omphalotus in 1994.

TREMELLA FUCIFORMIS

Tremella fuciformis is a species of fungus; it produces white, frond-like, gelatinous basidiocarps (fruiting bodies). It is widespread, especially in the tropics, where it can be found on the dead branches of broadleaf trees. This fungus is commercially cultivated and is one of the most popular fungi in the cuisine andmedicine of China Tremella fuciformis is commonly known as snow fungus, silver ear fungus, andwhite jelly mushroom.

Tremella fuciformis is a parasitic yeast, and grows as a slimy, mucous-like film until it encounters its preferred hosts, various species of Annulohypoxylon (or possibly Hypoxylon) fungi, whereupon it then invades, triggering the aggressive mycelial growth required to form the fruiting bodies.

TAXONOMY AND NAMING

Tremella fuciformis was first described in 1856 by English mycologist Miles Joseph Berkeley, based on collections made in Brazil by the botanist and explorer Richard Spruce. In 1939, Japanese mycologistYosio Kobayasi described Nakaiomyces nipponicus, a similar-looking fungus that differed by having scattered, dark spines on its surface.

Later research, however, showed that the fruit bodies were those ofTremella fuciformis parasitized by an ascomycete, Ceratocystis epigloeum, that formed the dark spines. Nakaiomyces nipponicus is therefore a synonym of T. fuciformis.

In Chinese, it is called ?? (pinyin: yín er; literally "silver ear"), ?? (pinyin: xue er; literally "snow ear"); or??? (pinyin: bái mù er, literally "white wood ear"), and in Japanese it is called shiro kikurage (??????, lit. "white tree jellyfish"). In Vietnam, it is called n?m tuy?t or ngân nhi.

In his book, Growing Gourmet and Medicinal Mushrooms, Paul Stamets lists the following common names for Tremella fuciformis (which he calls "White Jelly Mushroom"):

- Yin Er
- White Jelly Fungus
- White Jelly Leaf ("Shirokikurage")
- Silver Ear Mushroom
- Snow Mushroom
- Chrysanthemum Mushroom

DESCRIPTION

Fruit bodies are gelatinous, watery white, up to 7.5 cm (3 in) across (larger in cultivated specimens), and composed of thin but erect, seaweed-like, branching fronds, often crisped at the edges. Microscopically, the hyphae are clamped and occur in a dense gelatinous matrix.

Haustorial cells arise on the hyphae, producing filaments that attach to and penetrate the hyphae of the host. The basidia are tremelloid (ellipsoid, with oblique to vertical septa), 10–13 by 6.5–10 μm, sometimes stalked. The basidiospores are ellipsoid, smooth, 5–8 by 4–6 μm, and germinate by hyphal tube or by yeast cells.

HABITAT AND DISTRIBUTION

Tremella fuciformis is known to be a parasite of Hypoxylon species. Many of these species were reassigned to a new genus, Annulohypoxylon, in 2005 including its preferred host, Annulohypoxylon archeri, the species routinely used in commercial cultivation. Following its host, fruit bodies are typically found on dead, attached or recently fallen branches of broadleaf trees.

The species is mainly tropical and subtropical, but extends into temperate areas in Asia and North America. It is known throughout South and Central America, the Caribbean, parts of North America, sub-Saharan Africa, southern and eastern Asia, Australia, New Zealand, and the Pacific Islands.

ECONOMIC USAGE

Tremella fuciformis has been cultivated in China since at least the nineteenth century. Initially, suitable wooden poles were prepared and then treated in various ways in the hope that they would be colonized by the fungus. This haphazard method of cultivation was improved when poles were inoculated with spores or mycelium. Modern production only began, however, with the realization that both the Tremella and its host species needed to be inoculated into the substrate to ensure success. The "dual culture" method, now used commercially, employs a sawdust mix inoculated with both fungal species and kept under optimal conditions. The most popular species to pair with T. fuciformis is its preferred host, Annulohypoxylon archeri. Estimated production in China in 1997 was 130,000 tonnes. Tremella fuciformis is also cultivated in other East Asian countries, with some limited cultivation elsewhere.

In Chinese cuisine, Tremella fuciformis is traditionally used in sweet dishes. While tasteless, it is valued for its gelatinous texture as well as its supposed medicinal benefits. Most commonly, it is used to make adessert soup called luk mei (??), often in combination with jujubes, dried longans, and other ingredients. It is also used as a component of a drink and as an ice cream. Since cultivation has made it less expensive, it is now additionally used in some savoury dishes.

BEAUTY AND OTHER USAGE

Tremella fuciformis is also used as a beauty product by women in China and Japan as it reportedly increases moisture retention in the skin and prevents senile degradation of micro-blood vessels in the skin, reducing wrinkles and smoothing fine lines. Other anti-ageing effects come from increasing the presence of superoxide dismutase in the brain and liver; it is an enzyme that acts as a potent antioxidant throughout the body, particularly in the skin.

6

Composition Variability of Spent Mushroom

INTRODUCTION

Spent mushroom compost (SMC) is becoming available in increasing quantities with the Irish mushroom production industry producing an estimated 295,000 tonnes of SMC annually, a fact that poses a great environmental challenge in terms of its effective management. It is generally acknowledged that SMC is a valuable material for improving soil structure in tilled soils owing to its highly organic nature (Maher et al. 2000, amongst others) and increasing dry matter production on grassland soils. As 72 % of all SMC in Ireland is applied to land (Maher et al. 2000), it is therefore imperative that systematic analysis be carried out on its composition, in order to evaluate its merit as a fertilizer, so that it can be applied to land in a rational and informed manner.

The main objectives of this study were to identify the differences in nutrient composition of SMC in Ireland, in relation to selected physical and chemical parameters and to evaluate its overall potential when utilized as a fertilizer or soil conditioner.

MUSHROOM FARMING SYSTEM

The manufacture of mushroom compost in Ireland generally involves two stages, the first of which is performed outdoors or under a roof, in large heaps, where the raw materials are moistened and thoroughly mixed for up to 12 days. Raw materials are moistened in order to ensure that the different components are mixed uniformly, and more importantly, to encourage microbial activity.

However, this system may be susceptible to changes in the ambient temperature, especially outdoors. After this crucial pre-treatment phase, these stacks are placed in long windrows undercover, for seven to eight days and are mechanically aerated. These stacks heat up quickly and sometimes may reach temperatures as high as 80oC (Maher et al. 1993).

Phase two of this composting process is carried out in purpose built structures, which are generally well-insulated plastic tunnels with slatted floors. The environment is carefully controlled, where the compost temperature is allowed to rise to 57 – 60oC for up to 12 hours and subsequently reduced by the influx of air from the air plenum below the compost. This pasteurisation stage is essential for the control of diseases and unwanted organisms. This phase is continued until the temperature has dropped to around 30oC and the ammonium levels are below 10 ppm as at higher concentrations the ammonium would be toxic to the mushroom (Maher et al. 1993).

The compost is then mixed with spawn, which is a monoculture of mushroom mycelium on cooked and sterilised grain and then placed into plastic bags, or more economically on Dutch shelves which are then distributed to mushroom farms around the area. After about two weeks the compost is completely colonized by the mycelium and the final step in the preparation of the compost involves covering the mycelium with a layer of casing. This layer generally consists of peat and calcium carbonate, which initiates the formation of pinheads in a vertical direction.

Three weeks after casing, the first mushrooms can be harvested. The used compost is sometimes sterilised for 12 hours at 70oC or disinfected. This sterilised mixture of compost and casing soil is further available for beneficial use in agriculture and horticulture and is known as spent mushroom compost (Maher et al. 1993).

MATERIALS AND METHODS

Spent mushroom compost was collected from mushroom production units supplied with compost from each of the thirteen composting yards in Northern Ireland (5 yards) and the Republic of Ireland (8 yards), where the compost was initially manufactured from the raw materials wheaten straw, gypsum, poultry litter and/or horse manure, with cottonseed meal and mushroom spawn also supplemented. One bag of SMC was chosen randomly from each of five production units (growers) supplied by each yard and all of these bags originated from the same compost cycle and had produced 3 flushes of mushrooms. The total number of bags of SMC collected and analysed was 63 as only four SMC samples could be obtained from each of two production units.

Bags were cylindrical in shape and measured approximately 60 cm in diameter and 45 cm in height, about 22 kg in weight and included the casing layer. Segments of compost, 20 cm wide, extending from the surface to the bottom of the bag were cut along the diameter of each bag so as to achieve a representative sub-sample and these were subsequently removed for analysis. These were mixed thoroughly by hand and the dry matter (DM) content determined on duplicate sub-samples by drying in a forced draught oven at 105 oC. The remainder of each segment was air dried for one week and shredded using a JCB SS2400 shredder (Argos, Ireland). Representative sub-samples of the shredded material were then finely pulverized using a coffee grinder, which allowed the material to pass through small-aperture sieves as required by some of the analytical procedures.

Despite the fact that no standard analytical methods of compost or SMC analysis exist, methodologies chosen for this study were similar to those employed for analysis of SMC and dry plant material. No comparisons were made where different extraction methods were employed or where incomparable units were reported.

Plant nutrient and physical analysis

Twenty-five parameters were measured on the 63 samples and, in addition, associated mushroom yield data were obtained from each grower. Organic matter (OM) content was determined following overnight ashing at 500 oC (Gallenkamp muffle furnace). pH values were obtained in a 2:1 ratio with distilled water, using a Jenway 3010 pH meter in accordance with Hendershot et al. (1993) while the electrical conductivity (EC) of the composts was determined using a 5:1 ratio with deionised water, as per Bower and Wilcox (1965) using a Jenway 4200 portable conductivity meter.

Total phosphorus was measured colorimetrically by UV spectrophotometry while total potassium, calcium, magnesium and sodium levels were analysed by atomic absorption spectrophotometry (AAS) using an air-acetylene flame.

Filtrates for both phosphorus and total cations were obtained as per Rowell (1994). Plant-available soil phosphorus and potassium levels were also determined using AA spectrophotometry, following extraction with Morgan's solution, which is routinely used for agricultural analysis in Ireland.

Total nitrogen was determined using the Kjeldahl method and the C/N ratio was calculated from this value along with the associated organic matter value, on the hypothesis that organic matter contains 58 % carbon. The acid detergent fibre (ADF), acid detergent lignin (ADL) and hemicellulose components were analysed following a series of refluxing and ashing as per Goering and Van Soest (1970) and this analytical procedure was also employed by Sharma (1999) for mushroom compost analysis.

Heavy metal analysis

The filtrate obtained for the determination of the total elements copper, zinc, iron and manganese was extracted according to Richards (1993), while total cadmium, chromium, nickel and lead values were determined as per Soon and Abboud (1993). All element levels were determined by atomic absorption spectrophotometry. The appropriate standards were prepared within the range for optimum working conditions, as stated in the operator's manual.

Statistical analysis

Normality tests were conducted on all SMC samples and where data were skewed, they were transformed (log10). The data were then analysed statistically using analysis of variance and Pearson's bivariate correlations on SPSS version 11.0. The data were initially analysed using descriptive measures giving the mean, minimum and maximum values for each parameter analysed, along with the standard deviation and coefficient of variation.

Multivariate statistical analyses were carried out using a MultiVariate Statistical Package (MVSP) for windows version 3.0. Box and whisker plots were utilized to graphically summarize the array of values for each parameter about the median. Hierarchical cluster analysis (HCA) was also employed using Gower general similarity coefficients on MVSP, where the level of similarities between each yard are linked and presented on a dendrogram.

Principal Component Analysis (PCA) was also employed to analyze the relationships between the physical and chemical parameters measured for SMC supplied from each of the 13 compost production yards, with the resulting graphical analysis presented in ordination biplots in relation to the ordination axes. The correlation matrix for standardization was utilized as the parameters that were analysed were on different scales.

RESULTS

Nutrient composition of SMC

The nutrient composition and physical component description of the 63 samples are epitomized, where it is evident that SMC has a considerable yet varying supply of plant nutrients and a high organic matter content. The coefficient of variation, which is a measure of variation independent of the unit of measurement, is highest for bio-available phosphorous and total calcium, while the consistency of organic matter and pH are relatively uniform. Variability is within these parameters may be due to the varying mixes and types of ingredients utilized in the manufacturing of the selective mushroom substrate, while the supplementation of the digestive enzyme phytase in chicken feed may be a cause of the high variability within phosphorous concentrations as well as the varying rates of phosphorous uptake by the mushroom crop.

In a typical commercial growing medium, EC levels would be in the 1.2-1.5 mS cm-1 category (Maher et al. 2000), however a mean value of 10.5 mS cm-1 was obtained for the 63 growers. This fact has been reported to limit the further use of SMC as a potting substrate, soil amendment and organic manure (Maher et al. 2000, amongst others). This high salinity level is possibly due to the level of potassium present ($P<0.01$, $r=0.794$) and to a lesser extent total Na ($P<0.01$, $r = 0.428$). All C/N ratio values obtained for the 63 samples were below the recommended ratio of 25 and therefore indicate that SMC is relatively stable and this stability is reiterated in the fact that a further 6 weeks of composting would yield a completely stabilised SMC compost.

The composition of SMC nutrients determined within this study are compared to those of other studies, where it is notably evident that the EC, phosphorous and magnesium content of SMC are lower than all other SMC samples in Ireland, the UK, the Netherlands, Florida and Pennsylvania while the DM, potassium, calcium and sodium levels are appreciably higher. Values for total K obtained by Maher (1988), EC, N (Levanon and Danai, 1995 and Chong and Rinker, 1994) and total P are equivalent to those obtained in this study.

However, as a broad range of mushroom compost production systems are operating worldwide, the discrepancies between mean values obtained for various SMC characteristics between countries may be attributed to this fact.

Heavy metal content of SMC

The mean concentration of heavy metals in the 63 SMC samples are outlined, along with the maximum and minimum values, standard deviation and coefficient of variation for each metal. However, it is not known if these values are acceptable as no legal heavy metal limits or standards have been published for SMC or indeed for any general compost produced in Ireland, yet there are standards implemented in many other European countries for general compost.

These limits for lead range from 120-1200 mg kg-1, from 1-105 mg kg-1 for cadmium, 70-750 mg kg-1 for chromium, nickel from 20-400 mg kg-1, copper from 90-1750 mg kg-1 and zinc from 280 to 4000 mg kg-1. While the coefficient of variations for most of the heavy metals are passable, the values obtained are well within the recommended range in other EU countries and should not be a cause for concern when applied to land, as elevated heavy metal concentrations negatively affect plant growth.

According to Briton (2001), the cadmium levels obtained for SMC are significantly lower than the proposed legal limits for compost in some EU countries. However in comparison to values published by Hogg et al. (2002) in a review of compost standards in Ireland, a maximum limit of 1.5 mg kg-1 Cd was suggested for general compost thus signifying that the majority of SMC samples in Ireland are in excess of this concentration.

The heavy metal content of SMC determined within this study is compared to levels published in other studies, where it verifies that the copper and cadmium levels are elevated, while manganese, iron, chromium and nickel are invariably lower that those reported in other countries.

In summary, the range, skewness of each variable and outliers are identified and visually synopsized for the 63 SMC samples, but some variables should be looked at with scepticism as the magnitude of some of the parameters are dominated by larger valued variables. The hierarchical cluster dendrogram epitomizes the similarities between SMC supplied from each composting yard in regard to each of 25 parameters analysed.

SMC samples from Northern Ireland composting yards denoted by the letters A-E are evidently clustered together while SMC samples from the Republic of Ireland yards are also closely clustered together and are denoted by the letters F-M, illustrating that the closer the yards are linked together, the more similar they are.

The multivariate relationships between SMC nutrient content, physical composition and heavy metal content as determined by principal component analysis (PCA) on a standardised correlation matrix. The first two axes accounted for 53 % of the overall variation and are graphically displayed. The first axis differentiates between samples analysed from the Republic (to the left of the ordination diagram) and Northern Ireland (positioned to the right of the ordination diagram) and detailed 32 % percent of the total variation between SMC samples.

The differentiation maybe due to a number of parameters, predominately the pH and cellulitic values of SMC from the southern yards while the phosphorous, potassium and OM levels along with the mushroom yield data differentiate the northern yards. The second axis, which explicates 20.7 % of the total variation of SMC, differentiates SMC according to the lignolytic components and heavy metal content with the exception of manganese, from the chemical and nutrient properties.

IMPLICATIONS

1. When purchasing SMC as an organic fertilizer or for any agricultural or horticultural use, it is imperative to be assured that SMC will offer 'value for money' in terms of its adequate and reliable supply of plant nutrients. In general, the extent of nutrient variability in SMC is concerning, as these inconsistencies could lead to the surplus accumulation of plant nutrients in the soil, particularly if SMC is not analyzed prior to land application. Systematic consistent information regarding SMC composition must be available from each compost production yard. Centralized SMC handling depots as suggested by Maher et al. (2000) could facilitate such methodical analysis of SMC and may encourage landowners to utilize SMC beneficially as a soil conditioner or fertilizer as accurate nutrient values can be guaranteed.
2. Overall, the coefficients of variation should be improved for all parameters, in particular for plant nutrients. Until then, SMC should be analyzed prior to land application and subsequent application rates should determined from these analyses along with the nutrient content of the soil, in conjunction with the appropriate nutrient management plans.

3. National compost standards should be implemented for not only SMC, but for all general composts in Ireland for all plant nutrient and heavy metal concentrations. Such standards would ensure uniformity and consistency in all composts and may result in a market growth for SMC. National standard methods of analysis should also be purposed and enforced to enable an accurate and direct comparison between compost results and legal limits.

7

Button Mushroom Industry

INTRODUCTION

In a business sense there is nothing unique about the Agaricus spp (button mushroom) industry. We produce and deliver a product for which there is some demand. We market and sell that product for a profit. As such we are subject to the same business principles as any other industry, agricultural or otherwise. Even the common lament, that business is tough because our costs keep rising yet we rarely are allowed a price increase, is common to many industries.

I have been associated with mushroom businesses with very elaborate and complex accounting practices and mechanisms for data collection; however at the end of the day all the accounting practices can be reduced to a very simple calculation. Sales revenue generated minus cost to produce and distribute, equals profit, which in the end is the feature that determines the existence of any business. Because we are all part of this wonderful dynamic system that selects for the best competitor, which I call economic Darwinism, the best, the most intelligent, and the most progressive operations of each business survives.

Each business works to improve its operations in order to seek competitive advantage over the competition. This advantage is used to increase its profitability, or at least its viability, so that it can exist and finance further improvement or change. Unfortunately in many cases improvements or advances just seem to allow the business to exist and don't lead to expected increases in profitability, but this is an illusion.

In reality most enterprises are doing the same and improving their chances for survival. In essence the operations are peddling faster just to stay in the same place, but that is not necessarily a bad thing.

The reality is that the businesses that are not innovating, that are not improving, that are not progressing will not survive because they are loosing ground to the rest. In the end they are the equivalent of the dedicated buggy whip, telegraph, and abacus manufacturers. They are, or will be, out of business. In the button mushroom business intelligent innovation and improvement are necessary to achieve viability and at least consistent, if not spectacular profitability as opposed to the alternative, which is oblivion.

In the past our industry has been fortunate in that there has been sufficient funding and agencies to provide research and develop innovation. This has been partly due to the fact that most of the producers have been in developed economies where profit margins were large.

Agencies such as the Horst experimental station in Holland, the Glasshouse research Station and HRI in the UK, Penn State in the United States, and the Kinsealy Institute in Ireland fueled by government and industry funding developed many of the cultural practices and technologies that have come into prominence today. However in recent years support for research and development has not been forthcoming.

Because of spending cuts by the various governments and the effects of cheap imported mushrooms from developing economies on the developed industries, the above mentioned agencies are either closed or scaled back and the funding has been reduced to a trickle. Consequently we are currently riding the crest of a wave of technological advancements, but there should not be high expectations for similar advancements in the near term. Yes. change will occur, advancements will be made, but perhaps not with the frequency and significance we have seen.

As I review the performance of the Agaricus spp mushroom industry I have recognized two general characteristics that have impacted profitability and viability. They are efficiency, or whatever reduces the unit cost to produce, and marketing and sales, which creates demand and generates revenue.

This is an extension of the calculation I mentioned earlier. What I intend to present today, with the help of the reality of the past, an awareness of the present, and intuition of the future, is to explore the methods by which the button mushroom industry has, and will, address efficiency and sales. By no means am I a visionary or a fortuneteller and I have no particular insight into the future.

However, I do have global experience and have global contacts, some of which have offered suggestions or corroborated personal opinions. They are duly noted in the references. In some cases I have seen the future, and in others I will speculate what may occur by extending the economic principles just mentioned. Please bear with my simple speculations of the future and accept them as just that, simple. Any other opinions may be just as accurate, or more so, that the ones to be presented.

It should be highlighted that, although the business principles for the mushroom industry are the same as other industries, the mushroom industry is unique because of its complexity. As an agricultural business its productivity is limited by the requirements and limitations of the organism being cultured. This ag-business may be the most industrial in application of any agriculture and as such is very capital intensive for agriculture. It is a low profit margin industry so the requirements of the organism are often compromised because of the inability to afford the best of systems because of lack of funds. Because the mushroom requires large volumes of composted organic matter and much organic waste is generated, regulatory agencies must be dealt with merely to continue existence.

Finally because it is also a labor intensive industry, methods must be found to deal with employee relations, health and safety, and of course, wages. Given this complex matrix of challenges the industry faces, let's look at how the industry has addressed the major areas of efficiency and sales/marketing to deal with these pressures. Also how we will continue to address these economic challenges in the future.

EFFICIENCY

Operational efficiency in the Agaricus spp mushroom industry can be impacted in many ways. In general, efficiency is impacted positively or negatively by the way we do things that affect unit cost, reliability of production, or the ability to get product sold. For example doing more required work in less time (operations, harvesting, packaging, etc.) or with less energy decreases unit cost. Higher yield from the same growing area reduces unit cost.

Lower raw material usage and better raw material conversion into mushroom tissue also reduces unit cost. Reliability of production allows more efficient use of harvested mushrooms week in and week out. Good quality and timing of production allows maximum valuation of mushrooms and thereby efficient returns on product sold. Arguably the last two items are marketing/sales issues in nature, but it takes cultural improvement to achieve them. In recent years improved physical and cultural technology has been the driving force toward improved efficiency. There have been technological improvements throughout the Agaricus spp cultural process, but a few aspects of the process have provided the most significant impact. Following are the major areas that have provided the greatest impact in efficiency in the recent past. These areas will also be explored to imagine how efficiency will improve in the future.

1. Yields and Quality
2. Composting and Compost Processing
3. Growing Cell Improvements
4. Harvesting
5. The Mushroom Itself
6. Raw Materials and Additives

Yields and Quality

Yields of mushrooms per unit area climb inexorably higher every year. In the USA, national yields have increased from 26.2 kg/m2 (5.36 lb/ft2) in 1990/91 to 28.5 kg/m2 (5.83 lb/ft2) in 2000/01, an 8.8% increase. Similar yield increases have been noted around the world, but particularly in Europe and the south Pacific. The higher yields have been essential to reduce unit cost and increase revenue generated per unit area of growing space since sales price has only increased marginally. Interestingly, in the USA the 8.8% increase in yields was accomplished on only 2.7% more square meters (square feet) laid with an astonishing 42.8% fewer growers! This is also a global trend that will be addressed later in this presentation.

Table. USA Agaricus spp Production – USDA.

	Growers	Total Sales in Kg X 1,000	m^2 Cased X 1,000	Yield Kg/m^2
1990/91	238	340,523	13 016. 2	26.2
1995/96	180	353,577	12588.1	28.1
2000/01	136	381,187	13 370.9	28.5

Increases in yields have come from a variety of factors. A major boost to production was seen in the mid 1980's as a result of the first generation of hybrid spawn strains and a similar yield boost was noted in the early 1990's with the advent of the second-generation hybrids.

Beyond spawn some of the influential factors affecting the rise in yields are increasing dry matter per unit area, the wide spread use of supplementation, the use of bulk composting and compost processing systems, and the implementation of good growing practices. Good growing practices would include better environmental controls, better hygiene, less major disease problems, better casing practices, and better attention to detail. Although bulk phase III is not common in the USA, it still must be considered an influential factor for higher yields.

Yields in Holland where virtually all farms use phase III, average yields have climbed to ~30.8 kg/m2 (6.3 lb/ft2). It is important to note that with 42.8% fewer growers, slightly higher growing area, and 8.8% higher yields the validity of efficiency and economic Darwinism is demonstrated. It can be inferred from the data that the better growers survived, took over many of the under performers, and transferred their expertise to their new facilities.

Interestingly, improved quality has mirrored the increase in yields. Although we are approaching the point where yield may be limited by the number of quality mushrooms that can be harvested per unit area, we are not there yet.

Innovative pinning and growing practices have been implemented to produce more volume and more quality per unit area. Altered harvesting practices are also improving yields by harvesting larger mushrooms at peak maturity periodically through the day. All of these practices are adding another dimension to yields by allowing quality and quantity growing, simultaneously.

Composting and Compost Processing

Bulk composting and compost processing systems, and the reliability of which, have improved efficiency and productivity significantly. Although not a recent development, bulk phase II and phase III in tunnels were improved to the point where consistency and reliability surpassed traditional ways of performing the processes of pasteurization, conditioning, and incubation. In doing so, less labor and energy was required, better environmental control was achieved, and more growing space was gained by eliminating in situ tray or bed phase II/III. Also tunnel design and cultural practices have improved over the years so that the periodic outbreaks of virus disease have been largely eliminated.

More recently bulk phase I was developed as a result of a Dutch government mandate to eliminate odors and air pollution. The Italians did the initial work, but since 1995 the Dutch have taken the technology to its furthest extent. The process of bulk phase I produces compost in an enclosed vessel with aeration lines imbedded in the floor.

Computerized control regulates the amount of oxygen in the mass of compost, which maintains the optimum conditions for producing compost at all times. In Holland, the CNC operates a fully enclosed composting system that can produce phase I compost from stable bedding in less than one week. Other operations such as Walkro, Tunnel Tech, Meadow's, McGeary's, Rucklidge, and others have modified and simplified the process into a more cost effective alternative to the expensive, high tech, and fully enclosed Dutch and Belgian systems.

The concept and application is quite simple, although some dedicated equipment is necessary for maximum performance. The development of the bulk system composting has provided many important advances including shorter composting cycle, easier management, simplified processes, more reliability, less raw material usage, less influence of ambient climate, and less odor.

The odor issue is becoming a major issue in the mushroom industry and odor control alone has precipitated many to change to bulk phase I systems. These systems reduce odors because the fermentation process is totally aerobic and because the composting cycle is generally much shorter in duration, but the opportunities are much greater. All air supplied to the compost can be captured, scrubbed, and biofiltered thereby further reducing odor generation and air pollution. Although it must be said these systems are not yet completely effective.

Compost businesses have become more common. In areas where farms are in close proximity individuals have stopped making their own compost. Instead compost sites have been consolidated by growers forming cooperatives or by development of independent companies. Whereas once 10 compost sites may have produced 100 tons each, now one site produces 1,000 tons. This organizational advancement has eliminated redundant composting operations, especially in developed areas, and has improved efficiency. Cost per ton of compost has decreased because raw materials bought in larger quantities are cheaper, much less equipment and labor is used on one site than 10, and the sites are on cheap, marginal land where, in this case, isolation is an advantage.

The isolation presents a buffer against odor and noise complaints from neighbors. The central composting sites may produce more than 5,000 tons of phase I per week and the compost may be supplied in phase I, phase II, or phase III forms depending on the operation. Additionally the compost may be shipped to the grower in bulk, bags, or blocks.

Bulk phase III is characteristic of the Dutch industry whereas bulk phase I is produced in Australia and in the Kennet Square area of Pennsylvania, USA. Ireland had produced phase II entirely in bags, but blocks of phase II or phase III compost are increasingly common. Blocks are ~20-24 kg, 0.4 X 0.6 meter formed bags that can be placed on shelves or racks to provide increased operational efficiencies. Once again cost factors determines the direction of the business.

Growing Cell Improvements

Sophisticated air handling systems operated with computer control programs fully prioritize and integrate the environmental control parameters of temperature, relative humidity, air volume and velocity, and carbon dioxide. While most farms still have basic environmental control systems, the advanced systems are gradually gaining acceptance as a way to improve farm efficiency.

Improved quality is a noticeable benefit of the advanced systems since critical pinning regimes and evaporation rates can be successfully managed room after room. Yields can also be optimized. Energy conservation is another benefit of the systems.

Fresh air utilization can be automatically managed within CO_2 control parameters so that more or less fresh air is used depending on the suitability of that air to reduce air conditioning. Fan speed can be regulated to reduce electricity usage and reduce the volume of air that requires conditioning. Ground water can be used in preconditioning units to bring the air to a state that will cost less to final condition for use in the growing cell. This saves on power bills and reduces the cost of the final air-handling units. Design of growing cells themselves has improved to provide more lighting, space, and insulation.

There are systems being developed that fully automate watering. Computer controls store instructions to mechanically apply various volumes of water at different times during the day. The drying cycle automatically follows to dry the mushrooms also via the computer program. Premixed chemicals can also be applied in this way from a dedicated tank.

Harvesting

Harvesting is the most expensive cost center of button mushroom growing. This is one area that although there is a terrific need, there has been minimal progress. Fresh market mushroom harvesting is still largely a physically demanding, manual job, which is also considered undesirable work in developed countries.

The improvements that have been made are generally directed to making the harvesting job easier. This decreases harvesting costs by increasing picking speeds. In Holland, dedicated processed mushroom operations use a machine cutter to harvest 100% of their product, but aside these operations, little harvesting is done by completely mechanical means.

The picker assist and automatic cutter are two ways in which harvesting has been influenced towards faster speeds. The picker assist is a stationary item that allows harvesters to pick two handed, while the automatic trimmer is mechanical unit that allows two handed harvesting and trims the stem. Both are useful, but have their drawbacks.

Strategies have also been employed to improve harvesting efficiency. The picking parlor, which applies the principle of bringing the harvestable mushrooms to the harvester, has been implemented in a few cases. The concept requires growing in trays or some other mobile container, which are run via mechanical means through a gauntlet of harvesters. The harvesters pick and sort the mushrooms while the containers roll by. Increase of picking rates have been noted up to 50%, but this also seems to be determined by the type and motivation of the harvesters in question.

Manual labor still seems to be the best option for mushroom harvesting at this time. Neither sophisticated strategies nor current equipment surpasses the efficiency of motivated manual harvesters. That is, harvesters from less developed economies that find real financial advantages to harvesting mushrooms compared to their current lot in life. In the United States harvesting is virtually totally accomplished with the help of Latin American immigrants. In Eastern Europe mushroom operations are flourishing solely because of the availability of plentiful harvesting labor. This has developed to the extent that phase IV growing, the transport of fully pinned trays from Holland and Belgium to Eastern Europe for harvesting, has become a financial reality.

THE MUSHROOM ITSELF

The last significant improvement in the phenotypic expression of cultivated A. bisporus was in the early to mid-1980's when hybridization expanded the yield potential of the standard off-white strains while retaining quality. More recent hybridization resulted in a "second generation" of hybrids further increasing productivity. These second generation hybrids are nearly universally used throughout the white button mushroom industry.

These developments significantly improved mushroom farm efficiencies by producing a larger volume of product from the same fixed costs and raw materials, but little else has developed since.

Raw Materials and Additives

The use of wheat straw and poultry manure as composting raw materials has changed little in recent years. The only remote trend is working toward less expensive raw materials for composting.

Poultry manure as a cheap source of nitrogen is used exclusively in most countries, while the United States continues with seed meals, but is gravitating toward more poultry manure. Spawn has already been discussed. The addition of supplements or nutritional additives to compost post spawning has come to be common. There have been several types of supplements marketed, but the trend has been toward higher nitrogen formulations particularly in associated with lower nitrogen composts. Supplementation is integral to the Dutch strategy of mushroom production, particularly due to their low nitrogen compost. Addition of the materials tends to be at spawning on farms that produce or buy in phase I compost, but addition at casing is associated with farms that produce or buy in bulk phase III compost.

In recent years there has been considerable focus on casing soils. The general trend has been away from the brown (young) dried, milled peat and toward black (mature) wet, deep dug peat. The beneficial characteristics of black peat are better water retention, cleaner mushrooms, less bed damage, and easier watering.

Quality improvements are easily noted with the deep dug peat. Dutch and Irish ready-made casing soils are distributed all over the world because of their superior cultural characteristics. The use of sugar beet lime in conjunction with both black and brown peat has improved the properties of both. Because it serves to increase the density and water retention of both peats it makes the brown peat more similar to a black and improves the characteristics of the black further.

The use of chemicals for disease and pest control and for hygiene has come under continued pressure. There were few chemicals available in the first place for the control of fungal and bacterial pathogens and insect pests, but there are fewer now.

Because the mushroom industry is a comparatively small agricultural concern, chemical companies are reluctant to invest in the development and licensing of new chemicals, or even to renew the licenses of existing ones. An initiative toward biological control of pests and diseases has started.

A bacterial control for bacterial blotch was marketed for several years, but was dropped due to some production problems associated with it. A parasitic nematode marketed under the trade name Nemasys for mushroom flies has been marketed and is gaining some acceptance.

THE FUTURE

Efficiency with respect to being an innovative, creative, least cost producer of quality mushrooms will continue to be the driving force for operator viability. Yields will continue to increase because of improving cultural practices, increased reliability of production, and improved nutrition and nutrition availability.

In substrate preparation, bulk composting systems will gain dominance and eventually bulk composting processing systems will follow. Where multiple growing operations are in close proximity, consolidation of compost sites will continue, in bulk. Bulk procedures will be further refined and be more reliable.

Odor issues from compost fermentation will become an increasing worry for operators as the public and regulatory agencies become more critical and stringent. The odor issue will be an unrelenting challenge until odor is totally eliminated from the process. Consequently, the odor capturing properties of bulk phase I will be further refined and improved and biofilters will become more effective and more prominent. There is much opportunity in this area.

Raw material changes will be minimal and will be economically driven toward cheaper materials including inorganic nitrogen sources such as urea and ammonium sulfate. Seed meals will become less prominent in USA. Long-term, alternative substrates may become reality. The vision is that the nutrients necessary to grow mushrooms could be provided in a sterile and filtered nutrient broth that could be supplied to the mushroom through a sponge-like substrate.

This would be the solution (no pun intended) to many problems, but of course many new problems would also be created. Supplementation will evolve to more closely satisfy the actual nutritional needs of Agaricus spp. Currently seed meal or feather meal nitrogen is processed and used as a general nutritional boost, but eventually there will be supplements that specifically address the nutritional requirements of the mushroom.

In the mushroom growing sector, more and more growing cells will be fitted with sophisticated environmental control systems to improve yield, quality, and energy efficiency. Programmable watering systems will become common to reduce labor. Energy efficiency will become a higher priority because of higher fuel and energy prices. Heat exchangers will be developed to recover some of the energy currently vented during phase II, phase III, cookout, and even phase I if done on site.

Likewise heat, or cooling exchangers will be used to utilize vented air to precondition fresh air in growing cells. CO2 scrubbers will be used in exhaust ducts to "cleanse" vented air so that the conditioned air can be reused in the same cell. Additionally, irradiation or concentrated UV light may be used in place of absolute filters to clean fresh air which would save filter costs as well as reduce air handler costs. Inside the cell, aluminum shelves will replace trays on some farms to eliminate the cost of trays and to provide a better environment for the mushrooms and the harvesters.

Metal or plastic trays will also become an alternative particularly with parlor picking applications. In particular, USA mushroom farms will have to undergo significant upgrade of facilities to keep pace with employee health and safety requirements.

Many farms are of substandard condition and will require significant investment, or closure, in the coming years to stay ahead of customer and employee requirements for health and safety. The cropping cycle of the mushroom will continue to shorten. Whereas 4 and 5 flush cycles were common, most farms have reduced to 3 and 4 flush cycles. Eventually we will see many farms operate for only 2 flushes to maximize farm throughput, particularly if substrate is inexpensive. Additionally the short cropping cycle reduces the exposure to pests and diseases.

With regard to pests and diseases, the number of available chemicals for pest and disease control will continue to diminish as licenses for chemicals expire and are not renewed. This will eventually make the Agaricus spp mushroom an organic food by default. Cultural practices will change in order to operate without chemicals such as the short cropping cycle mentioned earlier as well as improved hygiene and the use of integrated pest management systems. Improved composting, compost processing, and the trend toward supplementation at casing will help reduce competitor molds. Bulk phase III, especially at remote sites, will reduce the exposure to mushroom flies. Biological controls such as Nemasys will experience growth in the disease control market. Indeed another product is currently being tested for control of Trichoderma spp.

Harvesting will continue to be a labor-intensive process and any improvement will only occur when technology, and the cost of that technology, make an interesting argument for change. Near term I believe that the dedicated, motivated harvesters from undeveloped economies will harvest the mushrooms in developed countries. In some cases the mushroom farms will move to the harvesters (eastern Europe), but more development of labor export or labor brokering will also occur. Many developed economies have a demand for people who are willing to perform manual labor. Likewise there are many people from developing economies that would be delighted to work under the favorable conditions and earn the money that is available in these countries.

This demand and supply will be satisfied. Of course the cost of this scenario is not fully inexpensive so eventually advanced strategies and technologies will prevail. One option that is currently available, if not economically so, is a completely automated harvesting and cutting system developed by the Silsoe Research Institute in England. It is a system by which computer mapped photos provide coordinates for a suction device that picks the mushrooms and then delivers it to a trimming machine. A parlor picking strategy is required for the system, and some growers are implementing this strategy now in the hopes that the system becomes for economically interesting soon. Eventually the concept may be applied to shelves as well since demand (many shelf farms in Holland and other countries) will spur the research. Once again the search for efficiency will drive the use of this technology.

The characteristics of A. bisporus are an area where the future holds great promise, but only if the political and ethical climate allows it. Gene splicing has been done.

There are no technical barriers to modifying A. bisporus in ways that would alter the biology of the organism as well as the composition of the sporophore, if it allowed. Greater questions must be answered before that time arrives, but some of the possibilities are certainly food for thought. Just a few of the characteristics that could develop are disease and pest resistance, increased flavor, increased shelf life, faster mycelial colonization, more forgiving environmental tolerances, more efficient utilization of substrate, etc. are all parts of the opportunities that modifying the genetics of the organism presents. Whether or not this will be allowed to occur is anyone's guess and is not appropriate for this chapter, but just imagine.

Even without modifying the genetics of A. bisporus there are some possibilities for change. Faster mycelial colonization can be accomplished with alternate carriers for the spawn. Smaller particle sizes with nutritional additives have been shown to reduce spawn run by 25%. They will become more reliable and widely used in the future. There are already opportunities for increased flavor, altered texture, and disease resistance, but poor yields limit the commercial viability of these characteristics at this time. The possibility of increasing the vitamin and trace mineral concentration in A. bisporus is also a possibility since mushrooms possess easier uptake characteristics than green plants. As such, essential elements such as Selenium can augment the nutritional characteristics of the mushroom.

Finally, the wastes from the mushroom growing process, stumps and spent compost, will become an increasing problem. Disposal of the large volumes of material produced on a sizable farm can present considerable environmental concerns from nitrate leaching into ground water to filling up landfills. Increasingly these materials are and will be used as soil conditioners for the nursery business and for agricultural crops. Some of the materials may be reevaluated for casing soil if peat supplies become scarce due to environmental concerns about peat harvesting. Spent compost has also been shown to absorb pollutants from mine tailing runoff so this use also will be expanded. Finally, the material could also be used for fuel.

BUTTON MUSHROOM

Button Mushroom (Agaricus spp.) is the most popular mushroom variety grown and consumed the world over. In India, its production earlier was limited to the winter season, but with technology development, these are produced almost throughout the year in small, medium and large farms, adopting different levels of technology. The species being grown in most farms is the white button mushroom (Agaricus bisporus) belonging to Class Basidiomycetes and Family Agaricaceae.

OBJECTIVE

The main objective of the exercise is to present a small scale viable bankable model production unit through adoption of appropriate technology, utilization of resources and suitable market strategy.

BACKGROUND

Origin

Cultivation of button mushrooms (A.bisporus) started in the sixteenth century. However, on a commercial scale, the cultivation was initiated in Europe around 17th Century. Many farms for production of button mushrooms were established and this variety still dominates the world production and consumption. India, with its diverse agroclimate conditions and abundance of agricultural wastes, has been producing mushrooms, mainly for the domestic market, for more than four decades. Commercial production picked up in the nineties and several hi-tech export oriented farms were set up with foreign technology collaborations. But major share of mushroom production is still on small farms.

Botanical Description

The vegetative mycelium is composed of many inter-woven sepatate hyphae. The reproductive phase is initiated by the formation of small knob like swellings at different points of interwoven mycelial strands.

These swellings increase in size and break through the surface of the substratum as small balls constituting the button stage. A matured basidiocarp (fruit body) is whitish in colour and consists of thick short stipe with an annulus.

The stipe supports the pileus which appears as a hat like expansion. On the underside of the pileus, a number of radiating gills or lamella are present which are pink when young but purple-brown when mature.

Production Status

Large scale white button mushroom production is centred in Europe (mainly western part), North America (USA, Canada) and S.E. Asia (China, Korea, Indonesia, Taiwan and India). The national annual production of mushrooms is estimated to be around 50,000 tonnes with 85 percent of this production being of button mushrooms.

Economic Importance

Mushrooms are highly proteinaceous and are used as food. The white button mushroom is sold as fresh mushroom or is canned and made into soups, sauces and other food products. Protein in mushrooms have 60-70 % digestibility and contains all the essential amino acids. It has medicinal properties also. A high amount of retene is present in the button mushroom which is supposed to have an antagonistic effect on some forms of tumours.

MARKET ANALYSIS AND STRATEGY

DEMAND AND SUPPLY PATTERNS

White button mushrooms are grown all over the world and account for 35-45 % of the total mushroom production. In India, large units with production capacities between 2000 – 3000 tonnes/annum, have been set up mainly as export oriented units in the southern, western and northern regions. A large number of small units without climatic control equipment exist throughout India and function during the autumn and winter months only.

A big gap exists between the demand and supply position of white button mushrooms in the United States and European market. India exports the highest quantity of the mushroom produced in the country to USA. Netherlands and China account for 60% of the export of mushrooms. Germany is the largest importer and France and UK are large producers as well as consumers.

The demand for fresh mushroom is increasing in the international market while that of preserved or canned mushrooms is decreasing. The possibilities of exporting fresh mushrooms to the markets in Middle East, Europe and USA need to be explored. Europe is a very large producer of fresh button mushrooms as such only some exotic varieties of mushrooms which are high priced can be exported to these countries. However, some inhibiting factors are high cost of transportation and absence of proper pre-cooling techniques and storage facilities.

Marketing problem is experienced in the winter months (December-February) when more than 75% of the annual production comes in market for sale in limited duration and market area. Farmers face the consequences of over-saturated market and are forced to sell their produce at a cheaper price. The commercial units need to establish mushroom processing unit so that during peak periods when there is glut of mushrooms in the market, the growers can resort to preservation of mushroom and as such fluctuation in prices will not affect the project economy.

The price of fresh mushrooms during May-June in different markets viz. Chandigarh, Delhi and Mumbai varies between Rs.50 and Rs.100/kg. Any mushroom unit located in and around the main markets should be able to make sufficient profit as they can save on transportation of produce.

Import/Export Trends

Netherlands is the leading exporter of button mushrooms (40% share) followed by China, France, Spain, Hong Kong, Taiwan, Indonesia and South Korea. USA is the largest consumer accounting for one third of World production. Other important consumers are Germany, UK, France, Italy and Canada. The quantity of mushrooms exported by India in comparison to the world export is almost negligible. The following tables gives the export status of fresh and dried mushrooms.

Table. Country-wise Quantity and Value of Fresh Mushrooms Exported from India During 2001 – 2002.

Country	Fresh Mushrooms	
	Quantity	Value
Ireland	40.80	14.55
Singapore	0.05	0.02
U.A.E	0.05	0.01
U.S.A	11756.73	5090.72
Total	11797.63	5105.30

Table. Country-wise Quantity and Value of Preserved/Dried Mushrooms Exported from India During 2001 – 2002

Country	Preserved/Dried Mushrooms	
	Quantity	Value
France	40.00	41.64
Japan	1.00	10.36
Nigeria	6.58	5.59
Russia	11.00	16.33
Switzerland	1.00	6.38
U.A.E	10.01	4.08
U.S.A	4029.66	2057.16
Total	4099.25	2142.25

The most important importers of white button mushroom are Germany, USA, France, U.K. and Sweden. Canned button mushrooms are imported by UK, Germany, France, USA, Sweden etc. Asian countries like China, Taiwan, Korea export their produce to the American and European countries in the form of canned mushrooms.

Analysis and Future Strategy

Marketing of mushrooms in India is not yet organized. It is the simple system of producers selling directly to retailer or even to the consumer. Wholesale distributor is mostly missing. However, trade in the processed (canned and dried) is sizeable and organized. In other countries 10% of the total cost is earmarked for marketing. Production of mushrooms, especially of the white button mushrooms, in India has gone up during recent years creating marketing problems.

The market for processed foods has yet to develop in the country and basically fresh fruits and vegetables are preferred. Per capita consumption of mushrooms in India is hardly 5g. as against over a kg. in developed countries. There has not been any serious effort to promote the product and to strengthen and expand the market in order to increase consumption. The marginal increase in demand is for fresh mushrooms instead of dried/preserved mushrooms. Fresh mushrooms have very short shelf-life and therefore cannot be transported to long distances without refrigerated transport facility. They are sold in the markets in and around the production areas.

The cultivation of white button mushrooms throughout the year under controlled condition is restricted to a few commercial units and much of the production is under natural conditions during the winters.

Majority of the growers in India do not have pasteurization facility and other sophisticated machinery/infrastructure for round the year production of white button mushroom. As such, button mushroom is cultivated seasonally when climatic conditions are favourable and production expenses are minimum.

Many growers in Haryana, especially in Sonepat, Ambala and Hisar have revolutionized the cultivation of white button mushroom by adopting very simple and cheap technology of construction of mushroom houses (mud houses with thathched roofs). Seasonal growing of white button mushroom in Haryana and Punjab has many advantages like nearness to market, easy and cheap availability of raw material coupled with utilization of family labour.

The growers in HP do not use compost prepared by long method because pasteurized compost is readily available from mushroom projects located at Solan and Palampur.

PRODUCTION TECHNOLOGY

Agro-climatic Requirements

In India, button mushrooms are grown seasonally and in environment controlled cropping houses. White button mushroom requires 20-28°C for vegetative growth (spawn run) and 12-18°C for reproductive growth. Besides that it requires relative humidity of 80-90% and enough ventilation during cropping. Seasonally, it is grown during the winter months in the north-west plains of India and for 8-10 months in a year on the hills. However, with the advent of modern cultivation technology it is now possible to cultivate this mushroom anywhere in India.

The growers can take on an average 3-4 crops of white button mushrooms in a year depending upon the type and varieties cultivated. Factors affecting the yield of the crop both in terms of quality and quantity are incidence of pests/pathogens and non-availability of pure quality of spawn.

Growing and Potential Belts

The major producing states are Himachal Pradesh, Uttar Pradesh, Punjab, Haryana, Maharashtra, Andhra Pradesh, Tamil Nadu and Karnataka.

Varieties/Strains

Ooty 1 and Ooty (BM) 2 (released in 2002) are the two strains of button mushrooms released for commercial cultivation by the scientists of Horticulture Research Station of the Tamil Nadu Agricultural University at Vijayanagaram, Ooty. The strains which are mostly cultivated in India are S-11, TM-79 and Horst H_3.

Cultivation Technology

The whole process of mushroom production can be divided into the following steps:

i. Spawn production
ii. Compost preparation
iii. Spawning
iv. Spawn running
v. Casing
vi. Fruiting

Spawn Production

Spawn is produced from fruiting culture/ stocks of selected strains of mushrooms under sterile conditions. Stock culture may be produced in the lab or may be obtained from other reputed sources.

Fruiting culture is mainly imported from various places including foreign sources which give higher yield than Indian strains and the spawn is produced in the lab. The spawn should be of good quality in terms of flavour, texture and size apart from having potential for high yield and longer shelf life.

Compost Preparation

The substrate on which button mushroom grows is mainly prepared from a mixture of plant wastes (cereal straw/ sugarcane bagasse etc.), salts (urea, superphosphate/ gypsum etc), supplements (rice bran/ wheat bran) and water. In order to produce 1kg.of mushroom, 220g. of dry substrate materials are required.

It is recommended that each ton of compost should contain 6.6 kg. nitrogen, 2.0kg. phosphate and 5.0kg. of potassium (N:P:K- 33: 10:25) which would get converted into 1.98% N, 0.62% P and 1.5% K on a dry weight basis.

The ratio of C: N in a good substrate should be 25-30: 1 at the time of staking and 16-17: 1 in the case of final compost.

Short Method of Composting

During the first phase of compost preparation, paddy straw is placed in layers and sufficient water is added to the stack along with fertilizers, wheat bran, molasses etc. The whole thing is mixed thoroughly with the straw and made into a stack (almost 5feet high,5 feet wide and of any length can be made with the help of wooden boards). The stack is turned and again watered on the second day. On the fourth day the stack is again turned for the second time by adding gypsum and watered. The third and final turning is given on the twelveth day when the colour of the compost changes into dark brown and it starts emitting a strong smell of ammonia.

The second phase is the pasteurization phase. The compost prepared as a result of microbe mediated fermentation process needs to be pasteurized in order to kill undesirable microbes and competitors and to convert ammonia into microbial protein.The whole process is carried out inside a steaming room where an air temperature of 60°C is maintained for 4 hours. The compost finally obtained should be granular in structure with 70% moisture content and pH 7.5. It should have a dark brown colour, sweet unobnoxious smell and free from ammonia, insects and nematodes. After the process is complete, the substrate is cooled down to 25°C.

Long Method of Composting

The long method of composting is usually practiced in areas where facilities for steam pasteurization is not available. In this method, the first turning is given about six days after preparation of the substrate for composting. The second turning is given on the tenth day followed by third one on the thirteenth day when gypsum is added. The fourth, fifth and sixth turnings are given on the sixteenth, nineteenth and twenty-second day. On the twenty-fifth day the seventh turning is given by adding 10% BHC (125g.) and the eighth turning is given on the twenty-eighth day after which it is checked whether there is any smell of ammonia present in the compost. The compost is ready for spawning only if it doesn't have any smell of ammonia; otherwise a few more turnings are given at an interval of three days till there is no smell of ammonia.

SPAWNING

The process of mixing spawn with compost is called spawning.

The different methods followed for spawning are given below:

i. *Spot Spawning*: Lumps of spawn are planted in 5 cm. deep holes made in the compost at a distance of 20-25 cm. The holes are later covered with compost.

ii. *Surface Spawning*: The spawn is evenly spread in the top layer of the compost and then mixed to a depth of 3-5 cm. The top portion is covered with a thin layer of compost.

iii. *Layer Spawning*: About 3-4 layers of spawn mixed with compost are prepared which is again covered with a thin layer of compost like in surface spawning.

The spawn is mixed through the whole mass of compost at the rate of 7.5 ml./kg. compost or 500 to 750 g./ 100 kg. compost (0.5 to 0.75%).

Spawn Running

After the spawning process is over, the compost is filled in polythene bags (90×90cm., 150 gauge thick having a capacity of 20-25kg. per bag)/ trays(mostly wooden trays 1×1/2m. accommodating 20-30kg. compost)/ shelves which are either covered with a newspaper sheet or polythene. The fungal bodies grow out from the spawn and take about two weeks (12-14 days) to colonise. The temperature maintained in cropping room is 23 ± 20 C. Higher temperature is detrimental for growth of the spawn and any temperature below than that specified for the purpose would result in slower spawn run. The relative humidity should be around 90% and a higher than normal CO2 concentration would be beneficial.

Casing

The compost beds after complete spawn run should be covered with a layer of soil (casing) about 3-4 cm. thick to induce fruiting. The casing material should be having high porosity, water holding capacity and the pH should range between 7-7.5. Peat moss which is considered to be the best casing material is not available in India, as such the mixtures like garden loam soil and sand (4:1); decomposed cowdung and loam soil (1:1) and spent compost (2-3 years old); sand and lime are commonly used.

The casing soil before application should be either pasteurized (at 66-700 C for 7-8 hours), treated with formaldehyde (2%), formaldehyde (2%) and bavistin (75 ppm.) or steam sterilized. The treatment needs to be done at least 15 days before the material is used for casing. After casing is done the temperature of the room is again maintained at 23-280 C and relative humidity of 85-90% for another 8-10 days. Low CO2 concentration is favourable for reproductive growth at this stage.

Fruiting

Under favourable environmental conditions viz. temperature (initially 23 ± 2°C for about a week and then 16 ± 2°C), moisture (2-3 light sprays per day for moistening the casing layer), humidity(above 85%), proper ventilation and CO_2 concentration (0.08-0.15%) the fruit body initials which appear in the form of pin heads start growing and gradually develop into button stage.

Pest & Diseases

The insect pests mostly observed are nematodes, mites and springtails. The crop is suspect to several diseases like Dry Bubble (brown spot), Wet Bubble (White Mould), Cobweb, Green Mould, False truffle (Truffle disease), Olive green mould, Brown plaster mould and Bacterial blotch. Professional help and extension advice will have to sought by the entrepreneur to adopt appropriate and timely control measures against pests & diseases.

Harvesting and Yield

Harvesting is done at button stage and caps measuring 2.5 to 4 cm. across and closed are ideal for the purpose. The first crop appears about three weeks after casing. Mushrooms need to be harvested by light twisting without disturbing the casing soil. Once the harvesting is complete, the gaps in the beds should be filled with fresh sterilized casing material and then watered.

About 10-14kg. fresh mushrooms per 100 kg. fresh compost can be obtained in two months crop. Short method used for preparation of compost under natural conditions gives more yield (15-20kg. per 100kg. compost).

POST HARVEST MANAGEMENT

PACKING AND STORAGE

Short Term Storage

Button mushrooms are highly perishable. Harvested mushrooms are cut at the soil line and washed in a solution of 5g. KMS in 10L. of water for removing the soil particles as well as to induce whiteness. After removing excess water these are packed in perforated poly bags each containing around 250-500 g. of mushrooms. They can be stored in polythene bags at 4-5°C for a short period of 3-4 days. The mushrooms are usually packed in unlabelled simple polythene or polypropylene for retail sale. Bulk packaging does not exist. In developed countries, modified atmosphere packaging (MAP) and controlled atmosphere packaging (CAP) are in vogue.

Long Term Storage

White button mushrooms are not usually dried by common procedures used in case of oyster, paddy and shitake mushrooms. Canning is the most popular method of preserving the white button mushrooms and sizeable quantity of canned produce are exported to international markets. Besides that, freeze drying, IQF and pickling are also practiced by some units.

SOURCES OF TECHNOLOGY

- National Centre for Mushroom, Chambaghat, Solan, Himachal Pradesh-173213, [Tel: (01792) 30451, 30767]

ECONOMICS OF A SMALL SCALE MODEL

The demand for Button mushroom is fast increasing in international markets and a big gap exists between supply and demand. There is need to take advantage of this situation by encouraging its production which is a highly viable venture as brought out below:

Costs & Returns

The minimum viable production unit will require a land site of 1.5 acres. The cost components of this model along with the basis for costing. Inclusive of contingencies, the project cost works out to Rs.107 lakhs as below.

Project Cost	Amount
Land & Site Development	5.15
Building	44.96
Plant & Machinery	47.00
Misc. Fixed Assets	0.75
Contingency	4.88
Pre-Operative Cost	4.25
Total	106.99

The major components of the model are:

- *Cost of acquiring land and its development (Rs.5.15 lakhs)*: The land would have to be acquired in areas well connected to urban markets. On an average the cost of land might be put at Rs.3 lakhs per acre.
- Cost of levelling the site (including fencing etc.) would be Rs.0.15 lakhs and cost of putting up guard rooms would be Rs.50 thousand.
- *Building (Rs.44.96 lakhs)*: The estimated cost of this component works out to around Rs.45 lakhs, major item being growing room at the cost of Rs.25.92 lakhs.
- *Plant & Machinery (Rs.47.00 lakhs)*: The cost of equipping the production unit works out to Rs.30 lakhs, that of compost and casing unit to Rs.7 lakhs and that of installing canning facilities, spawn Lab and other equipments to Rs.10 lakhs.
- *Miscellaneous Fixed Assets (Rs.0.75 lakhs)*: This is the estimated cost of building up a communication system and furnishing.
- *Pre-operative Expenses (Rs.4.25 lakhs)*: These include professional charges, administrative expenses and other start up expenses.

There would be three sources of financing the project as below:

Source	Rs. Lakhs
Farmer's share	53.50
Capital subsidy	21.40
Term loan	32.10
Total	107.00

Returns from the Project: The data on production cost and profitability. The yield from the Unit is estimated at 200 tonnes per annum. Valued at Rs.24,000 per tonne, the annual gross return would come to Rs.48 lakhs.

Financial Analysis

The project profit and loss account over a 10 year period. It would be seen that after accounting for all costs including depreciation, interest, taxes and retained profit etc., there are net cash accruals every year from year 1 to year 10. These, however, decline slightly over the 10 year period from Rs.20.70 lakhs in the first year to Rs.16.10 lakhs in the final year.

SALES AND MARKETING

As mentioned earlier, improving operational efficiency and expanding revenue generation determine viability in the Agaricus spp industry. Having addressed efficiency aspects of operations, retrieving revenue for the product is the other side of the equation. Mushrooms pricing, like any other saleable product, is subject to supply and demand.

Because of improved growing practices and technology, supply has been plentiful and demand has been more or less constant making price increases very rare. Consequently, the objective has been to increase overall demand for mushrooms through group marketing efforts and then use individual marketing and sales strategies to maximized the value of the product sold. The group marketing efforts have concentrated on identifying "what the customer wants" and then educating the grower and the consumer.

Knowing what the customer wants has directed the individual grower's efforts toward producing a higher quality product in a variety of product lines with convenience being an underlying factor. The grower then implements these details into individual sales strategies. Following are the ways in which these issues have been implemented in recent years to expand national, regional, and local consumption and sales.

1. Education
2. Quality
3. Variety
4. Convenience

Education

In recent years marketing organizations have been created to promote the use of mushrooms to the public in general and the restaurant trade in particular.

In the United States and Australia marketing orders have been established with each grower contributing funds consistent with the size of their operation. These organizations have increased the awareness of mushrooms in the public's eye from both dietary and nutritional perspectives.

The marketing organizations work through consumer public relations and food service contacts to achieve their ends. The consumer public relations angle is used to gain favor with newspaper and magazine editors for inclusion of mushroom recipes and dietary information that positively promote mushroom usage.

These initiatives are meant to expose the public to different ways of utilizing mushrooms as stand alone parts of meals or as enhancers to other dishes. Additionally the low calorie, low fat, high mineral content, vitamin B-12 message is promoted to the diet and nutritionally conscious consumer. Through food service contacts the marketing organizations attempt to make inroads into the restaurant trade.

They also work to increase exposure on various cooking television shows. Martha Stewart, Martin Yang, Opra etc. Since very little money is available for direct advertising all of these initiatives provide a subliminal, indirect advertising for the use of mushrooms. Finally, attempts have been made to increase consumption in various ethnic diets that traditionally do not include mushrooms. This type of marketing targets the low consumption end of the general population. Finally the buy fresh message has also been a result of consumer education.

Quality and Service

Quality sells. It has been determined that the consumer demands a fresh, healthy, and high quality product. In response to this demand, improvement in quality and service has increased sales for individual farms within a market. Quality also increases overall consumption, creating demand. In the recent past quality standards have increased in many ways from the actual quality of the mushroom harvested to the quality of packaging and delivery to facilitate sales and marketing.

Mushrooms sold in the United States, Africa, and Latin America are whiter, tighter, better shaped, and cleaner than they were 10 years ago. Correspondingly shelf life has increased because of the increased freshness and quality of the product on the shelf. In Europe and Australia quality standards have been and are much higher with competing retailers extracting progressively higher quality standards every year.

Improved mushroom quality has been achieved culturally by the use of sophisticated environmental control systems, improved nutrition, better casing soils, and controlled pinning techniques. One touch harvesting (growing surface to package) is now virtually universally used and post harvest handling has been improved to move the product to the chiller within one hour.

Vacuum cooling is becoming more prominent because of its ability to reduce pulp temperatures and remove surface moisture in a fraction of the time. Quality is also enhanced at the farm by packaging in controlled environment and getting the product out the door within one day. The cold chain from harvesting, packaging, distribution, through wholesaler and retailer handling, and on to the consumer has become a sophisticated exercise of precision.

Additionally, the concept of quality has gone beyond what meets the eye. The threat of illness and possible legal action upon any retailer, wholesaler and operator for any food contaminant has forced extreme measures to insure food safety.

As a result, product safety has become a major issue in all developed countries and most retailers require HACCP (hazard analysis critical control points) plans to insure the safety of the product they are purchasing. This includes, metal detectors for packaged product, chemical usage compliance, product track-ability, standard operating procedures, hazard identification, and regular biological assays. Random chemical and biological tests are also made at the retail level to insure farm compliance.

While all these improvements to quality and service have been required just to be viable in today's market, they have not generally increased revenue. Retailers are usually unwilling to pay for higher quality and in general higher quality is usually associated with lower yields. Therein lies the conflict. What quality and service standard allows a farm to remain viable in a given market? That is a complex issue to be resolved.

Variety

Research Item: The consumer wants variety, different options, something new and exciting. The A. bisporus industry has responded from selling mushrooms only in bulk in the distant past, to a very broad range of sales options including value added products. The variety of the packages in which mushrooms are sold is perhaps the greatest change that has occurred in the sales and marketing of mushrooms. In addition to consumer demand, competition for store shelf space has driven this change.

Bulk mushrooms are sold in 3, 5, 8, 10-pound sizes, prepack in 8, 12, 16, 18, and 24-ounce sizes. The packages and labels can vary in color, size, and shape depending on the customer. Packed mushrooms themselves vary in size from baby buttons, small, medium, large, to jumbos or giants. These package sizes are available in both brown and white Agaricus spp mushrooms. As an extension of the fresh and healthy image of mushrooms, organically grown mushrooms are being introduced to the market. Open mushrooms are sold in medium to large or Portabella sizes

Portabellas! The addition of brown, open cup Portabella mushrooms has been a magnificent addition to the button mushroom marketing arsenal. It has provided recent evidence of what the development of a new product line can do for a farm, and even an industry. In the USA, Portabella sales have skyrocketed since 1995 and arguably have kept some members of the Agaricus mushroom industry afloat. Although open cup mushrooms have been a long-term staple of the British industry, their recent appearance in the USA has dramatically increased revenue. Whether the idea was borrowed from the British industry or developed independently, those informed say it took at least 8 years to develop the product in the USA. This highlights the dedication and persistence required to develop a new product in any market.

To achieve another dimension of variety Agaricus spp producers also add specialty mushrooms to their product lines. This concept is usually used to provide a marketing advantage for certain producers to garner sales for button mushrooms. Critics of this practice have inferred that this will eventually reduce sales of A. bisporus, but this has not been the case.

Convenience

In today's world, convenience is a critical cornerstone to food marketing. People want delicious, fresh, healthy food prepared in a variety of ways, but do not want to work or spend the time to prepare it. As a result the producer or marketer must find ways of catering to those wants and needs, and profit from it.

The result is the new lines of value added products have entered the markets in recent years. Instead of the package of mushrooms left for the consumer to do something with, the progressive grower/marketer is doing it for them. Common items have been sliced and washed mushrooms, but there is more where that came from. Other value added packs I have seen are mixed brown and white packages, salad packs highlighted by mushrooms, mushrooms packs with enclosed marinades, microwaveable packages with additives, and even mixed packs of button mushrooms and specialty mushrooms.

Convenience extends from the kitchen to the restaurateur as well. In most cases the professional cooks do not want to chop or slice or whatever to the mushroom so the grower/marketer does it for them. In the case of a food processing organization, time is money and any way to make any job quicker and easier is a competitive advantage.

The Future

From the perspective of sales and marketing the future looks like much the same, except more and better. The problem is the source of information and the directional force is loosing impact. The marketing order in the USA has been challenged in the courts and the funding for this organization has been radically reduced.

Funding has also been reduced for industry funded marketing organizations in Australia and Britain. Therefore their role and influence will be reduced. As such the educational initiatives to consumers, restaurants, the media, and the growers about uses of the product and ways to market the product will slow and be less creative. Without the external perspective of an inter-industrial marketing organization we will be more introspective and our marketing ideas will be less imaginative. However we will see some change.

Education will continue and promotion through printed and screened media will continue. Quality and service will continue to improve, but particularly mushroom quality in the western hemisphere. As growing systems are renewed and rebuilt technology will improve quality. Also the retailers will pressure growers to provide better and better quality, which will require cultural changes. Black casing and pinning techniques such as described by Samp (1994) to control pin numbers will be used to improve quality. Product sizing will get larger because of the need to maximize yield and harvesting efficiency.

Product lines will continue to expand with convenience in mind. Baby buttons will become more common because of the number of consumer uses. Sliced mushrooms will expand and prewashed, diced, mashed, and quartered mushrooms will be seen. More value added packages featuring mushrooms will be sold with more options of marinade, salad packs, alternative flavor packets, pasta inclusion, and instant side portion possibilities. New options will be introduced from new strains of Agaricus spp with enhanced flavor, color, and keeping quality.

The health factor will be addressed by growing mushrooms that will possess more essential elements. Because mushrooms uptake basic elements more easily selenium and other minerals can be incorporated into the tissue, thereby presenting health advantages. Since the general population will trend away from red meats, the meaty texture of mushrooms will be viewed as a bulk additive for vegetarian diets. The high concentration of vitamin B-12, a vitamin found in meat but not in plants, will enhance that perception. Also related to health, product safety will become more of an issue in years to come, perhaps to the extent that an inspector will be required to give a seal of approval prior to sale. The issue will have international repercussions since a tainted mushroom grown and processed in China will become a marketing problem in the USA. The food safety consequences as they relate to mushrooms, Agaricus spp and otherwise, could be severe.

The future will see gradual increase of consumption, but unfortunately not as high as growers would like. Partially because of reduced marketing efforts by professionals, but also due to the gradual nature of change of the social structure in any country. Mushroom consumption has been seen to reflect the education, sophistication, and disposable income of a population, not necessarily a culture. These things do not change quickly so there is not much reason to believe mushroom consumption will jump significantly.

THE INDUSTRY

In recent years the industry has consolidated into fewer growers producing more mushrooms. Because of cultural factors and single farm expansions, production has increased faster than the rate of consumption. As a result, economic Darwinism has asserted itself causing the nonprogressive, noncompetitive mushroom businesses to cease operation. They have either closed or been purchased and reopened by existing competitors. Since these survivors are good competitors and because they can lower cost to produce by distributing fixed cost over more production, they are likely to grow and remain viable.

The wholesalers and retailers are also selecting for consolidation because they seek to reduce their cost and simplify their operations by dealing with fewer suppliers/growers. As such the large retailers are inclined to deal with the largest suppliers because they are the only ones that can supply the required volumes. Additionally the retailers prefer not to deal with more than two suppliers.

Consequently the small operators are relegated to the small independent retailers who are under pressure from their larger, more efficient, or at least more influential competitors. To keep pace the smaller growers will form strategic alliances to market larger volumes by pooling their resources. These strategic alliances, whether with groups of small growers or alliances between larger growers and a few smaller ones, will have mixed results. Leadership issues and differing opinions between independent entrepreneurs will have to be circumvented in order for these alliances to be successful. As a result the trend toward consolidation will continue until a critical mass of suppliers is established for any market.

Mushroom farms will exist in areas of low cost, low regulation environments. As such, flight to nearby, developing economies will continue. With that flight, import of processed mushrooms of all sorts to the developed economies will expand. Fresh mushroom sales support farms in developed economies, at least temporarily, because of the demand for safe, high quality produce.

The saving grace for button mushroom growers near undeveloped economies is that mushroom shelf life is relatively short. This will all change when mushroom strains are developed with longer shelf life and/or when irradiation becomes an acceptable way of "cleansing" fresh product. When either or both of these conditions occur the mushroom production industry will see a further shift to the developing economies such as Latin American, eastern European, and southeast Asian countries where labor willing to work on mushroom farms is plentiful. Unless, of course technology has progressed to the point where harvesting and packaging can be mechanized. Silsoe will see it's day. Technology is the key! Once again movement to advanced, efficient, cost effective systems will determine the viability of the mushroom grower in developed countries.

Finally as already mentioned, Agaricus spp consumption will increase at a steady, slow rate although specialty mushrooms as both food items and nutritional or medical supplements will expand at a much higher rate of growth. Specialty mushrooms will not transplant or replace button mushrooms. Button mushrooms are the introduction to fungal foods, the staple of the fungal food kingdom.

They are to other fungal foods as potatoes are to vegetables. I do not see specialty mushrooms crowding out button mushroom sales in the reasonable future. Since there is still such a large percentage of the consuming public that are infrequent mushroom eaters, there is still a large market to be realized. Additionally, in cookbooks and recipes button mushrooms are ubiquitous and interchangeable with any other specialty mushroom. Since it is always easily available, A. bisporus can gain as much from specialty popularity as specialty mushrooms gain as the next step beyond the button mushroom in the culinary adventure.

8

Identification and Control of Cassava Diseases

INTRODUCTION

Cassava is one of the most important staple food crops in Africa. Three continents, Africa, Asia and Latin America produce large amounts of cassava roots. Over 500 million people in the tropical world particularly Africa depend on cassava as one of their major staple foods. In Asia and Latin America, productions are largely used as raw materials for industries, as animal feed or for export markets.

In Africa, the bulk of production is depended on as food by humans. Cassava is one of the most significant food security crops in some parts of sub-saharan Africa and has proved to be the most dependable crop in a number of countries as the last line of defence against famine. In the last decade, cassava is cultivated not just for human consumption in sub-saharan Africa but also to provide raw materials for emerging industries that depend on products from the roots, particularly starch.

The ability of cassava to thrive or do well on poor soils gives it an advantage over yam and the other root and tubers, grains or legumes in Africa. For many years to come cassava will continue to be an important source of carbohydrate to millions of people, particularly the rural and urban poor in Africa. Cassava, therefore, has to be managed more effectively than it is currently experiencing to increase its yield per unit area to ensure that more than enough roots in particular are produced to satisfy domestic, industrial and food security requirements at all times.

Among the factors that affect cassava production, diseases and pests still remain the major constraints that can bring Africa's cassava production to a halt. The recent East African Cassava Mosaic pandemic and the food shortages that resulted from it adds value to the above statement. African cassava mosaic disease is still widespread and causes severe yield losses in production systems that depend on susceptible cultivars. Cassava bacterial blight, anthracnose, bud necrosis, leaf spots and root rot diseases affect yields of cassava in almost all producing countries in Africa. Information on yield losses due to diseases are often based on estimates but observations indicate that losses are significant in most of the cassava growing areas of Ghana.

What is the Importance of Cassava Diseases?

- Diseases cause low yields of edible roots.
- Low yields due to diseases affect incomes of farmers.
- Food security is reduced by diseases.
- Severe outbreaks of diseases such as cassava bacterial blight can result in famine (in whole communities or countries).
- Cassava diseases that affect stems can lead to loss or shortages in the supply of planting materials.
- Loss of leaves through diseases can affect the availability of leafy vegetables.
- Loss of leaves and poor yield of storage roots can affect livestock production in communities that use cassava as animal feed.

Unfortunately, however, cassava farmers in most producing countries in Africa do very little or nothing to control diseases and pests of the crop. An impression that exists among cassava farmers (particularly in Ghana) is that cassava cuttings will give some root yields no matter where they are planted even if no attention is paid to the plants. Also, it is common to meet farmers who regard symptoms of certain diseases of cassava as signs of plant maturity. These incorrect impressions need to be corrected to increase yields of cassava. Farmers must be made aware of diseases and their importance and why it is necessary that diseases must be controlled.

This text is, therefore, written to introduce cassava as a crop with diseases that need to be controlled to increase yields to meet demands for consumption, food security and raw material requirements of industry. Symptoms of diseases have been shown or described to make disease identification an easy exercise. Actions that can be undertaken to control specific diseases have been described. Agriculture extension agents, farmers and students of agriculture will find this small text a very useful guide to controlling diseases of cassava.

AFRICAN CASSAVA MOSAIC DISEASE

Africa cassava mosaic disease (ACMD) is the most important of all cassava diseases known in Africa. Almost all traditional cultivars of cassava cultivated in different countries on the African continent are susceptible to this disease. Yield losses due to cassava mosaic disease range between 20-95% in susceptible cultivars. On a continent that experiences food insecurity, losses of this magnitude in yield of such an important food crop need cannot be accepted. Most traditional farmers who constitute the majority of food producers in Africa do not control mosaic disease. In Ghana for example, yields of cultivars susceptible to mosaic disease are under 10 t/ha in most farming communities compared to yields of 30 t/ha or more that can be achieved with improved varieties resistant to mosaic disease.

Causal Organism and Symptoms of the Disease

Cassava mosaic disease is caused by a virus. The common visible symptom of the disease is the leaf mosaic. Leaves showing this symptom have patches of normal green colour mixed with different proportions of yellow and white depending on the variety. These chlorotic patches indicate reduced amounts of chlorophyll in the leaves, which affects photosynthesis and therefore yields. In some susceptible varieties, the leaf blades become distorted and are often reduced in size. Leaf production as a commercial activity can be severely affected when susceptible varieties are depended on.

In highly susceptible cultivars, stunted growth is common, especially in plants that experience early infections. These plants often develop poor stems that are not useful as planting materials. Poor root yield is associated with stunted growth.

Transmission of ACMD

Infected plants are the main sources of the virus responsible for the disease. The white fly Bemisia tabacci is the vector in the transmission of the disease from plant to plant through its feeding on cassava leaves. Virus numbers increase in leaves and stems of infected plants. The disease spreads largely through the use of infected stem cuttings as planting materials.

CONTROL

Use of Resistant Varieties

Improved varieties of cassava resistant to mosaic disease are available in production systems of a number of countries. These resistant varieties have been introduced consciously into areas with high disease pressures to improve yields. Significant increases in yield have been achieved through the introduction of improved varieties in some countries including Ghana. Agriculture extension agents must help farmers in their operational areas to access desired disease resistant varieties.

Farmers cultivating cassava on a large scale, to feed starch producing factories for example, need varieties that are not just high yielding but also mosaic disease resistant to maintain stable yields.

Observations indicate that some improved varieties of cassava lose their resistance after a number of years of planting in areas with high mosaic disease pressures. Performance of improved varieties introduced to control diseases therefore needs to be monitored continuously to detect loss of resistance and ensure early replacement with new cultivars.

Most of the traditional varieties of cassava cultivated extensively by farmers in Africa are susceptible to mosaic disease. Peasant farmers in most circumstances prefer their local traditional varieties despite being low yielding and susceptible to mosaic disease because of certain unique cooking qualities. It is necessary that yields and disease resistance attributes of these traditional varieties are improved in the interest of traditional cassava farmers who actually produce the bulk of the cassava consumed on the continent.

Use of Healthy Planting Materials

The spread of the disease as mentioned earlier is largely due to the use of infected cuttings as propagating materials. Mosaic disease can be controlled effectively through the use of healthy or virus free planting materials. Farmers must select stems from plants with no mosaic symptoms to produce cuttings. If the source of planting materials is from a branching susceptible variety, spread of the disease can be reduced if cuttings for planting are derived from the branches rather than the main stem. Cuttings from the main stem often sprout with the disease. In non-branching varieties it is preferable to avoid using cuttings from the basal portion of stems as planting material. Cuttings from the basal portions of stems give rise to young diseased plants at sprouting. Plants that develop from healthy cuttings often grow vigorously to escape early infections and give good leaf and root yields. Programmes of planting material multiplication that supply stems to large numbers of farmers must ensure that disease free stems are distributed to prevent large scale spread of diseases especially into new communities.

Roguing

The practice of removing the few diseased plants showing symptoms of the disease from a population of healthy ones and destroying them (roguing) reduces spread of diseases particularly on farms. Regular inspection of plants on a farm is necessary if effective disease control is to be achieved. Young plants from sprouted cassava stem cuttings showing mosaic symptoms can be replaced with new healthy ones to maintain high planting densities.

Fig. Cassava plants showing healthy leaves.
Note absence of chlorotic areas.

Fig. Cassava plant showing the typical leaf mosaic symptom. Note the yellow and green patches on leaf blades (chlorotic areas).

Fig. A severely infected plant of a highly susceptible cultivar showing distorted leaves and poorly developed stems.

Fig. Root yields of two plants planted on the same day and harvested twelve months after planting. The smaller plant is showing all the important features of the mosaic disease.

CASSAVA BACTERIAL BLIGHT DISEASE

Cassava bacterial blight (CBB) can be found in all cassava producing countries and in the opinion of the authors is the most devastating of all known diseases of the crop in Africa.

In susceptible cultivars, CBB can cause 100% yield loss when environmental conditions optimum for disease outbreaks occur. CBB causes death of leaves and stems and as such severe yield losses are often encountered when outbreaks of the disease occur. Severe outbreaks of CBB in epidemic proportions caused famine in Zaire (now Congo DR) and Nigeria in the early 1970s. In severe outbreaks of the disease shortages in the supply of planting materials may result.

ROOT ROT DISEASES

Root rot diseases are very important because rotten storage roots of cassava are unwholesome for consumption. Severe outbreaks of root rot diseases on a large scale may result in food shortages or even threaten food security in communities that depend very much on cassava as a major staple food.

Root rot diseases may lead to death of entire plants - a situation that can affect the availability of planting materials and leafy vegetables. Root rot diseases can also affect the supply of storage roots to large scale processing factories that depend on cassava as the only raw material.

Causes and Symptoms of Root Rot Diseases

Peasant farmers that cultivate cassava are often quick in attributing root rots to waterlogging and periodic flooding of land planted to cassava.

It is true that waterlogged soils are not good for cassava production because they promote rots. There are however other causes of cassava root rot that may be due to pathogenic microorganisms (fungi and bacteria) and some parasitic mushrooms. In most parts of Ghana root rot diseases are caused by microorganisms.

In the last fifteen years, however, a parasitic mushroom (Polyporus sulphureus), originally suspected to be pathogenic on woody plants, has been found attacking cassava plants and causing severe root rots in Ghana. This parasitic mushroom is capable of causing 100% yield loss on farms where susceptible cultivars are planted.

Another parasitic fungus that produces small whitish fruiting bodies at the distal end of attacked cassava plants was discovered in Ashanti region of Ghana in the last three years. The fruiting bodies of this parasitic fungus appear late in disease development and storage roots of attacked plants may be completely rotten by the time the whitish fruiting bodies become visible on stems.

The bases of attacked stems become weak, and lodging is very common in fields attacked by this parasitic fungus. An interesting feature of this rot disease is that certain flies use the rotten roots as breeding grounds for their larvae. A characteristic foul smell is associated with this root rot disease. Yield losses as high as 45% have been recorded in fields of susceptible cultivars.

Certain rot causing organisms actively attack storage roots when they overstay in the soil or when harvesting is delayed. A number of fungal species including Botryodiplodia theobromae cause rots of this kind in several soil types. An example of this rot where the roots on display were harvested 24 months after planting.

General symptoms of root rot diseases include wilting of leaves, which in most cases is accompanied by defoliation. Other symptoms include swollen roots with colored inner tissues.

Rotten roots may be soft and produce an offensive odour (this is often associated with rots caused by bacteria). Shoot or stem dieback is a feature of plants with underground rotten roots. Root rot diseases may lead finally to death of infected plants.

Methods of Spread of Root Rot Diseases

Root rot diseases caused by some microorganisms require water to spread. Reproductive or infective units of certain rot causing fungi have to swim to reach a new host to initiate a new attack.

Plant debris, especially rotten roots, left on fields after harvest are sources of spores or other infective structures that can cause new infections.

Root rot diseases can spread through the use of farm tools such as cutlasses and hoes contaminated with spores of fungal organisms or bacteria cells.

Fig. Bright yellow fruiting bodies of the parasitic mushroom Polyporus sulphureus that causes severe root rot of cassava.

Fig. The parasitic mushroom Polyporus sulphureus (arrowed) growing on a young cassava plant.

Fig. Rotten root of cassava (R) caused by the parasitic mushroom Polyporus sulphureus (M) (the fungus leaves a yellow pigment in the rotten storage roots).

Fig. Whitish fruiting bodies of a newly discovered root rot causing fungus growing at the base of a susceptible cassava plant.

Fig. A dislodged infected stem showing the whitish fruiting bodies of the rot causing fungus.

Fig. Rotten root of cassava harvested 24 months after planting. Note the inner colored rotten tissue.

CONTROL OF ROOT ROT DISEASES

Site and Land Selection

One important characteristic of land suitable for cassava cultivation is that it should not be subject to flooding. Waterlogged soils also promote root rot diseases and must be avoided at all times. Farming close to rivers and streams must be avoided as these areas are likely to be flooded at some time in the year. A sandy loamy soil that is well drained is a good soil type for cassava.

It is advisable not to cultivate cassava on land that has a history of root rots and other major diseases. Any land showing the presence of any of the root rot causing mushrooms described above should not be planted to cassava. If the only land available for cassava cultivation has a history of root rots, then good disease management practices must be maintained if good yields are expected.

Land suitable for cassava production must be fertile enough to give a healthy crop of plants. Healthy plants are not easily attacked by diseases. Fertility of poor soils can be improved through the addition of organic fertilizers such as poultry manure if inorganic fertilizers prove too expensive.

Disease Resistant or TolerantVvarieties

Farmers are always advised to plant disease resistant or tolerant varieties if they are available. In localities with a long history of root rot diseases, farmers must consult their Agricultural Extension agents for advice on the best varieties to cultivate to minimize losses in yields. Results of work in Polyporus endemic areas in Ghana indicate that some varieties tested give yields two times higher than the susceptible local cultivars.

Quarantine Measures

Cassava stems from fields with visible signs of root rot diseases must not be used as planting materials, even if they look healthy. Stems from such fields are likely to carry spores of root rot fungi.

Localized or national quarantine measures to check movement of planting materials from root rot endemic areas into new localities may be necessary to check the spread of root rot diseases.

Good Farm Sanitation

Destruction of plant debris including rotten roots and stems bearing fruiting bodies immediately after harvest is a good measure that destroys spores of pathogenic fungi. The leathery fruiting body after harvest can persist for over a year and is a good source of spores for new attacks in the subsequent season's crops. Disease severity on farms can be reduced through destruction of debris that carry spores into the next planting season.

Fruiting bodies of parasitic mushrooms such as Polyporus sulphureus start their development on cassava plants after the first few rains following the dry season. Regular harvesting and destruction of young fruiting bodies shortly after they appear and destroying them through burning reduces severity of rots on farms. Harvesting and destroying the fruiting bodies soon after they appear prevent them from producing spores required for the spread of the disease.

Fig. Rotten cassava roots left on a harvested field. This is a good source of spores and other infective structures of pathogens for new infections in the next season's crop of cassava..

Early Harvesting

Some root rot causing organisms actively invade and degrade storage roots when they are well developed and harvesting is delayed. Early harvesting therefore prevents or reduces incidence of rots in some varieties of cassava.

Fig. Stems of cassava with an attached old leathery fruiting body of the root rot fungus Polyporus sulphureus (arrowed).

Crop Rotation

Most root rot causing pathogens are soilborne and therefore continuous cultivation of susceptible varieties on the same piece of land may lead to a build-up of pathogen populations on a farm. Incidence and severity of diseases on the same field therefore increases year after year.

Rotating cassava with cereals or grains every three years can help reduce the effects of root rot diseases on a farm. It is advisable not to plant cassava continuously for three years or more on the same piece of land especially in localities with high disease pressures. The absence of host plants from a field for a reasonable period of time deprives pathogens of their nutrient supply and this often leads into a decline in pathogen populations.

Fallow

Fallowing of land after five or more years of continuous cassava cultivation for a period of three to five years is a good measure that can reduce incidence and severity of cassava diseases. When practised properly, fallowing can help eliminate a disease completely from a locality or reduce its incidence significantly. In localities where pressure on available land is high, crop rotation may be the better of the two options.

Clean Farm Tools

Farm tools such as cutlasses, hoes and ploughs used on fields with a root rot history must be cleaned immediately after use before being used on a second farm. This reduces the spread of diseases from farm to farm.

Avoid Planting Cassava as the First Crop after Clearing Woodlands or Forests

Certain parasitic mushrooms can grow on woody trees or cassava depending on which one is available or preferred. It is therefore not advisable to cultivate cassava as the first crop just after clearing forests or woodlands. In the absence of woody trees, introduced cassava plants will be attacked.

Woody stumps left on farms after clearing woodlands may serve as secondary hosts or reservoirs to fungal pathogens that attack cassava. It is therefore a good practice to remove stumps from cleared fields.

Host Range

Pathogenic organisms causing root rot diseases of cassava, particularly fungi, may have more than one host. This implies that a single pathogen can cause diseases in more than one species of plant. Some root rot fungi of cassava can attack soybean and sunflower. The Polyporus root rot mushroom can attack a number of crops including yam and citrus. Care should therefore be taken in the selection of crops for rotation or intercropping with cassava.

CAUSES AND SYMPTOMS OF DISEASES

The disease is caused by a bacterium (Xanthomonas campestris pv. manihotis). Distinctive symptoms of the disease include the appearance of water soaked spots or lesions on leaves of infected plants. The spots often start along the veins, margins and tips of leaf blades. As the disease develops, neighboring spots join together to form large brown patches or blights killing the leaf blade as it expands. The leaf dries or wilts and finally falls.

In some susceptible cultivars, creamy or yellowish brown gummy exudates are discharged on leaves or stems but often distinctively on leaf petioles of infected plants.

Petioles of blighted leaves are often horizontally orientated to the main stem axis. In advanced stages of the disease, dieback of stems is common. It is common also to find new shoots developing from dead ends of stems of severely infected plants.

Transmission of CBB

The spread of the disease occurs if the bacterial causal organism is transferred from an infected plant to a new susceptible plant. Often the bacterium gains entry into plants through wounds or openings or scratches on leaves and stems.

Farm tools particularly cutlasses can easily be used to transmit the disease from farm to farm if tools are not cleaned after work in an infected field.

Stems of infected plants are sources of the bacterium that causes the disease. The spread of the disease is largely through the use of cuttings derived from infected stems in starting new farms.

It is common to find grasshoppers on plants showing symptoms of CBB compared to healthy plants in the same area. This observation has been made in several disease documentation surveys. Grasshoppers and other insects that feed on cassava may therefore be involved in the transmission of the disease from plant to plant on the same farm or over long distances.

CONTROL

Resistant Varieties

In CBB endemic areas or localities with reported cases of the disease, farmers must consciously search for and plant CBB resistant varieties if economic yields of cassava are to be sustained.

Rouging of Plants

Farmers cultivating susceptible varieties regularly must inspect their plants and remove those showing symptoms of the disease and destroy them through burning. This practice of search and destroy must seriously follow the first few rains coming after the dry season. It is safe to eat storage roots from CBB infected plants. Early detection and destruction of plants showing symptoms of the disease can prevent or slow down the spread of the disease on a farm.

Fallow

If complete outbreaks on whole farms are observed, it may be necessary to harvest roots immediately and destroy stems and leaves and other plant debris through burning. Infected plant debris may also be ploughed deep into soil. In both situations the land must be allowed to fallow for few years (3 years minimum) before it is planted again to cassava. The bacterium responsible for the disease is unable to survive over a long period outside the host.

Crop Rotation

In communities where land for peasant farming is scarce, fallowing of land may not be a good disease control option. After destruction of infected plant debris as described in the preceding section, cereals, grains or legumes can be planted on the same piece of land. After three seasons the land can be returned to cassava.

Quarantine Measures

In cases of localized outbreaks of CBB it may be necessary for a localized quarantine measure to be implemented that ensures that planting materials from CBB outbreak zones are not moved into other communities. Farmers must be educated to appreciate the importance of such a measure.

Quarantine authorities must monitor movement of planting materials across borders and ensure that uncertified planting materials are quarantined to be sure of their safety.

Tissue culture materials from unreliable laboratories or sources must pass quarantine regulations before they are allowed into cropping systems of countries.

Use of Healthy Planting Material

Farmers must consciously harvest stems from healthy plants completely free of any of the described symptoms of the disease. It is generally wise to avoid using planting materials from any farm suspected to be under CBB attack even if symptoms of the disease have not been observed on plants.

Pest Control

Grasshoppers and other insects that can serve as carriers of the bacterium from farm to farm must be controlled using environmentally friendly measures. Controlling grasshopper movement after the early first rains of the wet season can reduce the spread of CBB.

Fig. A typical leaf from a CBB infected plant showing two important symptoms of the disease. A- blighted patch; B- a brownish gummy exudate deposited on the reddish leaf petiole.

Fig. A CBB infected plant showing severe dieback. Note the great loss of leaves.

Fig. A CBB infected plant showing wilting (arrowed leaf W) and grasshoppers (G). The grasshoppers are believed to be involved in spreading the disease from plant to plant.

CASSAVA ANTHRACHNOSE DISEASE

Cassava anthracnose disease (CAD) is widespread in most of the cassava growing regions of Africa. The disease is caused by a fungus (Collectothricum gloeosporioides) that is also capable of causing diseases on other food crops. It is estimated that CAD causes yield losses in the neighbourhood of 30% or more in susceptible cultivars. The disease affects both leaf and stem production. Severe anthracnose attacks can cause death of stems which can affect the availability of planting materials especially in large scale production systems.

Symptoms

The main distinctive symptom of CAD is the appearance of cankers or sore-like lesions on the stem of susceptible varieties. The cankers may be formed at the nodes bearing petioles or along any part of the stem depending on the variety.

Depending on varieties or existing environmental factors, cankers may be small or large. Young and older parts of stems may bear cankers. Cankers may develop cracks, exposing inner tissues of stems to the external environment. Cracks when present serve as entry points for other disease causing organisms. Development of cankers may result in distortions in the shape of infected stems.

Wilting is observed in infected plants and this is often accompanied by defoliation. Dieback of stems is an important symptom of the disease and in some varieties entire infected stems may die back and break off. The symptoms of the disease often start and develop rapidly in the wet season.

Fig. An infected cassava stem showing cankers or lesions (arrowed). Note that the main stem on display has lost its leaves.

Fig. A severely infected stem showing cankers (arrowed) and poorly developing young branches. This type of cankers could potentially produce cracks in the stem.

Transmission of the Disease

Spores of the disease causing fungus are spread by wind or rain splashes and may gain entry through wounds on stems to establish the disease. Feeding holes made by the sap feeding bug Pseudotheraptus devastans may also be the entry holes for the spores of the causal organism.

Planting stem cuttings bearing cankers of the disease is one of the means of spreading the disease into new areas. Shoots that develop from cuttings bearing cankers develop symptoms of the disease early and are likely to suffer higher yield losses.

CONTROL

Resistant Varieties

The most reliable control measure is to use desired anthracnose resistant varieties particularly in localities with high CAD pressures. Cultivation of disease resistant or tolerant varieties is even more important in large scale production systems that require stable high yields to feed industries that depend mainly on cassava as raw material.

Healthy Planting Material

In situations where desired varieties are susceptible to CAD, healthy stems free of cankers and dieback tissues must be selected to provide cuttings for new plantings.

Healthy cuttings sprout well and give rise to young vigorous growing plants that are likely to escape early infections. Where canker bearing stems are the only available sources of planting materials, stem cuttings must be dipped in appropriate fungicides recommended by extension agents in their operational areas. Spores and other fungal materials of disease causing fungi can be destroyed by a few minutes of dipping in suitable fungicides.

Farm Sanitation

Stems and leaves from infected plants after harvest must be destroyed by burning to reduce the amount of fungal spores and other infective structures that can cause infections in the next generation of plants.

Host Range of Causal Organism

The fungus that causes cassava anthracnose can also cause diseases on other food crops such as pepper, avocado, banana, pawpaw and yam. Spores therefore can be transferred from these plants to cause infections in cassava. Plant debris from plants suspected to be harboring the anthracnose causing fungus must be destroyed by burning, particularly during land preparation before cassava is planted.

CASSAVA BUD NECROSIS

Bud necrosis is a fungal disease usually found in cassava growing areas with humid environments. Incidence of the disease is therefore higher in the humid forest zones compared to the drier savanna areas. Observations indicate that poor farm sanitation (weedy fields) in high relative humidity zones promotes high incidence and severity of the disease.

Symptoms

The main symptom of the disease is the appearance of dark or grey patches or necrotic lesions on stem surfaces of susceptible cultivars. The necrotic areas are made up of fungal tissue of the causal organism. Necrotic areas often cover buds on the stem giving the disease its name.

Transmission

The disease spreads through spores that are carried by wind from plant to plant or from farm to farm. Bud necrosis of cassava, however, largely spreads through the use of infected stem cuttings bearing necrotic lesions in planting.

CONTROL

Healthy Planting Materials

In farming communities where the desired varieties grown are susceptible to the disease, farmers must use cuttings derived from healthy stems completely free from necrotic lesions.

Stem cuttings with infected buds often fail to sprout when planted, resulting in poor plant establishment on farms. In large scale commercial production farms, refilling or replacement of cuttings that fail to sprout increases production cost to farmers.

Good FarmPpractices

Incidence and severity of bud necrosis is significantly reduced on farms when good planting distances that allow free movement of air around plants are maintained. The disease is better controlled when weeds are also well managed. These good practices contribute effectively to disease control when healthy planting materials are always used to start farms.

Plant debris, especially stem pieces bearing necrotic lesions. must be destroyed by burning immediately after harvest to reduce sources of infective fungal spores.

Host Range

The fungus that causes bud necrosis can also live on other crops such yam, banana and mango. Debris from these plants suspected to be harboring disease causing organisms must be destroyed by burning, particularly during land preparation.

Fig. Cassava plant with bud necrosis lesions on stem. The dark patches are the necrotic areas.

Fig. A susceptible cultivar of cassava with grey necrotic areas on bud (arrowed).

BROWN AND WHITE LEAF SPOT DISEASES

Brown and white leaf spots are relatively minor diseases of cassava caused by fungi. White leaf spot is less frequently seen in most cassava growing areas in Ghana compared to brown spots. In Ghana, symptoms of brown spots are seen by some farmers as signs of crop maturity.

Symptoms

The key symptom of brown leaf spot disease is the appearance of few to several brown spots on the upper surface of leaves of susceptible varieties.

Margins of brown spots are irregular. The middle of brown spots may break given rise to 'shot holes'. White leaf spot disease is characterized by the presence of white spots on the upper surface of leaves of infected plants. Symptoms of both diseases may be found on the same leaf.

Control

As mentioned earlier, several farmers regard symptoms of brown leaf spot disease as signs of crop maturity because the spots according to these farmers show up when plants are fully grown. Very little or nothing is therefore done to control the disease.

Fig. Leaves showing brown spots.

Fig. Cassava leaf with white leaf spots.

Observations indicate, however, that in some susceptible cultivars brown spots appear early after planting. In such varieties large areas of the surface of leaves may be covered by brown spots reducing the total surface area available for photosynthesis. Yields will be reduced in situations of this nature. Efforts must therefore be made to control leaf spot diseases.

Infected leaves that drop from plants are sources of spores of leaf spot causing fungi. From infected leaves spores are carried by wind or rain splashes to cause new infections. Weeds can also serve as sources from which leaf spot fungi may spread. Good weed control practices can, therefore, reduce the spread of leaf spot diseases.

9

The Principal Cultivated Mushroom Species

MUSHROOM CULTIVATION

The commercial mushroom, Agaricus bisporus (Lange) Imbach, is the principal mushroom species cultivated in Canada, representing at least 95% of the production. Canada produces about 85 000 tonnes of mushrooms annually at a farm gate value ranging between $250 and 300 million. Ontario continues to cultivate over 50% of the nation's mushrooms, followed second by British Columbia at about one-third. Two varieties are cultivated, a hybrid off-white and a brown. The brown variety, depending on the degree of its maturity at harvest, is known in the market as portabella (open with gills exposed) or cremini (closed with no gills exposed). Ten to fifteen per cent of the total Canadian production is the brown variety. Other species, such as various oyster mushroom species, shiitake and enoki mushrooms, are also cultivated in Canada.

Agaricus is a saprophytic fungus and must obtain its nutrients from the materials on which it is growing. The basic ingredient is wheat straw, which is formulated with horse, chicken or turkey manures or waste grain residues to increase the total nitrogen value. Gypsum (calcium sulfate) is added to buffer the pH during composting and to improve the compost texture. Mushroom compost is prepared either in long windrows (approx 1.8-2 m wide x 2-2.4 m high) or in bulk chambers (approx 6 m wide x 7 m high, with or without doors or a roof).

The composting process includes 2 stages. The first composting stage begins with a thorough mixing and hydration of the dry ingredients. Over the next 2 weeks the raw materials are transformed through aerobic biological and chemical activities. Once the straws are soft, well hydrated, dark-chocolate brown in colour, and rich in microbes, and the compost odour is strong in ammonia, the compost is ready for the second stage of composting. In this stage the substrate is pasteurized and then held at specific temperatures that favour conversion (aka conditioning) of residual nitrogen compounds into microbial protein, later to be used by the mushroom fungus. This process usually takes between 5 and 10 days.

Once the composting process is complete, the substrate is seeded with a pure culture of the mushroom fungus. The mushroom seed, known in the industry as "spawn," is prepared in an expressly designed facility by inoculating hydrated and sterilized cereal grains (eg, wheat, rye or millet) with pure mycelia of the mushroom fungus. This spawn is thoroughly mixed into the compost. During the two-week spawn-run period the substrate temperature is maintained between 24 and 27ºC with a high relative humidity, and a carbon dioxide (generated by the fungus) level between 10 000 and 20 000 ppm.

The substrate, although it may be perfectly colonized by the mushroom fungus, will not produce mushrooms unless the surface is covered with a layer (aka casing layer) of wetted loam soil or peat moss, buffered with lime (calcium carbonate) to a slightly basic pH.

To stimulate normal looking mushrooms to appear, the microenvironment on the surface of the casing is changed within about 5 days of casing by reducing the air temperature to about 17ºC, the compost temperature to about 20ºC, the carbon dioxide to about 1000 ppm and the relative humidity to about 85%. In 10 days mushrooms will be ready for harvest.

Mushrooms grow in cycles, known as breaks or flushes. The environmental conditions maintained for production are similar to those used to stimulate the mushrooms to form. Industry practice is to harvest for 2 or 3 breaks. Each break is harvested over 3 to 5 days with a non-harvesting period of about 2 days. As the white or cremini mushrooms reach market maturity they are manually picked before the gills are exposed, with growers calculating that the mushrooms will remain closed for several days under refrigeration. Portabella mushrooms are allowed to "open," exposing the gills, and are harvested with the maximum diameter but with the margin of the mushroom slightly curved toward the gill tissue. The stem is trimmed and each mushroom is gently placed into the consumer packaging. The delicate mushrooms, except for adjusting package weight, are not touched again. Promptly after harvest, the mushrooms are cooled to 2ºC using passive (refrigerator-like environment), forced air or vacuum cooling. They are maintained at refrigeration temperature until they are placed on the warmer display counter.

The used compost is pasteurized prior to its removal from the growing rooms to manage any PEST problems that may have developed during mushroom production. This material can be used to grow earthworms, as a potting soil mix, to assist in cleaning up mine drainage or break down pesticides, or used as a casing material or in land reclamation. Principally, it is recycled as a soil conditioner.

GROWING MUSHROOM

Mushrooms are our most unique growing vegetable, and mushroom growing is one of the most unusual stories in agriculture.

White Mushrooms

White mushrooms, like all mushrooms, grow from microscopic spores, not seeds. Plants growing from spores are called fungi. A mature mushroom will drop as many as 16 billion spores. Spores must be collected in the nearly sterile environment of a laboratory and then used to inoculate grains or seeds to produce a product called spawn (the mushroom farmer's equivalent of seed).

Because mushrooms have no chlorophyll, they must get all their nutrients from organic matter in their growing medium. The medium, called compost, is scientifically formulated of various materials such as straw, corn cobs, cotton seed and cocoa seed hulls, gypsum and nitrogen supplements. Preparing the compost takes one to two weeks. Then it's pasteurized and placed in large trays or beds. Next the spawn is worked into the compost and the growing takes place in specially constructed houses where the farmers can regulate the crucial aspects of heat and humidity.

In two to three weeks, the compost becomes filled with the root structure of the mushroom, a network of lacy white filaments called mycelium. At that point, a layer of pasteurized peat moss is spread over the compost. The temperature of the compost and the humidity of the room must be carefully controlled in order for the mycelium to develop fully. Eventually, tiny white protrusions form on the mycelium and push up through the peat moss. Farmers call this pinning.

The pins continue to grow, becoming the mushroom caps, which are actually the fruit of the plant, just as a tomato is the fruit of a tomato plant. It takes 17 to 25 days to produce mature mushrooms after the peat moss is applied. Size is no indication of maturity in mushrooms. Perfectly ripe ones vary from small buttons to large caps.

Each crop is harvested over a period of several weeks and then the house is emptied and steam-sterilized before the process begins again. The remaining compost is recycled for potting soil. The harvested mushrooms are set in carts, refrigerated and then packaged and shipped quickly to supermarkets, food processors and restaurants. The entire process from the time the farmer starts preparing the compost until the mushrooms are harvested and shipped to market takes about four months.

Crimini Mushrooms

Crimini mushrooms are grown and harvested in the same manner as the white mushroom. The reason they have a darker color and slightly denser texture is that they come from a different strain of spores.

Portabella Mushrooms

Portabella mushrooms are also grown like the white mushrooms. Actually, the portabella is a mature crimini. It's usually three to seven days older than the Crimini when harvested. As a result of their longer growing period, portabellas develop much larger caps, ranging up to six inches in diameter.

Oyster Mushrooms

Oyster mushrooms, like other mushrooms, are grown in mushroom houses, but they require a bit more humidity and fresh air than the white variety. They grow well on a range of agricultural and wood waste products, including hardwood chips, chopped cereal straws or corn cobs. After the growing medium is pasteurized and cooled, it is inoculated; that is, mixed with spawn and packed into long, tubular shaped plastic bags. Holes are punched in the bags to allow the mycelium to breathe and the bags are hung up or set on racks in the growing rooms. After about 14 days, the mushrooms pop out through the holes and can be harvested. If straw is used as a growing medium, the substrate can be used as fertilizer after mushroom production is completed.

Shiitake Mushrooms

Shiitake mushrooms were originally cultivated on natural oak logs, a process which took two to four years before the mycelium colonized the wood sufficiently to produce fruiting. Shiitakes were harvested on a seasonal basis (spring and fall) for about six years.

Now, however, oak sawdust is packed into poly bags, sterilized, inoculated with spawn and placed in environmentally controlled rooms. These man-made "logs" produce shiitakes in seven weeks. The total process, from spawning to the end of harvesting, takes about four months as compared to the six-year cycle on natural logs.

Enoki Mushrooms

Current technology uses automated systems to fill plastic bottles with substrate usually ground corn cob pellets along with other ingredients such as wheat bran and soybean meal. The bottles are sterilized, inoculated with the mushroom culture and placed in growing houses. When the substrate is fully colonized with mycelium, the bottles are moved to an area where a plastic collar is attached to the mouth of the bottle.

This collar guides the forming mushrooms to grow straight up to help control carbon dioxide. enokis require a colder environment, 45 degrees, compared to growing temperatures of about 60 degrees, which other varieties require. After about 90 days, the mushrooms are harvested. The collars are removed, the Enokis plucked from the mouth of the bottle and usually packaged in shrink-wrapped bags. The remaining substrate is recycled, since enokis only produce one set of fruiting bodies per crop.

Beech Mushrooms

In some ways, growing beech mushrooms is similar to growing enokis. Plastic bottles are sterilized, inoculated with mushroom culture and then placed in growing houses to allow the substrate to colonize with the mycelium. However, beeches require a temperature of 60 to 64 degrees in order for the culture to fully develop. It takes about 100 days to produce a mature crop. Afterward, the mushrooms are harvested and packaged for sale. Since beeches only produce one set of fruiting bodies per crop, the remaining substrate is recycled for agri-business products.

Maitake Mushrooms

The cultivated maitake starts out as a mushroom "culture"- a piece of mushroom tissue grown on special sterile media in a petri plate in a laboratory. The culture is used to make mushroom spawn- a series of steps to make a lot of mushroom tissue out of a little. The mushroom spawn is used to inoculate maitake production logs, which are made out of sawdust supplemented with grain byproducts such as bran.

The logs go through a "spawn run" where the mushroom spawn colonizes the sawdust and supplements and knits them together in a solid mass. This takes about 30 days.

The logs are incubated in special mushroom houses with temperature, humidity and air flow carefully controlled. Once the logs start to pin (small mushrooms begin to form) the logs are moved into "fruiting" houses which are also very carefully controlled to provide the best environment for mushroom formation.

Like the enoki mushroom, maitake produces only one time, then the substrate is recycled into agri-business products. The whole process from lab to table takes from 10 to 14 weeks.

AGARICUS BISPORUS

The commercial mushroom, Agaricus bisporus, represented about 32% of the world mushroom production in 1997. This species is cultivated typically on a straw or hay base, amended with animal manures and gypsum. The materials initially undergo a two-phase composting process, one at high temperature (up to 85°C) and another for pasteurization and conditioning (beginning at 60°C and decreasing to about 45°C).

The colonization stage by this mushroom fungus is followed by covering the surface of the colonized compost with a layer of peat, top soil or other suitable material. Within two weeks mushrooms are visibly ready for harvest. After about three weeks of mushroom harvest, the growing material is considered spent. After usually undergoing a post-crop heat treatment, the growing material is removed and the chamber is ready for a new crop.

Pleurotus spp

The oyster mushroom consists of a number of several edible Pleurotus species. This species represented 14% of the world production in 1997. Pleurotus can be cultivated on wood sawdust, on various plant fibres or plant residues, which are amended with locally available proteins and carbohydrates to optimize its growth requirements. The materials are generally not composted previous to inoculation.

The wood sawdust may be aged or the plant fibres hydrated for several days. The growing materials are treated with either heat or chemicals to augment the selectivity of these materials for the oyster mushroom fungus. After colonization is complete, the colonized substrate is subjected to conditions suitable to initiation and maturation of fruiting bodies. At the end of several mushroom harvests, the growing material is considered spent. It may be heat treated before being removed from the growing chamber.

Lentinula edodes

Shiitake mushrooms, Lentinula edodes, represented 25% of the 1997 world mushroom production. This species is either cultivated on natural logs or on a 'synthetic' logs. Natural log production utilizes various species of trees, especially oak.

Trees are cut down after leaf fall and the wood cut in lengths of about one meter. Within one month these logs may be inoculated with the shiitake fungus. After up to one year of incubation, the colonized logs are brought under conditions that initiate fructification. Mushrooms are harvested about twice per year for several years. Once production ceases, these logs are considered spent. 'Synthetic' logs for production of shiitake mushrooms are formed from sawdust, straw, corn cobs or mixtures thereof. Starch-based additives from cereals are often added to optimize the nutritional needs of the fungus. The growing materials are generally sterilized. After colonization is completed, conditions are changed to initiate the formation of mushrooms. After several harvests, these synthetic logs are considered spent.

The utility of spent mushroom substrate. Characteristics of spent substrate are outlined, and the following uses for spent substrate are detailed: Bioremediation, crop production, re-use in the cultivation of mushrooms, food for animals and fish, and pest management. Each of these uses is noted in association with one of the particular mushroom species noted above. The environmental impact of weathering spent compost is also discussed.

CHARACTERISTICS OF SPENT SUBSTRATE

Agaricus bisporus spent substrate: Microbiology of composted (Raymond et al. 1997) or steamed material; physical and/or chemical characteristics of fresh and/or weathered material (Beyer 2001, Gerrits 1997a, Iiyama et al. 1995, Lemnaire et al. 1985, Levanon and Danai 1995, Lohr et al. 1984b, Maher et al. 2000, Szmidt and Chong 1995).

BIOREMEDIATION

Purification of air

Agaricus bisporus spent substrate: As mix with other materials for removal of H2S or volatile organic compounds.

Purification of water

Agaricus bisporus spent substrate: Treatment of metal-contaminated water from coal mines (Anon 1997, Dvorak et al. 1992, Stark et al. 1994); treatment of acid mine drainage (Chang et al. 2000) in wetland environments (Karathanasis and Thompson, 1990, Manyin et al. 1997, Stark and Williams 1994, Stark et al. 1995, Stark et al. 1996, Tarutis and Unz 1995, Vile and Wieder 1993, Wieder 1993); treatment of nickel-contaminated mine water (Hammack and Edenborn 1992); biological treatment of sewage (International Organic Solutions Corp. 1996); treatment of waters polluted with radioactive elements and heavy metals (Groudev et al. 1999).

Agaricus waste mushroom/tissue: Production of phenoloxidases (Steffen et al. 1995).

Pleurotus spp spent substrate: Reduction of phenol content and toxicity in olive mill waste (Martirani et al. 1996).

Lentinula edodes spent substrate: Treatment of acid mine drainage (Chang et al. 2000); treatment of effluents from olive mill.

Purification of soil

Agaricus bisporus spent substrate: Effect on zinc distribution (Shuman 1999a, 1999b), cadmium and lead among soil fractions; amelioration of zinc toxicity; degradation of chlorophenols, polycyclic aromatic hydrocarbons or aromatic monomers (Semple et al. 1995, Semple et al. 1998, Fermor et al 2000, Staments 2001); inhibition of nitrification (Bazin et al. 1991); treatment of hazardous wastes; stabilization of disturbed and commercial sites.

Pleurotus spp spent substrate: Blend of fish oil and spent substrate for degradation of polycyclic aromatic hydrocarbons in age-creosote contaminated soil; removal/degradation of pentachlorophenol (P.CP).

Lentinula edodes spent substrate: Removal/degradation of pentachlorophenol (PCP).

Purification of substrates contaminated with pesticides

Agaricus bisporus spent substrate: Degradation of carbaryl, 1-naphthol and carbamate (Kuo and Regan 1998, Regan 1994); sorption and movement of atrazine and 2,4-D by soils.

CROP PRODUCTION

Greenhouse crops - flowers

Agaricus bisporus spent substrate: Production of Chrysanthemum and Easter lilies, Helleborus (Richter et al. 1980); petunias and poinsettia; problems in use.

Greenhouse crops - vegetables

Agaricus bisporus spent substrate: Production of vegetable transplants (Lohr 1983, Lohr et al. 1984a, Lohr and Coffey 1987, Wang et al. 1984a), cucumbers, tomatoes (Celikel and Tuncay 1999a, Rathier 1982, Steffen et al. 1994, 1995,Vavrina et al. 1996) and eggplant; impact on post-harvest quality; general evaluation.

Field crops - vegetables

Agaricus bisporus spent substrate: Production of asparagus, beet root, cauliflower, cabbage, capsicums, celery, cucumber, lettuce, mustard, onion, potato, radish, snap bean, spinach, sugar beet, tomato (Abak and Gul 1994, Anon. 1979, Faassen et al. 1992, Kaddous and Morgans 1986, Maher 1994, Maher et al. 2000, Male 1981, Massi, A. 2001, pers. comm., Maynard 1989, Maynard 1991, Maynard 1994b, Nguyen et al. 1987, Pill et al. 1993, Ranganathan and Selvaseelan 1997a, Rhoads and Olson 1995, Selvi and Selvaseelan 1999, Sochtig and Grabbe 1995, Stephens et al. 1989, Stewart et al. 1998b, 1998c, Schwank 1985, Wang 1983, Wang et al. 1984)

Pleurotus spp spent substrate: Interplanting with cabbage and eggplant; wood shaving substrate for cultivation of lettuce (Batista et al. 2000); cucumber production.

Lentinula edodes spent substrate: Production of tomatoes.

Other species spent substrate: Production of cabbage (Lin 1993).

Field crops - fruit

Agaricus bisporus spent substrate: Mulching applied to "Italian" prunes (Robbins et al. 1986), apples (AntSaoir et al. 2000, Delver 1982, Delver and Wertheim 1988), apple seedlings, grapes; peaches (Derkacz, M. 2001, pers. comm.); organic alternative to methyl bromide in strawberries.

Field crops - other

Agaricus bisporus spent substrate: As a soil amendment for tea (Manivel et al. 1994); effect on green gram (Ranganathan and Selvaseelan 1994); as soil amendment for field corn (Weber et al. 1997, Wuest and Fahy 1991, Wuest et al. 1991, Wuest et al. 1995); effect on perennial rye grass, wheat (Maher 1994, Maher et al. 2000).

General soil amendment

Agaricus bisporus spent substrate: Effect on soil physical and physico-chemical properties (Ranganathan and Selvaseelan 1997b); as organic fertilizer.

Agaricus blazei spent substrate: As organic fertilizer (Dias, E. S. 2001, pers. comm.).

Pleurotus spent substrate: Cotton seed substrate pelletized for organic fertilizer or mixed with Agaricus spent substrate for organic fertilizer; sawdust substrate as organic fertilizer (Anderson, D. 2001, pers. comm.).

Lentinula edodes spent substrate: Pelletized for organic fertilizer or mixed with Agaricus spent substrate for organic fertilizer.

Nursery and landscape

Agaricus bisporus spent substrate: Production of foliage crops as potting mix; Chong et al. 1987, Chong and Wickware 1989, Chong et al. 1990, 1991a,b,c,d,e, Chong and Hamersma 1996a, b, Chong and Rinker 1994a,b, Chong 1991, 1999, Devonald 1987, Eames 1977, Henny 1980, Poole and Conorer 1974, Raymond et al. 1998, Smith 1982, van Keulen, H. 2001, pers. comm.); production of foliage crops in the field; improving turf.

Pleurotus spp spent substrate: Production of nursery crops (Quimio et al., 1990).

RE-USE IN THE CULTIVATION OF MUSHROOMS

Casing material for Agaricus bisporus

Agaricus bisporus spent substrate: Comparisons with peats and/or other local materials (Eicker and van Greuning 1989, Garcha and Sekhon 1981, Happ II 1974, Nair 1976a,b, Nair and Bradley 1981, Seaby 1999, Shandilya 1989a, b, Singh et al. 1992, 2000, Stoller 1979); leaching experiments (Riahi et al. 1998) or treatment with chelating agents; recomposting and leaching (Szmidt 1994, Szmidt et al. 1995); handling and use (Kinrus 1976, Schisler and Wuest 1982, Wuest 1976); separation and reuse of casing from spawn-run compost (Hesling 1981, Jablonsky and Srb 1989, Nair and Bradley 1981, Nair 1985). Pleurotus spent substrate: Composted sawdust media as casing (Kim et al. 1998).

Casing material for Agaricus bitorquis

Agaricus bisporus spent substrate: Comparisons with local materials (Guleria et al. 1989).

Cultivation of other species

Agaricus bisporus spent substrate: Cultivation of 11 species cultivation of Agaricus bisporus (Rinker and Alm 1990, Schisler 1988, Till 1963), Auricularia (Sharma and Jandaik 1994), Lentinula, Pleurotus (Mueller et al. 1984, Sharma and Jandaik 1994); Volvariella.

Pleurotus spp spent substrate: Cultivation of Pleurotus spp (Nakaya et al. 2000, Sharma and Jandaik 1985, 1992), Stropharia.

Lentinula edodes spent substrate: Cultivation of Pleurotus (Jaramillo, C. 2001, pers. comm., Royse 1993); mixed into Agaricus substrate (Yeatman, J. 2001, pers. comm.).

Spent substrate from other species: Volvariella substrate for Pleurotus production (Chang and Miles 1989, Quimio 1988); Flammulina or Ganaderma substrate for Coprinus comatus.

FOOD FOR ANIMALS AND FISH

Agaricus bisporus spent substrate: Feeding studies with sheep.

Pleurotus spp spent substrate: Cattle feed from spent wheat straw compost (Adamovi? et al. 1998, Jaramillo, C. 2001, pers. comm., Kakkar et al. 1990, Keil, C. 2001, pers. comm.); spent sugarcane bagasse compost in a dietary blend for ruminants (Permana 1990, Zadrazil and Puniya 1995) adult and young buffaloes fed spent wheat or rice straw from Pleurotus cultivation (Kakkar and Dhanda 1998, Bakshi et al. 1985); feed for lambs and sheep (Calzada et al. 1987a, b, Sanchez, J.E. 2001, pers. comm.); degradation studies.

Lentinula edodes spent substrate: Ground waste logs from natural log shiitake cultivation (Yoshida et al. 1978); rice straw fermented with waste shiitake sawdust media, corn and molasses; degradation studies (Braun et al. 2000, Zhang et al. 1996).

Other species spent substrates: Volvariella volvacea grown on rice straw or banana leaves for sheep (Sevilla et al. 1989); Coprinus fimetarius grown on rice and oat straws for goats.

Aquaculture

Agaricus bisporus spent substrate: Wheat straw substrate as a component in the diet of carp (Cirrhina mirigala) (Sehgal and Thomas 1987, Sehgal and Simmi 1991, Sehgal et al. 1993).

PEST MANAGEMENT

Insect management

Agaricus bisporus spent substrate: Effects on Colorado potato beetles populations (Stoner et al. 1996, Gent et al. 1998).

Disease management

Agaricus bisporus spent substrate: Effect of water extracts (Yohalem et al. 1994, 1996) and mechanism and dynamics of inhibition on apple scab; effect on: damping-off and root rot of creeping bentgrass (Craft and Nelson 1996); Pythium damping-off disease of tomatoes (Reigner et al. 2001); Verticillium disease in commercial mushrooms (Guardino 1998, Labuschagne et al. 2000, Wuest et al. 1996); root-knot nematode, Meloidogyne incognita (Kaul and Chhabra 1993, Verma 1986, 1993); chilli leaf and stem necrosis; wilt of carnation and black root rot of cucumber; suppression of turfgrass diseases; potato early dying disease caused by V. dahliae and P. penetrans (Gent et al. 1998, LaMondia et al. 1999); Rhizoctonia in cucumbers; Fusarium wilt of tomato; predaceous nematodes; influence on gas exchange in potatoes in presence of Verticillium dahliae or Pratylenchus penetrans.

Pleurotus spp spent substrate: Attacks nematodes (Hibbett and Thorn 1994, Thorn and Barron 1984).

Lentinula edodes spent substrate: Suppression of Rhizoctonia damping-off of cabbage (Huang 1997, Huang and Huang 2000); disease incidence of tomato.

MISCELLANEOUS USES

Agaricus bisporus spent substrate: Used in airlift bioreactor used to assess plant available nutrients (Velthof et al. 1998); used in heat resistant formulas (Donnelly and Busta 1980); as a alternative fuel (Maher et al. 2000); used as bedding for hogs (Beattie et al. 2001, Durrel et al. 1997); recovery of lignocellose-degrading enzymes (Ball and Jackson 1995); monitoring fate of entomopathogenic nematodes; carrier material for preparation of bio-inoculants (Bahl and Jauhri 1986, Bahl et al. 1989); production of biogas (Tumwasorn et al. 1980); vermiculture (Edwards et al. 1985, Massi, A. 2001, pers. comm.).

Pleurotus spp spent substrate: Production of biogas (Bisaria et al. 1983, 1990, Mehta et al. 1990); as alternative fuel; extracellular enzyme production; vermiculture (Rahman, H. 2001, pers. comm., Sanchez, J.E. 2001, pers. comm.).

Lentinula edodes spent substrate: As alterative fuel (Dias, E.S. 2001, pers. comm., Pauli 1999); vermiculture.

Other species spent substrate: Mushrooms in general as animal feed (Sova and Cibulka 1980); cellulolytic bacteria from Volvariella volvacea; Volvariella as alternative fuel and vermiculture.

ENVIRONMENTAL IMPACT OF WEATHERING SPENT COMPOST

Spent mushroom substrates are often spread onto land and allowed to weather for several years. This allows salts and nitrates to leach from the spent materials. The impact of storage and leaching has been explored.

Weathering process

Agaricus bisporus spent substrate: Organic matter transformations during weathering process (Chefetz et al. 2000).

Impact on ground water

Agaricus bisporus spent substrate: Nitrates in ground water beneath sandy terrace soil in intensive vegetable production (Maynard 1993a, b, 1994a); impact on water quality through applications to agriculture land (Kapland et al. 1995, Pannier 1993, Wuest 1992, Wuest and Fahy 1992, Wuest et al. 1991); release of sulfate-sulfur, potassium, calcium, magnesium (Stewart et al. 2000) and inorganic-N (Stewart et al. 1998).

Impact on surface water

Agaricus bisporus spent substrate: Effect on adjacent surface water.

Impact on air quality

Agaricus bisporus spent substrate: Odorous components; effect on health.

AGARICUS SUBRUFESCENS, A CULTIVATED EDIBLE AND MEDICINAL MUSHROOM, AND ITS SYNONYMS

Agaricus subrufescens Peck was first described in 1893 by C.H. Peck, the New York state botanist, from two collections. The first was of two mushrooms from a crop being cultivated at "Dosoris", New York (sent 15 Oct 1892). Because these arrived in poor condition, additional specimens found growing "in our [W. Falconer's] leaf pile in old leaf mold" then were sent (apparently on 24 Oct 1892) (Peck 1893; Falconer to Peck, in lit. [NYS]).

The mushroom, called the "almond mushroom" or "almond-flavored mushroom" due to its fragrance and taste, was widely cultivated, sold and eaten in the Atlantic states of the United States from at least Massachusetts to Washington D.C., from the late 19th century into the 20th. Spawn (inoculum culture for farming) of A. subrufescens was even offered for sale. As late as 1918 Kauffman (1918) reported it to be in cultivation. Commercial production of A. subrufescens subsequently declined as market trends changed; soon the related "button mushroom" species Agaricus bisporus Imbach appears to have been the only mushroom species being regularly cultivated in the United States.

Agaricus subrufescens often occurs in domesticated or semidisturbed habitats, including leaf piles. It has been recognized occasionally growing "wild" outside northeastern North America, for example in California, Israel (R. Kenneth, personal communication 1984–85), Taiwan and Hawaii, where it grows under forest trees.

Brazilian examples in the past three decades have entered commerce and (not having been recognized as A. subrufescens) raised questions, discussed below, about nomenclature and identity. In addition, the recently described A. rufotegulis Nauta from the Netherlands, the United Kingdom and Portugal is also extremely similar and considered here to be conspecific with A. subrufescens.

The history of A. subrufescens was reviewed by Kerrigan (1983a); updated and extended information follows. A discussion of its properties as an easily cultivated mushroom was presented by Kerrigan (1983a, 1984); notably, very similar outdoor methods are typically employed in Brazil today. A culture (RWK 1185; voucher at SFSU) of A. subrufescens was isolated by me from basidiomata growing in rich compost covered with sandy soil for raspberry culture in California in 1981. This culture was sold commercially to hobbyist mushroom growers (it recently has been cultivated at commercial scale in the United States and, based on sequence and other data, abroad). Reproductive micromorphology and genetic behavior of this strain were investigated by Kerrigan and Ross (1987a, b, unpublished).

Mushrooms originating in the Atlantic region of Brazil and agreeing closely with Agaricus subrufescens have begun in recent decades to be cultivated on a broad scale as "medicinal mushrooms" that are marketed primarily in Japan (Kerrigan 1983a, Wasser et al 2002). However, in this context the mushroom typically is referred to (incorrectly) as A. blazei Murrill, "A. blazei ss Heinem." or, in some commercial literature and product packaging, "A. sylvaticus".

The conventional account of the origin of 'Agaricus blazei Murrill sensuHeinemann' and its arrival in Japan is related by Wasser et al (2002). It is consistent with the account given to me by Mr Shusuke Minoura in Hiroshima, Japan, in 1981. His account and my conclusion that the Brazilian Agaricus then cultivated in Japan was "almost certainly" A. subrufescens were published shortly thereafter with one of Minoura's photographs (Kerrigan 1983a).

The conventional history also agrees with a specific and plausible account by Mr. B.-A. Eckart (personal communication) of Brazil and Germany, related to him by Mr Ernesto Noburo, which attributes the discovery of the Brazilian mushroom and its distribution to Japanese researchers to the late Mr Takatoshi Furumoto, an immigrant from Japan to Piedade, Brazil. Details in the report of Heinemann (1993) indicating that a culture was isolated from a collection made at São Paulo, Piedade, Brazil, in Feb 1973, and cultivated in Japan by Iwade, from which specimens (at BR) were preserved by Hongo, are also concordant.

Controversy has existed regarding the correct name of the Brazilian species. A search of the World Wide Web and a review of diverse commercial product literature indicated that association of the name A. blazei with the Brazilian mushroom is attributed to P. Heinemann. Minoura used this name in 1981; the published taxonomic determination appears in Heinemann (1993).

The nameA. sylvaticus Schaeff. sometimes is associated with the species, and this is said to have resulted from a determination of Brazilian cultivated material made by a European mycologist at the request of a Brazilian producer (R. Maziero personal communication). Agaricus sylvaticus customarily is placed in section Sanguinolenti Singer, while A. subrufescens(under any name and including Brazilian material) is certainly a member of section Arvenses Konrad & Maubl. (Kerrigan 1982, 1986).

Wasser et al (2002) rejected the name A. blazei for the Brazilian mushroom, correctly in this author's opinion, and recognized the latter as a new species,A. brasiliensis Wasser et al. Wasser et al also rejected conspecificity between Brazilian mushrooms and A. subrufescens, based on features of spores and cheilocystidia, although they wrote that the two species seemed to be each other's closest relatives.

However, new data presented below indicate that the medicinal mushroom from Brazil and Japan is biologically and phylogenetically the same species asA. subrufescens from North America. I will review features that have been emphasized in the literature on the taxa involved. Because Peck's name A. subrufescens is older than A. brasiliensis, it has priority and therefore is the correct name of the species. A. rufotegulis Nauta equally belongs to A. subrufescens, based on overall morphological and sequence criteria. The rDNA ITS1 + 2 sequences from Hawaiian specimens of A. subrufescens are the most divergent of those studied.

MATERIAL AND METHODS

All cultural and analytical methods were routine and have been described in earlier publications (Challen et al 2003, Kerrigan et al 1996). For microscopy, excised dried material was wetted in 95% ethanol, then mounted and measured in 3% KOH; spore length excludes the apiculus. Cultures of commercial samples of "medicinal agaricus" of Chinese and Japanese origin were obtained from spores aseptically washed from lamellae of dried mushrooms, in the form of single spore isolates (SSIs).

The karyotic status (n versus n + n) of each SSI was determined from potato-dextrose yeast broth (PDYB) grown samples using allozyme markers including peptidase and esterase. Heteroallelic SSIs were assumed to be heterokaryotic, while homoallelic SSIs were of uncertain status. Crosses were attempted between homoallelic SSIs on PDA, transferred to grain spawn medium, then compost (for cropping); successful hybrid cultures were isolated and cultured in PDYB for genetic analysis.

Some samples (A. rufotegulis, A. brasiliensis [Isotype], A. subrufescens DEH 1073, 513; KRP 070) were available only as herbarium specimens, from which DNA was isolated using the DNAEasy Plant Miniprep Kit (Quiagen). Living cultures were grown in PDYB, harvested, lyophilized and extracted for DNA using the CTAB miniprep procedure (Zolan and Pukkila 1986).

Amplification of the ITS1 + 2 region of the rDNA, sequencing of the products and subsequent alignment and analysis was done as described in Challen et al 2003. Normally primers ITS1 and ITS4 (White et al 1990) were used to produce a full-length ITS1 + 2 PCR product; however, some herbarium material provided DNA that only produced shorter PCR products, using primers ITS1 and ITS2, or ITS3 and ITS4. In this project it was routine in sequencing full-length products to use internal primers ITS2 and ITS3 in addition to terminal primers ITS1 and ITS4 due to length heterogeneity which often was present in both ITS segments 1 and 2 in this species. The sequence analyzed begins with ggaaggat in the 18S gene and ends with gaacttaa in the 25–28S gene.

Sequencing was performed on the most current equipment available at the time at either the Pennsylvania State University or at the University of Pittsburgh. Output was ABI trace files; these were inspected, corrected and assembled using the Seqman module of the Lasergene version 5 package (Dnastar). A sequence from A. urinascens Singer (=A. macrosporus [F.H. Møller & Jul. Schäffer] Pilát, nom. illeg.; non A. macrosporus Mont. [1837], per Nauta [2000]) (GenBank AF432878) was used as outgroup. Alignment was done using the Clustal W algorithm of the Megalign module of Lasergene, followed by inspection and manual correction. All sequences comprise data from both strands, although in the 18S, 5.8S and 25–28S genes short regions of single strand data are present. A few 5.8S sequences (which are almost invariant within Agaricus) are incomplete. Sequences were deposited in GenBank (AY818646-AY818660).

It was apparent that the distance matrix generated from the alignment by Megalign was treating heteromorphic characters as ambiguous data, which then were excluded from similarity calculations. The DNADIST program of PHYLIP also ignores heteromorphic data. Consequently, I manually constructed a pairwise distance matrix in which each pair of identical characters was scored as 0.0, each pair of fully dissimilar characters was scored, as 1/n, where n = character positions scored, and a pair consisting of one heteromorphic character and one of its constituent characters was scored as 0.5/n.

Both character and length heteromorphisms were scored in this way. Total pairwise distance was the sum of scores over all (nominally 711) positions. The matrix file was evaluated using both FITCH and the UPGMA method in NEIGHBOR (PHYLIP; Felsenstein 2004) to produce a graphical representation of similarity, rather than a phylogenetic hypothesis, because the presence of numerous heteromorphisms and the hypothesis of population-level hybridization in this species are not compatible with the usual assumptions of character state evolution and radiating phylogenetic lineages.

To evaluate the phylogenetic unity of A. subrufescens and putatively conspecific taxa, the sequences described above were compared to others of species in several sections of Agaricus, primarily section Arvenses. Sequences from GenBank included AB113576.1, AF161013, AJ131126.1 and AY484697.1 (as A. blazei, deposited by four research groups), AY484671.1, AY474672.1 (asA. augustus), AY484690.1 (as A. arvensis), AF482834.1 (as E. depressum, =

A. inapertus), AY484670.1 (as A. nivescens), AY 484686.1 (as A. macrocarpus), and AY484675.1 (as A. albolutescens), all in section Arvenses. Names associated with GenBank deposits were accepted provisionally. Other sections were represented as follows: Agaricus: A. campestris: W1H (M. Challen, HRI: includes AJ418775); Xanthodermatei: A. xanthodermus W3I (M. Challen, HRI: includes AJ418776); Duploannulati: A. bisporus RWK 1885 (AF432886);Sanguinolenti: A. pattersonae RWK 1415 (includes AJ418715); other: A. subrutilescens (in or near section Spissicaules) RWK 1940. The alignment file was prepared as described above and was evaluated under maximum parsimony using PAUP* version 4.0b8 (Swofford 2000).

RESULTS

Marker-assisted analysis of reproduction

Single spores were isolated and germinated from several samples of A. subrufescens, including I-101, a strain developed from Brazilian germ plasm and cultivated and sold commercially in Japan (as 'Iwade 101', per the provider of the sample) and from SBRFG, a subculture of the RWK 1185 isolate made by Kerrigan in California in 1981. These SSIs then were propagated in broth and subjected to allozyme analysis (Kerrigan et al 1992).

Segregation of alleles in offspring occurred at the PEP1 and PEP2 loci (Kerrigan et al 1996, Royse and May 1982) in progeny of I-101 and at an esterase locus in SBRFG. This demonstrates that meiosis, recombination and partitioning of recombinant nuclei into spores is occurring in these isolates of A. subrufescens, therefore the species is not homothallic. Furthermore, some SSIs had heteroallelic genotypes, proving that multiple nuclei were present in heterokaryotic spores, while other spores were homoallelic, implying that they could be homokaryotic.

All these observations are consistent with the presence of a basic system of amphithallic reproduction in which both uniparental reproduction (via intramixis) and outcrossing (heteromixis) is possible. The tendency of at least some strains of A. subrufescens to produce substantial numbers of bi- and tri-sporic basidia under some conditions also is consistent with the presence of an amphithallic life cycle.

An interesting property of SSIs of SBRFG is that they varied with respect to reproductive ability (as expected among amphithallic offspring). Although the SBRFG parent had a pigmented pileus, some fertile SSI offspring produced basidiomata with white pilei.

The latter observation could be explained by the presence of a Mendelian determinant for pileus color located at sufficient distance from the centromere to allow frequent crossing over, and the presence of one recessive allele in the parent, leading to a minority of homoallelic recessive heterokaryotic offspring (cf. Kerrigan et al 1993). These observations were first noted in work at UCSB in 1986 (Kerrigan and Ross unpublished). Some SSIs of I-101 (e.g., -s1) also were fertile.

Interfertility and hybrid analysis

All tested SSIs from the BS1 (Brazilian commercial) and CS4 samples were heteroallelic in allozyme analysis, so no crosses from these SSIs were attempted. Homoallelic SSIs from the I-101 and SBRFG stocks were selected to be the progenitors of a series of hybrids. Hybrid cultures were isolated for each pairing. The hybrid between SBRFG-s1 and I-101-s1, called H1X1, will serve as an example.

The hybrid status of the putative new hybrids was verified by allozyme analysis. In the case of the hybrid H1X1, the progenitor I-101-s1 carries allelePep2-s, while progenitor SBRFG-s1 carries allele Pep2-f. Both SSIs are fertile, therefore either or both might be heterokaryotic. The hybrid H1×1 between these two SSIs has the expected genotype Pep2-s/f, demonstrating that this isolate incorporates DNA from each parent. The simplest and most conventional explanation is that H1×1 received one nucleus from I-101-s1 and another nucleus from SBRFG-s1.

A set of 25 A. subrufescens hybrids between parents I-101 and SBRFG were grown on small containers of compost under standard conditions, with the SBRFG parent also present as a control. The phenotype of H1×1 serves as an example of how morphological and cultural traits may be inherited from the progenitors of such a hybrid.

Parent SBRFG had a thick-fleshed, wavy pileus with a brown pigmented surface and robust basidiocarps. SSI SBRFG-s1, progenitor of the hybrid, was similar but white and fruited a few days later than its parent. SSI I-101-s1 had a thin-fleshed, narrowly convex pileus with a brown pigmented surface and gracile basidiocarps that fruited about 10 d later than SBRFG. H1×1 produced robust mushrooms that fruited concurrently with those of SBRFG, with brown-pigmented pilei that were convex and not (or only obscurely) wavy. The several traits described here were inherited and expressed in different modes from the two SSIs; for example the pileus color trait exhibited classic Mendelian dominant/recessive behavior.

ITS1+2 DNA sequences

For available isolates and specimens, the sequences of the ITS1+2 regions of the nuclear rDNA were aligned and compared. The samples studied had an rDNA ITS1+2 sequence with nominal length of 711 nt; however, due to frequent length polymorphisms at either of two positions, the actual sequence lengths ranged from 710 to 712 or 713 nt and a majority of samples yielded sequences of more than one length. These length polymorphisms occurred at positions 49–51 (ttt versus tttt) and at or near position 485 (tttt versus tttttt versus ttttttt) in the nominal 711 nt sequence. They were commonly heteromorphic within single isolates (downstream from the indel, two distinct peaks were superimposed at each position when the output trace file was examined), which interfered with sequencing and necessitated bidirectional sequencing using four primers. The sequences were otherwise identical except at 16 other variable positions.

At a number of positions (ranging from four to nine in single sequences), nucleotide heteromorphisms always were present in North and South American samples and these pairs always corresponded to alternate nucleotides seen in some samples (e.g., a versus g versus r at position 601). The term heteromorphism should not be equated automatically with heteroallelism (because the ITS region is moderately or highly repeated), although equivalence in this instance would be the simplest possibility and is supported by the sequence of H1×1.

The sample from the UK, identified by M.M. Nauta as A. rufotegulis, fits this sequence pattern, although no heteromorphisms were present. The three successfully amplified sequences from Hawaii were identical among themselves and were similar to non-Hawaiian sequences but had slightly different sequence characteristics.

Like A. rufotegulis, Hawaiian sequences lacked both compositional and length heteromorphisms. They had two sequence characters, at positions 281 and 478, not found in any of the other non-Hawaiian sequences. Finally, their lengths were one nucleotide shorter than all other "nominal" sequences, at a third position (~485), where other sequences either were nominal or one nucleotide longer. DNA extracts from three other Hawaiian specimens of A. subrufescens (DEH 337, 527, 1452 [SFSU]) unfortunately failed to amplify.

Excluding several GenBank sequences identified as Agaricus blazei, mainly deposited by laboratories in Asia, the public sequences with the greatest affinity to the A. subrufescens samples all belong to taxa in section Arvenses.One of these is GenBank AF432878, deposited as A. macrosporus RWK 1925 but correctly named A. urinascens.

The A. urinascens sequence was 2.9–3.2% divergent from the A. subrufescens samples (using Megalign), while distances among A. subrufescens samples ranged from 0 to 0.27% (hand calculated), with Hawaiian isolates having the highest divergence scores.

In the FITCH and UPGMA trees derived from the distance matrix, Brazilian sequences always were interspersed with those from other regions. No phylogenetic signals associated either with geographical regions (other than Hawaii) or with recently proposed taxa were evident. In contrast, in an MP analysis of A. subrufescens sequences within Agaricus, particularly within section Arvenses, all A. subrufescens sequences (including several deposited in GenBank as 'A. blazei') formed a monophyletic unit within Arvenses. Bootstrap values for the A. subrufescens clade and the Arvenses sectional clade were both 100%. Within A. subrufescens, a clade formed by the three identical

Hawaiian sequences received 88% bootstrap support. Taken together results from both distance and parsimony analyses indicate the presence of a single phylogenetic species.

Study of the type of A. subrufescens

The material of the holotype is now more fragmented than it appeared to be in the photograph of Didukh et al (2003). Referring to their photograph, I was able to segregate and label specimens and fragments assigned by Didukh et al as "type A" and "type B", with an additional upper stipe fragment now assigned to element B. Element A comprises two basidiomata, in agreement with Falconer's letter to Peck (21 Oct 1892 [NYS]), which are relatively gracile and have dark brown pileus pigment. Lamellae of these basidiomata are fused and their cellular structure is collapsed and indistinct.

Element B comprises four basidiomata, based on stipe apices, not two as reported in Didukh et al (2003), in fragments. The B specimen fragments are in better condition and have a slightly more robust aspect and less pronounced pileus pigmentation, relative to the A specimens. Spores of the B element are larger, on average, than those of A, as reported by Didukh et al (2003). However, in both elements the spore lengths span similarly broad ranges (5.1–7.5 or -8.3 μm).

The distribution of lengths in element A is clearly bimodal, and it appears to be bimodal or multimodal in element B. Element B has a greater proportion of large spores (ca. 50%) relative to A (=10%). Developing spores were observed on the hymenium of the B element; while spore tetrads were most common; triads, diads and occasional monads also were observed at progressively lower frequencies.

Cheilocystidia could not be observed in element A, as expected given the condition of the lamellae. Irregular to semiglobose, catenulate cheilocystidia ca. 7.5–13.5 μm broad were observed in element B. Inflated elongate cells and occasional subglobose elements 10–26 μm broad were observed among narrower hyphae of the pileal disc of element B. No velar material could be identified with certainty in any part of the holo-type.

One loose lamellar fragment that fell from one of the basidiomata of element A had a spore size distribution like that of element B, indicating at least minor cross-contamination of the two formerly mixed elements due to the large number of loose fragments present.

DISCUSSION

This study demonstrates interfertility between North American A. subrufescens and a "medicinal Agaricus", an isolate made from cultivated Japanese material but believed to be of Brazilian origin, enabling the production of a first interpopulational hybrid generation. The presence in hybrids of genetic material from the two progenitors, and of novel phenotypes, was documented. This indicates that members of these geographically distant mushroom populations might constitute a single "biological species". The reproductive system is believed, based on a concordance of early data, to be amphithallic with heterothallic and pseudohomothallic components.

The data presented here further show that the DNA sequences of the ITS1+2 regions of geographically diverse members of this species are very similar. Three Hawaiian samples had no heteromorphisms but three otherwise unique polymorphisms, while one UK sample also had no heteromorphisms. Heteromorphisms always are present and frequent in the North and South American isolates and specimens studied to date. These data suggest an interpretation, developed below, based on the possibility of interpopulational hybridization; this hypothesis is speculative but useful in providing guidance for further studies.

No geographical population (with the exception of the Hawaiian samples) could be distinguished uniquely by sequence characters; the data provide no justification for recognizing distinct North American, South American or European taxa (some heteromorphisms were unique to the California + "Chinese" samples, but because only a single genotype might be represented, the significance of those characters cannot be assessed). FITCH and UPGMA phenograms derived from the distance matrix showed American, Brazilian and European sequences intermingled, while the Hawaiian sequences formed a distinct branch.

With respect to Hawaii, the question of how levels of sequence divergence relate to taxonomic rank-relationships arises. Some rough benchmarks for taxonomic rank relationships in Agaricus, appropriate to various degrees of ITS1+2 sequence divergence, are beginning to emerge. Two varieties of A. bisporus, distinguished by morphological characters and reproductive behaviors, each exhibited single unique sequence character differences from var. bisporus (Callac et al 1993, 2003). An alpine relative of A. devoniensis P.D. Orton that has two unique sequence characters currently is considered to be a subspecies (Challen et al 2003, Kerrigan unpublished). The homothallic "highland" and "lowland" entities (Kerrigan et al 1999) of A. subfloccosus (J. Lange) Hlavác ek s. l., arguably either subspecies or sister species, differ at only one position in the ITS1+2 sequence (Challen et al 2003, Kerrigan unpublished). Other "sister species" have greater ITS1+2 divergence (e.g., about 1.4–1.9% in A. bisporus versus A. subfloccosus, which corresponds to about 10–14 character differences.

However some species in sectionXanthodermatei Sing. might differ by smaller numbers of ITS1+2 sequence characters (Kerrigan et al unpublished, Callac et al unpublished) By comparison with these observations any taxon that might be proposed for the Hawaiian A. subrufescens could be argued to deserve either infraspecific or specific rank, presumably depending upon other observations that hopefully would include interfertility data.

Phylogeographic structure and dispersal

The distribution of A. subrufescens is documented only patchily, because the species appears not to have been well recognized in some regions (Europe, South America). However, it appears to have a tropical or subtropical to temperate zone distribution.

Agaricus subrufescens is the only species ofAgaricus known to be harmed or killed by prolonged exposure to temperatures of ca. 4 C or lower (Kerrigan unpublished, cf. A. brasiliensis in Wasser et al 2002). Wasser et al understandably were unaware of this trait of A. subrufescens when they attempted to use it to distinguish A. subrufescensfrom A. brasiliensis. It is also remarkably tolerant of high temperatures (Kerrigan 1983a). It is unusually versatile nutritionally, having been observed to have spontaneously colonized a bag of wet sawdust on one occasion (Kerrigan unpublished). The most "natural" habitat reported for the species is piles of leaves.

The Hawaiian Islands are geographically isolated. Relatively more sequence divergence might be expected within small island populations (Johnson and Seger 2001). The UK is less isolated but might be near the limit of the natural range of the species in the Eastern Hemisphere, which currently remains unclear. The samples from these localities might represent "pure" members of relatively isolated or marginal populations. Their lack of sequence heteromorphism is consistent with this theory. Conversely, samples from Brazil (and Japan by extension) and California are highly heteromorphic. Some sequences in GenBank also exhibit this characteristic. The Americas samples might represent examples of natural or accidental hybrids between formerly "pure" populations, assuming that the dual peaks and sequence length differences arise from allelic variations at the haplotype level (which is supported by the implicit allelic segregation needed to produce the H1×1 sequence).

The observation that heteromorphisms including length polymorphisms are relatively uncommon among species of sectionDuploannulati Wasser emend. Challen et al (2003) supports this hypothesis. A. devoniensis is the exception to this pattern, appearing to exhibit diverse aspects of recent population level hybridization (Callac et al unpublished).

To confirm the potentially allelic nature of the observed heteromorphisms it will be necessary to isolate haplotypes from SSIs or deheterokaryotized cultures or to clone PCR products amplified from heterokaryotic genomic DNA. Once haploid sequences are obtained, and if the heteromorphisms are allelic rather than interrepeat variants, it should be possible to construct gene genealogies that might provide better insight into the hypothesized hybridization among populations. This will be a goal of future studies.

Contemporary documents show that spawn of A. subrufescens was being sold commercially, sometimes as 'A. fabaceus', about a century ago (Falconer 1894a, b; Anonymous 1909). At that time the two species names were considered to be synonymous by B.M. Duggar, a USDA BPI collaborator involved with the developing mushroom spawn industry in the USA (Duggar 1905, 1920).

A. fabaceus is an older American name dating from 1847. It was described having a pileus that was white becoming yellow, and viscid when moist. It appears unlikely to be the same species as A. subrufescens. The type of A. fabaceus is at Kew. Spawn distribution is a documented route for geographically broad dispersal of Agaricus germ plasm into the environment (Kerrigan et al 1999). In addition, any organism that can use composted manure and wood as a substrate, and is thermotolerant, potentially could cross oceans on a traditional wooden sailing ship. When the vigor and amphithallic reproductive versatility (including single-spore fertility) of A. subrufescens is factored in, dispersal, establishment and gene flow in this species is not surprising. A quote from a Boston Mycological Club bulletin (Anonymous 1904) illustrates the reproductive potential of this species: "Its spontaneous appearance in various greenhouses in widely separate localities has brought it to notice at various times because it forced itself so persistently and abundantly on the owners that they have sent in specimens to the Club exhibitions in order to learn whether the visitation was to be regarded as a curse or a blessing.... When it appears it comes with a rush, having previously, with its strong growing, strand like mycelium, taken possession of some rich portion of soil, and then it sends its abundant fruits to the light, undaunted by any overlying difficulties."

In Santa Barbara, California, I encountered A. subrufescens growing on a lawn about 200 m from a laboratory where I had cultivated it the previous year (Kerrigan and Ross 1987a). The possibility that this represented an escape from cultivation was not contradicted by allozyme data I obtained from both isolates (Kerrigan unpublished). This was the second and only other time I ever encountered the species in nature.

Morphology of basidiomata

Although the present study did not primarily emphasize morphological criteria, a discussion of some points is in order. The basidiomatal morphology of A. subrufescens is somewhat variable. This would not be surprising in a situation where populations had diverged in isolation and were now interbreeding. Sporocarps can be robust or gracile, both due to genotype and environmental influences (Kerrigan unpublished).

Cuticle pigmentation and background yellowing are also variable (the degree of analogous reddening of the tissues of A. bisporus is under genetic control and both traits are managed actively in mushroom breeding programs [Kerrigan 2004, unpublished]). Although Peck noted that the lamellae could be yellowish-white, he reported the flesh to be "white, unchangeable". Wasser et al have emphasized this as a point of distinction between A. subrufescens andA. brasiliensis. However, this variation does occur naturally within member species of section Arvenses (Kerrigan 1982, unpublished).

Furthermore, the specimens Peck received had traveled more than 300 km (the straight-line distance between Glen Cove and Albany) in 1892 before he saw them and did not arrive in the best condition— "Dear Sir: I am glad you rec'd the mushrooms, but sorry they were so long delayed and in such poor condition. I sent them to Dr L(-) to forward to you as I did not know your proper address." (Falconer to Peck, 21 Oct 1892 [see also 15 Oct 1892] [NYS]).

Even the second shipment apparently suffered. Peck (1897) wrote that "From some of these specimens kindly sent me by the discoverer the original description was derived, but the specimens were not in satisfactory condition to figure."Kauffman (1918) wrote that "The original description was made from old material.... Peck's description of this species is, therefore, misleading." Color changes in Agaricus diminish in time after harvest as well as with age and deteriorating condition of basidiomata. Finally, the man who obtained and sent the type material of A. subrufescens to Peck, Mr W. Falconer (editor of the journal "Gardening" and subsequent author of the 1897 USDA Farmer's Bulletin 53, "How To Grow Mushrooms"), reported that the species had a "lemon-tinted neck", indicating that Peck's description was at least incomplete (Falconer 1894a). In my experience the cap shape also is variable, ranging from narrowly convex through cuboidal to broadly convex. However, two characters unusual in other species may sometimes be present: (i) a transient concave shoulder or bell-shape to the pileus as expansion in young pilei begins first near the margin; (ii) radially oriented folds or "pleats" of the pileus. Both features are illustrated in Kerrigan (1986). Falconer even included a tiny sketch of a pleated pileus in his first letter to Peck (15 Oct 1892). The elastic veil, which usually remains attached to the pileus margin during expansion, stretching while the lower layer breaks up into a large number of small cottony floccules, is a fairly consistent feature of the species.

Agaricus subrufescens is a widely illustrated species. The range of gross morphologies can be seen in these references: Peck 1897; Anonymous 1904;Anonymous 1909; Duggar 1905, 1920 (Pl. VI); Kauffman 1918; Tu and Lin 1981; Kerrigan 1983b, 1984, 1986; Nauta 1999; Hausknecht 2002; Wasser et al 2002; Peterson et al 2000. In its heyday the mushroom was described as "uncouth looking" (Falconer 1894a). The figure and description furnished byHotson and Stuntz (1938) probably refer to A. augustus Fr. Microscopic features have been described by Kerrigan (1982, 1986),Heinemann (1993), Nauta (1999), Peterson et al (2000), Hausknecht (2002) andWasser et al (2002), among others. The type of A. subrufescens has been examined and described by Freeman (1979), Wasser et al (2002) and by Smith (1940), who could not "add any information to that found in Kauffman's account." Some authors, particularly Wasser et al, have emphasized points of distinction among the entities they recognize. Spore size variability deserves some discussion.

Heinemann (1993) found the sizes of spores to be heterogeneous within single collections of cultivated Brazilian stock. He suspected the presence of bisporic basidia among the tetrasporic ones but was unable to verify this. Kerrigan and Ross (1987a, b) did document the presence of dynamically varying numbers of bi-, tri- and tetrasporic basidia in field and cultivated specimens of A. subrufescens, leading to an expectation of variation among spore size measurements. Kerrigan also presented data on variation in spore size from single sporocarps at different developmental stages. Occasional North American collections of A. subrufescens have been observed to have relatively longer spores (e.g., Smith 6789 [MICH], Rives, Washington D.C. [NYS]; the latter specimens were illustrated by Peck [1897]). We should expect considerable variation in spore lengths within and among collections of A. subrufescens, given the bimodality or multimodality observed in the distributions of spore sizes in the two elements of the holotype and the known dynamic variability in proportions of n-spored basidia that results from temperature shifts or other diurnal cues.

Cheilocystidia in A. subrufescens are usually reported to be variable: cylindrical to clavate or swollen, with few to many catenulate-globose cells (Kerrigan 1982, Heinemann 1993, Nauta 1999, Wasser et al 2002, Hausknecht 2002). However, Wasser et al (2002) did not observe cheilocystidia in element A of the type of A. subrufescens. Freeman (1979) also reported cheilocystidia to be absent in the type. By contrast, Kauffman's (1918) description of Michigan collections noted numerous subcylindrical sterile cells on edges of gills, and Peck authenticated at least some of Kauffman's A. subrufescensmaterial. Typical cheilocystidia are present in element B of the holo-type. Unfortunately, given the condition of the element A type specimens (discussed above), it is unlikely that cheilocystidia will be observed therein.

Two observations on this species argue against overemphasizing morphological features evaluated from dried specimens. First, observations and experience show that morphology within the interfertile group is rather diverse because of underlying genetic variation and is additionally plastic in response to environmental influences. Second, this is perhaps the easiest species of Agaricus to cultivate and, as shown above, is amenable to outcrossing. There are compelling advantages to studying the expression of morphological traits in living material under standard (and possibly nonstandard) conditions and to investigating trait expression when genomes from putatively distinct taxonomic entities share a common cytoplasm. For example, distinctive cells of the veils and/or cuticle of this species have been discussed by Nauta (1999), Heinemann (1993), and Wasser et al (2002). I have observed that SBRFG has sausage-like chains of cells in the universal veil of the annulus, but not in velar patches on the pileus. Similar cells have been observed in A. subrufescens from eastern North America (O.K. Miller personal communication). The best way to assess the taxonomic and/or phylogenetic significance of any differences in velar cells among populations would be to study expression of the trait in hybrids and their offspring. If, as in studies of some other basidiomycetes, barriers to gene flow were discovered within the

A. subrufescens phylogenetic unit, that might indicate that a more elaborate taxonomic arrangement could be appropriate. For these reasons living cultures from European, Hawaiian and other populations will be of great interest to future studies.

Other notable reports

Agaricus subrufescens first was reported from Brazil by J. Rick (1930). However, Rick gave the spore size of material from São Leopoldo as 5 × 3 μm, so Peck's name is unlikely to apply to these specimens. Later, Rick (1939)suggested the existence of a 'varietas microspora' with spores 3 × 2 μm; however this is not a validly published name and is unlikely to be phylogenetically congruent with the species. In the photographic collection of the late W.F. Isaacs, one transparency of A. subrufescens is labeled "from Argentine". The slide, which shows the mushrooms growing indoors in wooden boxes, was processed in the USA in Mar 1963. This suggests that some aspects of the cultural history of A. subrufescens in South America remain incompletely known.

A European culture identified as A. purpurascens (Cooke) Pilát (nom. illeg., non A. purpurascens Fr.; see A. porphyrizon Orton 1960) was cultivated experimentally at INRA Bordeaux, France (Brian et al 1981). Based on experience and on published and unpublished photographs, these mushrooms agree with A. subrufescens (J. Guinberteau and P. Callac personal communication). This report indicates that European strains should be amenable to cultural and hybridization studies.

Nomenclature and typification

Peck's publications and correspondence from Falconer to Peck at NYS make clear that the holotype of A. subrufescens comprises two separate collections. Under the circumstances lectotypification of A. subrufescens is appropriate.Didukh et al (2003) concluded from a study of the type that two different elements were present. They also concluded that two different taxa were present; however I disagree. Elements A and B fall within the range of variation known for A. subrufescens. This can be seen in the spore-size data. Didukh et al formally designated element B to be the lectotype. Peck (1897) indicated that the description of the species was based on specimens from Falconer's "compost heap composed chiefly of decaying leaves." Based on the numbers and condition of basidiomata in the two elements of the type, Peck was referring to the B element as the basis for his concept. Although spores from the B element are long relative to Peck's description (and spores from the A element are short), both elements have spore length ranges that bracket Peck's measurement. Didukh et al have selected the best element for the lectotype of A. subrufescens. The A element has now been segregated and should be considered an authenticated collection of the species. The synonymy of the species is:

Agaricus subrufescens Peck New York State. Mus. Ann. Rep. 46:105. 1893

- = Psalliota subrufescens Kauff. The Agaricaceae of Michigan 239. 1918.
- = Agaricus rufotegulis Nauta Persoonia 17:230. 1999.
- = Agaricus brasiliensis Wasser, Didukh, de Amazonas & Stamets. Int. J. Med. Mush. 4:274. 2002.

Misapplied names:

- – Agaricus blazei Murrill sensu Heinemann Bull Jard Bot Belgium 62:365–368. 1993.

SCIENTIFIC AND COMMON NAMES OF MUSHROOMS

Not all mushrooms have common names. Some have more than one. Scientific names are sometimes changed but mushroom enthusiasts frequently refer to them as they were previously known. We have listed some of these alternate names. The mushrooms in this list include those in the main body of the book as well as those listed under "More Edible Mushrooms".

Genus	Species	Common
Agaricus	*arvensis*	Horse Mushroom
	augustus	The prince
	bernardii	
	bisporus *brunnescens*	Common store mushroom button mushroom commercial mushroom
	bitorquis *rodmanii*	Spring agaricus
	campestris	Field or meadow mushroom
	crocodilinus	Crocodile agaricus
	fuscofibrillosus	Bleeding agaricus
	haemorrhoidarius	Bleeding agaricus
Amanita	*phalloides*	Death cap
Armillaria	*matsutake*	Matsutake
	mellea	Honey or oak mushroom
	ponderosa	American *matsutake* or pine mushroom, recently renamed *Tricholoma magnivelare*
Auricularia	*auricula*	Cloud ear mushroom or Judas' ear
	polytricha	Wood ear mushroom, tree ear, or black fungus
Boletus	*aereus*	
	appendiculatus	Butter bolete
	badius	Bay bolete
	barrowsii	Barrow's bolete
	bicolor	Two-colored bolete
	edulis	*Porcini, cèpe,* or king bolete
	mirabilis	Admirable bolete
	pinicola	Variant of *B. edulis*
	regius	Regal bolete
	zelleri	Zeller's bolete

Bovista	various	Puffball
Calbovista	various	Puffball
Calvatia	*gigantea*	Puffball
Cantharellus	*cibarius*	Golden chanterelle or egg mushroom
	cinnabarinus	Cinnabar-red chanterelle
	lateritius	Smooth chanterelle
	subalbidus	White chanterelle
	tubaeformis	Trumpet chanterelle
Chlorophyllum	*molybdites* *morgani*	Green-spored parasol mushroom
Clitocybe	*fragrans*	Fragrant clitocybe
	odora	Anise-scented
	nuda	Blewit
Clitopilus	*prunulus*	Sweetbread mushroom
Coprinus	*atramentarius*	Alcohol inky cap
	comatus	Shaggy mane, lawyer's wig, or inky cap
	micaceus	Mica cap
Cortinarius	*armillatus*	Bracelet cortinarius
Craterellus	*cornucopioides*	Horn of plenty, trumpet of death, or black chanterelle
Entoloma	*abortivum*	Aborted entoloma
Flammulina	*velutipes*	*Enoki*, velvet foot, golden needle, or winter mushroom
Gomphus	*clavatus*	Pig's ear
Grifola *Polypilus*	*frondosa*	Hen of the woods
Gyromitra	*gigas*	Snowbank false morel
Helvella	*lacunosa*	Black saddle mushroom
Hericium	*coralloides* *caput ursi* *americanum*	Coral hericium
	erinaceus	Bear's head, monkey head, or pom-pom
	ramosum	Comb tooth mushroom
Hydnum	*repandum*	Hedgehog mushroom or sweet tooth
	umbilicatum	Belly-button mushroom
Hygrophorus	*russula*	Russula like waxy cap
Lactarius	*deliciosus*	Delicious milky cap
	fragilis	Candy cap
	indigo	Blue milky cap
	rubrilacteus	Bleeding milky cap
Leccinum	*aurantiacum*	Orange-capped scaber stalk
	insigne	Aspen scaber stalk
	manzanitae	Manzanita scaber stalk
	scaber	Scaber stalk
Lentinus	*edodes*	*Shiitake*, black forest mushroom
Lepiota *Chlorophyllum*	*molybdites*	Green-spored parasol

Lepiota	*procera*	Parasol mushroom
	rhacodes	Shaggy parasol mushroom or drumstick mushroom
Lepista Clitocybe	*nuda*	Blewit
Lycoperdon	various	Puffball
Marasmius	*oreades*	Fairy-ring mushroom
	scorodonius	Garlic marasmius
Morchella	*angusticeps*	Morel or sponge
	conica	Morel or sponge
	deliciosa	Morel or sponge
	esculenta	Morel or sponge
Phlogiotis	*helvelloides*	Apricot jelly mushroom
Pholiota	*nameko*	*Nameko*
	aurivella	Butter mushroom
Pleurocybella	*porrigens*	Angels' wings
Pleurotus	*ostreatus*	Oyster mushroom
	sajor-caju	Oyster mushroom
Pluteus	*cervinus*	Fawn mushroom
Polypilus Grifola	*frondosa*	Hen of the woods
Polyozellus	*multiplex*	Clustered blue chanterelle
Polyporus	*umbellatus*	Umbrella polypore
Ramaria	*botrytis*	Red-tipped coral mushroom
Rozites	*caperata*	Gypsy mushroom or chicken of the woods
Russula	*aeruginea*	Tacky green russula
	cyanoxantha	Charcoal burner
	delica	Short-stem russula
	nigricans	Blackening russula
	vesca	Bare-toothed russula
	xerampelina	Shellfish-scented russula
Sparassis	*crispa radicata*	Cauliflower mushroom
Strobilomyces	*confusus floccopus*	Old man of the woods
Stropharia	*rugosoannulata*	Wine-cap stropharia
Suillus	*brevipes*	Short-stalked slippery cap
	granulatus	Dotted-stalk suillus
	pictus	Painted suillus
Terfezia	*bouderi*	Black *kame*
	claveryi	Brown *kame*
Tremella	*fuciformis*	Snow mushroom, white jelly fungus, or silver ear mushroom
Tricholoma	*flavovirens equestre*	Man on horseback
	magnivelare	Pine mushroom or American *matsutake*
Tuber	*aestivum*	Summer truffle
	gibbosum	Oregon white truffle
	magnatum	Italian white truffle
	melanosporum	French black truffle
	texensis	Texas white truffle

PSYCHOACTIVE MUSHROOM SPECIES

Psychoactive mushroom Species are

Genus Conocybe

Conocybe is a fairly large genus with over 50 species in North America alone. At least one species in this genus, Conocybe filaris (= Pholiotina filaris), is deadly poisonous. Conocybes are often called dunce capsor cone heads because they usually have a conical or bell-shaped cap. They are mostly fragile, often ephemeral, Mycena-like mushrooms with a long, thin and fragile stem and rusty-brown to ochre-brown spores.Conocybes are largely differentiated on microscopic characters.

They are sometimes confused with genus Psilocybe mushrooms, but have brighter brown spores. Among the brown-spored mushrooms, they are easily to be confused with Bolbitius, which usually have a distinctly viscid, striate cap, and Galerina, which have a filamentous rather than cellular cap cuticle (it looks like weaved fibers under the microscope whereas those of Conocybe are composed of inflated round cells resembling cobblestones) and an often viscid and/or translucent-striate cap. These mushrooms are partial to warm weather and fruit in great abundance on watered lawns. Some, such as Conocybe lactea, are so frail that they shrivel up or topple over a few hours after appearing.

- Conocybe cyanopus
- Conocybe kuehneriana
- Conocybe smithii

Genus Copelandia

According to Rolf Singer's interpretation of the Coprinaceae family, genus Copelandia which includes more than 10 different species is one of at least three (sub)genera stemming from the traditional notion of the genus Panaeolus. Although some American mycologists strictly refer to the genus as Copelandia, most European mycologists prefer Panaeolus. At the moment the names of the species in both genera are used as synonims (e.g. Copelandia cyanescens = Panaeolus cyanescens etc.).

The genus Copelandia was named by Italian mycologist Abbé Giacomo Bresadola (1847-1929) in honour of Edwin Bingham Copeland (1873-1964), an American research associate in botany who gathered fungi in the Philippines and presumably sent his collections - among which happened to be a bluing Panaeolus species - to Bresadola.Copelandias are black spored dung inhabiting tropical and subtropical mushrooms that readily bruise blue and feature a characteristic form of pleurocystidia.

- Copelandia affinis
- Copelandia anomala

- Copelandia bispora
- Copelandia cambodginiensis
- Copelandia chlorocystis
- Copelandia cyanescens
- Copelandia lentisporus
- Copelandia mexicana
- Copelandia tirunelveliensis
- Copelandia tropica
- Copelandia tropicalis
- Copelandia westii

Genus Gymnopilus

This genus contains around 200 rusty-orange spored mushroom species formerly divided among Pholiota and the defunct genus Flammula. The fruiting body is typically reddish brown to rusty orange to yellow, the cap is dry with small reddish fibers, taste is bitter and a veil is often present. The vast majority of species grow on wood but at times may appear terrestrial if it's buried or decomposed.

Pholiota and Cortinariusare the genera most often confused with Gymnopilus. Pholiota, however, usually has a viscid cap and duller (brown to cinnamon brown) spores, and Cortinarius grows on the ground. To an untrained eye there are also similarities to the genus Galerina which contains some deadly poisonous mushrooms.

- Gymnopilus aeruginosus
- Gymnopilus luteofolius
- Gymnopilus spectabilis (= Gymnopilus junonius)
- Gymnopilus purpuratus

Genus Inocybe

With Inocybe, you are truly dancing with danger in a mycological minefield of edible, psychoactive, and toxic (primarily of the muscarinic type) mushrooms. In fact, Inocybe contains a higher percentage of poisonous species than any other major mushroom genus, including Amanita! Also, species in this genus are some of the most difficult to identify accurately, even for the most experienced mycologists.

The late Dr. Daniel Stunz spent several decades studying this genus, and estimated 400-600 species, of which approximately 150 are recognized. Most Inocybes have not been tested for their edibility, toxicity, or psilocybin activity. Of those that have been tested, five species tested positive for psilocybin. Many species, including I. sororia, I. maculata, I. pudica, and I. geophylla, contain toxic levels of muscarine. None have yet been found to contain both psilocybin and muscarine, but there is no reason to believe that the compounds should be mutually exclusive. The best means of recognizing an Inocybe is by its characteristically silky, fibrillose, minutely scaly, and/or wooly cap which is often umbonate and seldom viscid.

The spore colour is some shade of brown, and is generally duller than that of Cortinarius. In addition, most Inocybes have a noticeable odor - occasionally sweet or fruity as in I. pyriodora, but more often unpleasant (pungent, spermatic, fishy, or like fresh green corn but not often radishlike as in Hebeloma).

Like Cortinarius, Inocybesare lárgely terrestrial and mycorrhizal and are a major fungal facet of temperate forests. Unlike Cortinarius, they are not the least bit colourful. They come in an endless, senseless procession of boring browns, yucky yellows, gratuitous grays, and wishy-washy whites, with only I. lilacina (among the common species) deviating from the norm. Extreme caution is advised when dealing with this genus, as you are more likely to find one that is toxic before you will find one that is psilocybin active or innocuous.

- Inocybe aeruginascens
- Inocybe coelestium
- Inocybe corydalina
- Inocybe haemacta

Genus Panaeolus

Genus Panaeolus belongs to the family Coprinaceae. It is a relatively small genus of black spored little brown mushrooms with a bell shaped to conical cap and thin, brittle stalk. The sides of the gills often have a mottled or spotted appearance due to uneven maturation of the spore producing cells (basidia), but they do not deliquesce (a process of autodigestion whereby the cap is reduced to a black liquid) as in Coprinus.Psathyrellas are similar but do typically grow in decayed wood substrata and in soils, and those that grow in grass tend to have a convex cap and/or dark brown spores. Psilocybes and Conocybes are common in dung, but do not have black spores. Panaeolus is abundant in pastures, lawns, and manure heaps, fruiting whenever it's moist. It often mixes company with other species. There are no known poisonous mushrooms in this genus.

- Panaeolus africanus
- Panaeolus castaneifolius
- Panaeolus papilionaceus (probably inactive)
- Panaeolus subbalteatus

Genus Pluteus

These pinkish-spored mushrooms have a central ringless stem that can be broken away from the cap with ease, and close gills, free at maturity. Being wood decomposers they grow almost exclusively on wood. The wood, however, may be buried or decomposed, making the mushrooms appear terrestrial.

Most species have soft flesh and they decay rapidly. They are segregated primarily on microscopic features such as structure of the cap cuticle and the the shape of cystidia (sterile cells on the gills). Worldwide, there are over 100 members in this genus.

Edibility of the five inactive Pluteus species described in David Arora'sMushrooms Demystified is either edible and good (P. petasatus, P. cervinus, P. lutescens) or unknown (P. longistriatus, P. flavofuligineus). Pluteus is frequently encountered but rarely abundant. They are most often confused with the pinkish, angular spored Entolomataceae, which are usually terrestrial with gills attached to the stem.

- Pluteus cyanopus
- Pluteus glaucus
- Pluteus salicinus
- Pluteus villosus

Genus Psilocybe

The genus Psilocybe contains roughly 180 small to medium-sized saprophytic mushroom species that can be found in a wide range of habitats: dungs, mosses, soils, grasslands, or decaying wood debris. When moist, most species have viscid, deep-brown caps that fade in drying to yellowish brown (i.e., are hygrophanous).

The more active species, particularly those high in psilocin, bruise bluish where injured. The gills are usually dark brown in color with whitish edges, and range from being subdecurrent to acutely ascending in their attachments. Almost any LBM (Little Brown Mushroom) can be mistaken carelessly for a Psilocybe - with potentially disastrous results! A good spore print is crucial, as it will eliminate the brown spored genera (Galerina, Inocybe, Conocybe etc.), which contain many poisonous species.

Among the dark-spored genera, Coprinus has deliquescing gills, Psathyrella typically has a non-viscid cap and never stains blue, Panaeolus species with a viscid cap grow on dung and have black spores, and Hypholoma(= Naematoloma) and Stropharia species are usually brightly coloured, while the cap colour in Psilocybe (with the notable exception of P. cubensis) is typically some shade of brown, gray, or buff.

- Psilocybe antioquensis
- Psilocybe arcana
- Psilocybe atlantis
- Psilocybe aucklandii

- Psilocybe australiana
- Psilocybe aztecorum
- Psilocybe azurescens
- Psilocybe baeocystis
- Psilocybe bohemica
- Psilocybe brasiliensis
- Psilocybe caerulescens
- Psilocybe caerulipes
- Psilocybe columbiana
- Psilocybe cubensis
- Psilocybe cyanescens
- Psilocybe cyanofibrillosa
- Psilocybe fimetaria
- Psilocybe heimii
- Psilocybe hispanica
- Psilocybe hoogshagenii
- Psilocybe mammillata
- Psilocybe mexicana
- Psilocybe moravica
- Psilocybe natalensis
- Psilocybe pelliculosa
- Psilocybe ovoideocystidiata
- Psilocybe portoricensis
- Psilocybe quebecensis
- Psilocybe samuiensis
- Psilocybe sanctorum
- Psilocybe semilanceata
- Psilocybe sierrae
- Psilocybe silvatica
- Psilocybe strictipes (= Psilocybe callosa)
- Psilocybe stuntzii
- Psilocybe subaeruginosa
- Psilocybe subcubensis
- Psilocybe tampanensis
- Psilocybe uxpanapensis
- Psilocybe weilii
- Psilocybe xalapensis
- Psilocybe zapotecorum

Genus: Weraroa

This genus of fungi are referred to as sequestrate fungi which means that they have lost there ability to forceful eject there spores. In stead they relies on insects and birds to eat and disperse them.

- Weraroa novea-zelandiae

Index